TEXAS, COTTON, AND THE NEW DEAL

NUMBER SEVEN:
Sam Rayburn Series on Rural Life
Sponsored by Texas A&M University–Commerce
James A. Grimshaw, Jr., General Editor

Texas, Cotton,
and the New Deal

KEITH J. VOLANTO

TEXAS A&M UNIVERSITY PRESS
College Station

The paper used in this book meets the minimum requirements
of the American National Standard for Permanence
of Paper for Printed Library Materials, z39.48-1984.
Binding materials have been chosen for durability.

Library of Congress Cataloging-in-Publication Data

Volanto, Keith Joseph
Texas, cotton, and the New Deal / Keith J. Volanto.— 1st ed.
p. cm. — (Sam Rayburn series on rural life ; no. 7)
Includes bibliographical references and index.
ISBN 1-58544-402-2 (cloth : alk. paper)
1. Cotton growing—Government policy—Texas—History. 2. Cotton trade—Government
policy—Texas—History. 3. New Deal, 1933–1939—Texas. 4. United States. Agricultural
Adjustment Act 1933. I. Title. II. Series
HD9077.T4V65 2005
338.1'7351'0976409043—dc22
2004009055

CONTENTS

ILLUSTRATIONS

TABLES

SERIES EDITOR'S FOREWORD

James A. Grimshaw, Jr.

John Steinbeck's 1939 novel, *The Grapes of Wrath,* contains poignant descriptions of tenant farmers and sharecroppers throughout the Southwest during the Dust Bowl period. His story of the Joad family's move to California and the privation of the migrant workers, whom they represented, was challenged by critics as gross exaggeration and irresponsible reporting. Then a reporter for *Life* magazine investigated the matter. The reporter's subsequent article and accompanying photographs revealed that the actual conditions were worse than Steinbeck had depicted in his fictional account. In this seventh book in the Sam Rayburn Series on Rural Life, Keith J. Volanto writes another chapter about that era.

Texas, Cotton, and the New Deal focuses on the Franklin Delano Roosevelt administration's assistance programs to Texas cotton farmers during the Great Depression. Under the Agricultural Adjustment Administration (AAA), farm subsidy programs were introduced for the first time in the United States. They were seen, at least according to the theory of M. L. Wilson, as "agrarian democracy in action." Volanto's study provides a crucial insight into the background of the programs, the difficulties encountered in their implementation and administration, and the results that were attained in Texas, which was the largest cotton-producing state in the mid-1930s. What Volanto reveals sheds new light on the New Deal and its effects on the economic recovery from the Great Depression. For example, the issue of tenant and sharecropper displacement was controversial and debated nationally. In the February 13, 1934, issue of *The Nation,* William R. Amberson's article, "The New Deal for Share-Croppers," addresses the injustices created by the government and the landowners who kicked tenant farmers off their land and by the government's failure to come up with adequate alternatives for displaced families, which Amberson posits as a national rather than a regional responsibility. Volanto offers statistics and examples of specific cases in Texas of individual injustices and suffering, documented by quotations from selected letters written by displaced tenants to AAA and USDA officials.

Volanto's writing provides a chronological inquiry into the AAA's efforts in Texas from the 1920s through the 1930s. His style is very readable, a fact that should put those readers not familiar with this topic more at ease. An element of intrigue can be found here, too, as Volanto discusses the bureaucratic give-and-take and the conflict between those landowners who willingly participated in tenant displacement and those who chose not to participate in it. Indeed, without the cooperation of the farmers, a governmental aid program was doomed to failure. The farming difficulties of the 1920s were only exacerbated in the 1930s by the Great Depression. Not until World War II was a remedy found, but it, too, was temporary at best. Volanto's well-documented discussion, though, gives a clearer picture of how Washington's bureaucracy affected rural life in Texas during that period, and it shows as well the impact of mechanization in agriculture. For those interested in learning more, a part of the history of cotton in Texas is preserved in the Audie Murphy American Cotton Museum in Greenville, Texas, a city once thought of as the cotton capital of the region.

The purpose of the Sam Rayburn Series on Rural Life is suggested partly in the series title, "rural life." The scope of the series, however, is broad, encompassing any aspect of rural life that bears witness to the patterns of a lifestyle that some twenty-first century observers say is dying. Aspects such as agriculture, women's rights, civil disputes, entertainment, religion, education, prairie grasslands, and literary lives are but a few of the many possibilities to which authors in this series are contributing. It is an ever-evolving mosaic, and Keith Volanto's book is a welcome addition to this composite picture.

PREFACE

This book chronicles the efforts of the Agricultural Adjustment Administration (AAA) to aid Texas cotton farmers during the Great Depression. The AAA was created at the outset of Franklin Roosevelt's New Deal to administer the first farm subsidy programs in American history. Using the inducement of cash payments, government officials hoped that growers of a variety of crops, including cotton, would reduce production to alleviate burdensome surpluses, which collapsed prices and threatened farmers with economic ruin. The cotton programs were especially important for Texas—the nation's leading cotton-producing state.

During the 1930s, cotton was central to the Texas economy. Raising the annual crop provided a livelihood for close to two million Texans, approximately one-third of the state's population. An equal number of nonfarming Texans were involved in picking, ginning, shipping, and financing the crop. Any major upheaval in the cotton market would obviously have destabilized the entire economy of the Lone Star State. The arrival of the Great Depression provided just such a disruption.

For all its sudden fury, however, the Depression merely accentuated the hard times that growers had been experiencing since the mid-1920s. As was the case with most other major agricultural commodities after World War I, huge production gains coupled with decreased domestic and foreign consumption had already driven prices down to damaging levels for southern cotton producers. The Depression threatened to make a dire situation much worse. As the economic downturn deepened, calls from farmers and politicians for direct action by the federal government gained momentum, paving the way for FDR's decision to experiment with an idea that had emerged from agricultural circles during the 1920s, the Voluntary Domestic Allotment Plan. This plan served as the AAA's foundation.

Federal government action did not arrive in the form of dictation to the growers. Quite to the contrary, M. L. Wilson, an agricultural economics professor and the person most responsible for developing and promoting the Voluntary Domestic Allotment Plan, envisioned an active role for producers. Farmer referendums were to be held to approve the programs. Elections were to determine membership in producers' committees, which would aid Extension Service agents in overseeing implementation at the local level. Wilson touted these aspects of the programs as democracy in action—a grand cooperative effort between the government and the people to solve one of the nation's gravest problems.

Although this cooperation would be tested regularly as the programs changed in reaction to farmers' discontent, political pressures, and court actions, continued grower support was always key to any success the AAA achieved in stabilizing prices and boosting farm income. Without farmers' cooperation, the programs would have failed completely, and Texas would have plunged farther into economic chaos.

Despite the Roosevelt administration's tremendous importance to Texas history, the study of the New Deal in the Lone Star State has been limited mostly to simple political accounts. Writing in 1991, Robert Calvert described this topic of research as "almost virgin territory." His evaluation remains largely true, especially with regard to the New Deal's agricultural programs. Although recent scholarship, such as Thad Sitton and Dan Utley's *From Can See to Can't,* Rebecca Sharpless's *Fertile Ground, Narrow Choices,* and Neil Foley's *The White Scourge,* has rekindled interest in aspects of Texas' cotton culture on the eve of the Great Depression, this is the first book-length examination of the AAA's important efforts to assist the state's ailing farmers during the New Deal.[1]

A study of the AAA's cotton programs in Texas can serve as an important inquiry into New Deal agricultural-policy implementation at the grass-roots level. The most noteworthy works to examine southern agriculture during the Depression years, namely, Gilbert Fite's *Cotton Fields No More,* Pete Daniel's *Breaking the Land,* and Jack Kirby's *Rural Worlds Lost,* employ a broad regional approach, focus on changes in southern agriculture, and largely ignore Texas. Other important works on New Deal agricultural agencies, such as Theodore Saloutos's *The American Farmer and the New Deal* and Van Perkins's *Crisis in Agriculture,* are "top-down" studies of government policy. The methods employed in these works neglect many significant topics, especially the numerous problems involved in policy implementation at the local level, not to mention the valuable perspectives of the farmers themselves.

Investigation of the AAA's cotton programs has additional significance as a case study of the New Deal itself. The AAA provides an excellent example of how the New Deal attempted to solve national problems in a largely experimental fashion. The Roosevelt administration launched its farm programs, as it did many other New Deal efforts, without any foundation or reference point. Never before had the federal government undertaken such an endeavor. Along the way, the AAA faced political, social, economic, and legal challenges that threatened the agency's mission—just as many other New Deal agencies did. Further, FDR typically prioritized his efforts in a "broker state" fashion by tending to address the concerns of highly organized groups, often to the detriment of unorganized individuals and groups lacking a large support base.

In this book I explore how the AAA's cotton programs fit these general patterns. What were the major problems encountered in carrying out these experimental programs and how were they solved? What forces influenced or constrained the AAA's efforts? How did underrepresented individuals fare under the AAA's cotton programs in Texas?[2]

With the exception of chapter 6, dedicated to the controversial issue of tenant and sharecropper displacement, I have adopted a chronological approach. I begin with a background chapter introducing Texas cotton culture, the problems of Depression-era cotton farmers, the origins of the AAA, and important agricultural and political leaders. In chapter 2, I describe the passage of the Agricultural Adjustment Act of 1933 (which served as the statutory basis for the AAA) and document the 1933 program, emphasizing its famous plow-up campaign. Chapter 3 examines the 1934 and 1935 programs, including the movement of cooperating producers to support the Bankhead Cotton Control Act, which in essence established compulsory controls on production through heavy taxes on production over established quotas. In chapter 4, I explain the 1936 and 1937 programs that operated under the auspices of the Soil Conservation and Domestic Allotment Act (SCDAA)—the temporary alternative created when the Supreme Court ruled in January 1936 against the constitutionality of the Agricultural Adjustment Act of 1933. Chapter 5 relates efforts to overcome the incredible surplus produced by the ineffective crop controls of the 1937 program, details the creation of a new AAA under the Agricultural Adjustment Act of 1938, and describes the 1938 and 1939 programs. In chapter 6, I analyze the negative impact of the AAA cotton programs on the state's tenant farmers and sharecroppers, noting particularly the AAA's inadequate attention to the problem. Chapter 7 contains my conclusions and some final observations.

In exploring the workings of the AAA's cotton programs, I have used a large array of primary and secondary sources in an effort to understand the perspectives of policy-makers and Texas farmers. Of paramount importance are the AAA's papers housed at the National Archives II in College Park, Maryland. Among these records is the invaluable correspondence of AAA personnel, U.S. Department of Agriculture (USDA) officials, members of Congress, and the White House. The records also contain countless letters from Texas cotton farmers to the government; these reveal extensive information about individual cases and farmers' opinions on a variety of policy matters. I have delved extensively into these letters, more so than has any previous researcher on New Deal agriculture, in order to gain information and perspectives on local conditions in Texas.

My access to the Texas Agricultural Extension Service county agents' annual narrative reports, housed at Texas A&M University, also greatly aided my understanding of the implementation stage of the cotton programs. After the Extension Service was drafted to help with implementation, the county agents became the vanguard of the ground forces assisting America's farmers. Their work was vital to the programs, and their reports have priceless historical value.

Only one study of a AAA commodity program at the state level exists: Anthony Badger's *Prosperity Road,* which examines the tobacco programs in North Carolina. In the introduction to that exceptional book, Badger bemoans the fact that the AAA's effort to aid America's cotton farmers "still awaits its historian." Although I did not intend this work to be a complete history of the AAA cotton programs—a task that would have required significant attention to all aspects of the agency's operations in Washington and intense study of its efforts in every cotton-producing state—I hope it contributes to the understanding of the major cotton-policy issues that confronted the Roosevelt administration and how the cotton programs operated.[3]

The saga of the AAA cotton programs in Texas is a multifaceted story involving great men and common people coming together to overcome an alarming economic emergency. In addition to being a fascinating tale of cooperative experimentation in the face of tremendous uncertainty, it is also a compelling chronicle of competing ideologies and clashing interest groups. In the case of tenant farmers and sharecroppers, it is also a story of people clinging to the soil during desperate times while others, supposedly acting in their interests, were ushering them off the land in the name of progress. It is an interesting story covering an important aspect of the New Deal well worth telling.

I owe a great debt to many people who made the telling of this story possible. First, I would like to thank my graduate committee. Larry Hill gave me constant encouragement and helped me immensely with my dissertation and many nonacademic matters. He has been an inspiring figure, both in and out of the classroom. While sharing with me his great knowledge of the New Deal, he has also been a caring and understanding friend. I hope to do my best to emulate his example with my own students.

The late Robert Calvert taught me much about Texas agriculture and was as fine a teacher of Texas history as I will ever know. Gracious thanks to my racquetball competitor Walter Kamphoefner, and to Henry Schmidt and William West.

My work was made much easier by generous help provided by Joseph Schwartz at the National Archives II, Mark Renovitch at the Franklin D. Roosevelt Library, and Mattie Sink at the Mitchell Memorial Library at Mississippi State University. I also received friendly and professional aid from the fine archivists and staffs at the Southwest Collection at Texas Tech University in Lubbock, the Texas State Archives in Austin, the Sam Rayburn Library in Bonham, the Special Collections Department at the University of Houston, and the Center for American History at the University of Texas at Austin. I would especially like to express gratitude to Fred Mitchell of the Texas Agricultural Extension Service, who allowed me generous access to the county agent reports in his office at Texas A&M University.

The research for my doctoral dissertation, on which this book is based, was aided by grants from the Franklin and Eleanor Roosevelt Institute, the Texas A&M University history department, and the Texas A&M University Office of Graduate Studies.

Part of the second chapter was published as an article entitled "Burying White Gold: The AAA Cotton Plow-Up Campaign in Texas," in the January 2000 issue of the *Southwestern Historical Quarterly*. I would like to thank Ron Tyler for granting permission to reproduce large portions of the article from that fine journal.

Finally, I would like to thank my parents, Joseph and Josephine Volanto. Without their continued love and support this book would never have been written. I dedicate it to them with love and appreciation for all they have done for me.

TEXAS, COTTON, AND THE NEW DEAL

CHAPTER I

BEFORE THE NEW DEAL

"Land just catches the culls that can't do no good in cities. Cept me. I wasn't culled here. I blong. But there's too much cotton and too much corn. Ain't no secret from nobody. We go on raisin it cause it's all we know." So ponders Sam Tucker, an East Texas tenant farmer in George Sessions Perry's classic novel, *Hold Autumn in Your Hand.* During his contemplations, Sam correctly discerns that overproduction is the main problem facing cotton farmers during the post–World War I years. Still, he has trouble coming to terms with the possibility that, despite all his hard work, the solution to his plight might be life off the farm: "It just seems strange when you know this year's cotton'll be just as good, just as white, an a better staple than it ever was; just as much work to raise. Except there ain't no use for but half of it. Ain't nobody's fault, I guess, but ourn for raising cotton. More of us got to crowd into the factories, looks like."[1]

As the 1920s progressed, many cotton farmers, like other agricultural producers, faced the possibility of losing their jobs and their way of life if something was not done to improve their worsening situation. In the decade before the New Deal, the declining cotton market led many Texans to support various proposals to aid American agriculture. Although ultimately unsuccessful, these earlier campaigns laid the necessary groundwork for acceptance of the Roosevelt administration's bolder production-control efforts under the supervision of the Agricultural Adjustment Administration. They also propelled into the national spotlight important farm leaders, such as George Peek, Chester Davis, M. L. Wilson, and Henry Wallace—men destined to have a tremendous impact on New Deal agricultural policy.

Texas Cotton Culture

The Lone Star State has had a long association with cotton. Before cattle grazed on the plains, before railroad tracks were laid to link burgeoning settlements, and before men punctured the earth searching for oil, cotton was growing wild in Texas. Native Americans living in the region at the time the Europeans arrived had long gathered varieties of the plant to utilize its snowy fibers for clothing and other needs. In his famous narrative, shipwrecked Spanish conquistador Alvar Núñez Cabeza de Vaca describes native women wearing cotton shifts and how tribesmen gave him cotton blankets as gifts. As the Spaniards advanced northward from Mexico, their missionaries and Indian converts became the first Texans to cultivate cotton actively.[2]

Cotton became a major crop in Texas with the appearance of American settlers. Beginning in the 1820s, prime cotton-growing land lured mostly southern Americans with their slaves, at the invitation of the new Mexican republic. The Mexican government, in an effort to develop Texas economically and to protect the sparsely populated area against Native American raiders and foreign intruders, offered extensive land grants to empresarios such as Stephen F. Austin as compensation for recruiting and delivering settlers.[3]

Cotton production in Texas increased rapidly after the state was annexed by the United States. The 1860 census listed the state's harvest at 431,645 bales. The Civil War caused a decline in output (to approximately 200,000 bales), but production figures rose every decade after Lee's surrender at Appomattox until the 1930s.[4]

During the first three decades of the twentieth century, Texas cotton growing expanded dramatically beyond its traditional base in the east-central counties. The southern High Plains near Lubbock, the newly irrigated farmland outside El Paso, and the Gulf Coast region surrounding Corpus Christi all saw a tremendous increase in cotton acreage. At the onset of the Great Depression, growers throughout the state were mining the white gold, with 223 of 254 counties devoting at least some acreage to cotton. Texas had also become America's leading cotton-producing state, raising over one-third of the national crop on two-fifths of the total acreage.[5]

In order to comprehend properly the New Deal's efforts to help Texas cotton farmers, it is first necessary to take a brief look into Sam Tucker's world. Basic knowledge of Texas' cotton culture in the early decades of the twentieth century not only is essential to understanding important terminology, it also helps one gain a greater appreciation for the hard life of Depression-era cotton farmers.

By 1930, fewer than half of Texas' cotton growers owned their farms. The majority fit into one of three broad categories of nontenured operators: cash renters, share tenants, and sharecroppers. At the top of the "agricultural ladder" of nonowners were a relatively small number of cash renters—growers with good capital resources, a full stock of work animals and cultivation equipment, and the ability to pay cash for use of the land. They retained full managerial control over the land under their supervision, generally without any landlord restrictions.

The majority of tenant farmers were share tenants who owned work animals and equipment, but lacked the capital to pay cash rent. Share tenants paid rent with a portion of the crop at harvest, typically one-third of their grain and one-fourth of their cotton. Because they were chronically cash starved, share tenants (and many small farm owners) relied on credit advances for needed supplies and living expenses from local furnishing merchants, who charged very high rates of interest for the services they provided. As collateral, merchants held a lien on the farmer's crop. The crop lien was a legal device used by creditors to guarantee first access to the proceeds of a crop at market. Merchants deducted the amount received for the crop from the farmer's account and refunded the difference, if any, to the grower.

The lowest farm operator on the tenure scale was the sharecropper. Not legally a tenant, the sharecropper was actually a wage laborer who worked a section of a plantation or farm. The impoverished cropper offered the landlord only his and his family's labor in exchange for feed, tools, seed, implements, use of the land, a run-down cabin, and advances for living expenses. Sharecroppers had no managerial functions—the landlord told them what to plant, how much to plant, where to plant, and how to raise the crop. As legal owner of the crop, the landlord sold the cotton and gave the cropper one-half of the proceeds as wages. Before paying out any cash, however, the landlord deducted the amount advanced over the growing season plus interest. If the sharecropper ended up in debt, because of the true economics of the situation or because of the proprietor's questionable mathematics, the landlord could legally demand that the laborer remain on the land for another year until the debt was paid off. Many unethical landlords and plantation companies used this form of debt peonage to exert social control and to guarantee their labor supply.[6]

In the postbellum years, as land values and credit costs continued to rise and cotton prices leveled off, the steady increase of farm tenancy and share-cropping developed into a statewide problem. As table 1 indicates, the percentage of Texas non–farm owners increased every decade after the Civil War until the 1930s. By 1930, over 60 percent of all Texas farmers were either tenants or sharecroppers.[7]

Cotton growing remained an immensely labor intensive operation until after World War II. Most phases of the cotton-raising process required nearly constant activity from dawn until dusk, "from can see to can't," as the expression went. More often than not, the new season started too soon after the old one was completed.

The first step in raising the coming year's crop was to dispose of the stalks left over from the previous crop, usually in early winter, before Christmas. Although some poorer planters still used such antiquated techniques as pulling up old stalks by hand, knocking them down with hoes and clubs, or bowling them over with heavy logs attached to work stock, most farmers employed mechanical stalk cutters pulled by mules. The rotation of the cutter's sharp knives acted much like a push mower cutting a lawn and broke the old stalks into small pieces. Growers then usually disposed of the stalks by gathering them into piles, drying them out, and burning them.[8]

After removing the old stalks, farmers arose early on many cold November and December mornings to prepare initial rows of seedbeds, which would support the new cotton plants during spring planting. Growers made ridges by attaching either a simple turning plow or a lister (double moldboard plow) to a mule and running this implement through the previous year's rows. Each pass threw soil to form a new row where a furrow had stood the previous season.[9]

Shortly after the rows were rebedded, farmers looked down to their almanacs, looked up to the sky, and then used their intuition to determine whether the last frost and heavy rains had passed, which would signify that planting time had arrived. Planting usually began in the middle of March in South Texas, and was under way elsewhere in the state by mid-April. Most farmers planted their crops with mechanical planting implements pulled by work stock.[10]

If the weather was cooperative, a farmer could expect the planted seeds to take about ten days to germinate. Anxious growers like John Skrabanek, a Blacklands Prairie farmer, visited the fields every day, digging into beds to examine the progress of germination, and wait "like a nervous husband outside a delivery room" for the crop to sprout up.[11]

Table 1

Texas Tenant and Sharecropper Statistics, 1880–1959

Year	Total Operators	% Nonowners	Total Owners	Nonowners	White Tenants	Nonwhite Tenants	White Croppers	Nonwhite Croppers
1880	174,184	37.6	108,716	65,468	*	*	*	*
1890	228,126	41.9	132,616	95,510	*	*	*	*
1900	352,190	49.7	177,199	174,991	129,685	45,306	*	*
1910	417,770	52.6	198,195	219,575	170,970	48,605	*	*
1920	436,033	53.3	203,724	232,309	177,198	55,111	40,382	27,999
1930	495,489	60.9	193,829	301,660	236,321	65,339	68,874	36,248
1935	501,017	57.1	214,914	286,103	235,162	50,941	50,793	25,675
1940	418,002	48.9	213,540	204,462	171,852	32,610	24,949	14,872
1950	331,567	30.4	230,740	100,827	86,791	14,036	9,935	4,928
1954	292,947	26.3	215,778	77,169	68,293	9,560	6,272	3,288
1959	227,071	21.7	177,907	49,164	45,567	3,597	*	*

Sources: For 1880–1930, 1940: Joseph R. Motheral, "Recent Trends in Land Tenure," 10; for 1935: U.S. Department of Commerce, Bureau of the Census, Sixteenth Census of the United States: 1940, Agriculture, 378; for 1950: U.S. Department of Commerce, Bureau of the Census, Census of Agriculture: 1950, Counties and State Economic Areas, 107; for 1954–59: U.S. Department of Commerce, Bureau of the Census, Census of Agriculture: 1959, 214.

Note: The "tenant" category combines cash renters, share tenants, and sharecroppers. The U.S. Bureau of the Census did not distinguish between the three when compiling its data, although it counted the number of nonwhite and white sharecroppers from 1920 to 1954.

*NA

If enough plants emerged from their dens so major replanting would not have to be undertaken, farmers immediately began to eradicate unwanted vegetation. Up to this point in the growing cycle, most growers handled matters with only minimal help while their wives and daughters carried on such traditional duties as food preparation, clothing production, and child care. But in the battle versus weeds, farmers had to call up all available family members as reinforcements. In addition to performing their normal household work, many wives came into the fields to help their husbands "chop" cotton. They brought their children into the fields during chopping and often placed those too young to chop into carts or tethered them to a cotton stalk or nearby tree.[12]

Chopping cotton required long hours of stooping with a hoe and using rhythmic motions to cut up weeds and grass, remove excessive cotton plants, and break up hardened soil. It was the most labor-intensive part of the cotton-growing process, yet absolutely essential in the days before chemical herbicides to keep down unwanted vegetation such as Johnson grass, to aerate the soil, and to make the soil more capable of absorbing moisture. In addition to chopping, farmers made several passes between the rows with a cultivator plow to kill weeds and deepen water furrows. Farm families repeated this exhausting chopping and cultivation ritual from sunup to sundown in the broiling summer heat until the cotton stalks grew to such height and thickness that a plow could no longer make it through the rows and they shaded and stunted further weed growth.[13]

At that point, usually around the Fourth of July (outside of South Texas), "laying-by" time commenced, when growers could do little more than hope that the crop would thrive. During the next four months, the cotton plants grew stalks, which bore squares that turned into blooms. Eventually, the blooms developed into bolls that opened to display the precious white fiber.

Farmers knew that a host of calamities could occur to severely damage or ruin maturing cotton plants. They prayed every day that such threats as flood or extended drought, a host of fungi, bacteria, or diseases, and a slew of insects, including the granddaddy of all cotton pests—the Mexican boll weevil—would not ruin all the work they had accomplished.[14]

Boll weevils are cotton-eating machines that feed on the pollen of the unopened flower buds of cotton plants. The insects spread rapidly once they infest an area; under ideal conditions, a single pair of weevils can produce over 100 million progeny in a single season, leaving growers with catastrophic losses if they do not harvest their crop in time. By the early 1920s, boll weevils were "the world's largest consumer of raw cotton," in the words of rural sociologist Rupert B. Vance. Native to Central America, the weevils migrated northward, reaching Brownsville in South Texas by 1892. From that entry point, boll weevil infestation spread throughout most of Texas (except for the arid western regions) and the rest of the Cotton Belt by 1920.[15]

Farm families used the opportunity presented by the break to socialize, play, and perform a variety of essential work in preparation for the harvest. It was a time for religious revivals, visiting friends and family, and getting some good hunting and fishing done. It was also a time for men to cut hay and mend fences while women preserved produce and made new cotton sacks, bonnets, and knee pads in preparation for the long cotton-picking season to come.[16]

Because of the availability of cheap labor and the lack of a practical picking machine, most cotton harvesting in Texas was done by hand until after World War II. Picking was usually well under way by the beginning of August in South Texas. By mid-September, all cotton-growing areas of the state were animated by the movement of bodies in the fields picking cotton. A farmer needed every able-bodied family member to harvest the crop, including women and young children. Wage laborers were also in high demand to help cotton farmers pick the crop as quickly as possible before weather and weevil damage took their toll. Truckloads of urbanites poured into rural districts to provide sorely needed labor. In addition, thousands of seasonal laborers from Mexico crossed the border to aid in the annual ritual of the fall harvest.[17]

Pickers harvested cotton in most areas of Texas by stooping over, plucking the fibers out of the opened cotton bolls, and depositing the fibers in a heavy sack slung over a shoulder and dragged through the fields. It was grueling work by any standard. As one man who picked cotton in Texas later recalled: "You'd pick standing up until your back hurt so bad you could hardly stand it, and you'd get down on your knees and go along until your knees got to hurting so bad you couldn't stand it, and you'd get back up and bend over again. Something was always hurting." Picking commenced at first light and continued all day long under a sizzling Texas sun for months, until the workers completed their task. Because of "late bloomers," cotton fields would have to be combed through many times for several weeks before the harvest was complete.[18]

After the exhausting harvest, small Texas market towns jumped to life as farmers came to town seeking the fruits of their labor. The first step was to gin the cotton. Ginning is the machine process that separates the debris from

Texas cotton pickers filling their sacks. USDA photo, National Archives II.

picked cotton, removes the seeds, and presses the remaining fiber into bales for easy transportation. Growers needed about fifteen hundred pounds of seeded cotton to make one five hundred–pound bale. If a farmer did not get his crop to town early, he joined a line forming at one of the local gin buildings. There he waited for his wagon's turn under the gin's suction pipes, which transferred the cotton directly out of the cart and into the gin. He often passed the time by socializing with fellow farmers amid the noise and billowy exhaust of the gin.

Growers often sold a portion of their seed to the gin to defray the ginning cost and retained the remainder for animal feed and for use in the next year's planting. Ginners held a separate financial interest from their customers. They profited irrespective of cotton prices, thus overproduction was not a direct problem for them. While producers always wished for high prices, ginners favored high volume. A catastrophic hit to the markets that threatened to put most of their customers out of business, on the other hand, would not be in their interests.[19]

G. H. Benton's cotton gin, Lawrence, Texas, ca. 1900. Courtesy Center for American History, University of Texas–Austin, Prints and Photographs Collection, CN No. 11637.

After ginning, farmers loaded bales into their wagons and tried to sell their product in the town market. A producer with a lien on his crop had to give the lienholder first chance to buy the cotton in order to settle the grower's debts. If the farmer was an independent owner without a lien against the crop, he often hauled his bales to a local warehouse to be stored, cut out some fiber, and carried the samples around town to show interested buyers. If the town did not have a warehouse, he simply took his wagon to the market area and looked for potential bidders.[20]

Cotton buyers analyzed the farmer's cotton for staple length and overall quality before offering a price for the entire bale. Buyers were either local men who had connections with large handling firms or were traveling representatives of these purchasing and shipping businesses. By the 1930s, Houston-based Anderson, Clayton and Company dominated the lucrative handling trade in Texas. As the world's largest cotton merchant, Anderson, Clayton and Company purchased and shipped over a million bales of southern cotton annually to American and European mills. Collectively, buyers exported over 90 percent of Texas' cotton out of the state for processing.

As was the case with ginners, cotton handlers held a separate financial interest from farmers because shippers also profited in high-volume seasons, regardless of cotton prices. Although shippers realized that extremely low prices could put producers out of business, they almost unanimously argued that expanding markets was the key to farmers' prosperity and abhorred any scheme that tried to save farmers (and hurt the shippers) by reducing cotton production.[21]

By the 1930s, Anderson, Clayton and Company was the most visible symbol of Texas agribusiness and a powerful reminder that cotton meant more to the state than simply a means of support for growers. According to the 1931 *Texas Almanac and State Industrial Guide,* over 70 percent of Texas' population by 1930 depended on cotton for its livelihood. Not just farmers, but also the various merchants, bankers, ginners, buyers, shippers, and the employees of these agribusinesses all relied on a stable cotton market for their continued prosperity.[22]

The Economic Problems of American Cotton Farmers, 1919–29

Although the Great Depression was a potential disaster for Texas, it merely accelerated pernicious economic trends that had begun after the end of the First World War. The "Roaring Twenties" were hardly roaring for a majority of American farmers. Agriculture in postwar America suffered through a decade-long price slump in most commodities before the infamous stock market crash. Cotton prices remained relatively higher than other farm products in the years immediately following World War I. As the 1920s advanced, however, the cotton market became increasingly unstable and finally collapsed in 1929. By the end of the 1920s, cotton growers were susceptible to the same economic problems affecting the producers of other agricultural commodities, namely, underconsumption, overproduction, and the increasing cost of living.[23]

Consumption of American cotton failed to keep up with supply for a number of reasons. In the postwar period, American consumers turned increasingly to newer synthetic products, such as rayon, thus reducing the demand for cotton. Foreign competition, especially from Egypt and India, began to eat into the United States' position in the world market. The war's high cost and devastation, high American tariffs, and the increasing reluctance of American bankers to provide loans to European nations all combined to hinder Europe's ability to purchase American cotton during the 1920s. American cotton exports all but dried up as a result of the Great Depression, but the problem of decreased sales to Europe appeared long before 1929.[24]

The drop in cotton consumption intensified the problem of overproduction during the 1920s. Overproduction existed before World War I, but the postwar decrease in consumption highlighted the worsening problem of over-supply. Because of insufficient organization, America's agricultural producers, unlike its manufacturers, could not adjust supply to match demand. American cotton producers were no exception. Despite lagging demand, American cotton production steadily increased after the war. While farmers in most cotton-growing regions increased plantings during the 1920s, no location experienced a greater increase in cotton acreage than the western areas of the Cotton Belt, especially Texas and Oklahoma. By the late 1920s, increased production from these new areas, when coupled with deceased domestic and world demand, inevitably helped depress the entire American cotton market.[25]

High state and local taxes, along with high industrial tariffs, further harmed American cotton farmers in the postwar years. An increased state and local tax burden drained purchasing power and thereby hampered the efforts of many producers to work through the depressed markets. Extremely high tariffs heaped another liability on farmers. Although growers sold their products in a highly competitive world market, they had to purchase needed industrial goods in a heavily protected home market. With foreign industrial goods effectively kept out, farmers paid higher domestic prices for such goods as tools, implements, automobiles, and a myriad of home products.[26]

Proposed Solutions before the New Deal

New Deal efforts to aid American cotton farmers did not develop in a vacuum. Rather, they represented the consummation of attempts begun a decade earlier. Beginning in the mid-1920s, the increasing hardship placed on growers led many to support a host of proposed remedies, ranging from voluntary cotton-acreage reduction to major marketing reforms. Although none proved to be satisfactory in solving the farmers' plight (or received enough support to be attempted), these pre–New Deal endeavors succeeded in greatly publicizing American agriculture's problems.

The wake-up call for American cotton farmers occurred in September

1926, when prices went into a tailspin. While the price decline had numerous secondary causes, the primary factor was the great expansion of cotton acreage, which resulted in a record-breaking crop of 17,977,000 bales. In 1925, southern growers had produced a large crop of 16,105,000 bales, but still received close to twenty cents per pound. By late 1926, however, the enormous new crop, when added to the 5.6 million–bale carryover from the previous year, began to drive prices below ten cents per pound and threatened many growers with financial ruin.[27]

On September 24, 1926, a group of Texas bankers met in Dallas to plan a course of action. At this assembly, the financiers pledged to underwrite private pools to purchase one million bales of Texas cotton and keep the fiber off the market. As a condition, the bankers stated that the pooling efforts had to be supplemented with a plan that would reduce the 1927 crop by 25 percent. They also urged local Texas bank managers to organize efforts in their communities and beseeched bankers in other states to join the movement.[28]

Leading growers, bankers, and businesspeople in other cotton states duplicated the efforts of the Texas bankers, calling for the establishment of pools backed by acreage-reduction pledges. Major newspapers endorsed the movement, urging their farmer-readers to participate. On receiving a favorable response, southern bankers in all the major cotton-growing states proceeded to establish private cotton pools.[29]

Despite much expended energy, efforts to persuade farmers to plant only three-quarters of their 1927 cotton acreage ultimately failed. Texans did cut their cotton acreage by 11 percent, and the South in 1927 cut its total cotton acreage by 12.4 percent from the 1926 total. Still, these figures represented no greater decrease than normal after a low-price year. Partly as a result of the limited acreage reduction, farmers saw the return of twenty-cent cotton in 1927, but this price would not last. Despite warnings of a return to 1926 conditions or worse, each year between 1928 and 1932, Texas farmers increased the acreage planted in cotton.[30]

In the aftermath of the 1926 season, the focus of aid for American cotton producers shifted for a time from voluntary acreage reduction to marketing reforms. The first attempt along these lines showed up in the various McNary-Haugen bills. The McNary-Haugen movement became the first national effort to address agricultural problems in the postwar era. The movement's catch phrase—"Equality for Agriculture"—resonated with many Texas growers, who supported the program's goal of restoring farmers' purchasing power.

As will be seen, the income goals of McNary-Haugenism would eventually seep into New Deal agricultural policy.

The principles embodied in the McNary-Haugen bills originated with a forceful plow company executive, George Peek, and his aide, Hugh S. Johnson. Soon after Peek became president of the Moline Plow Company of Illinois, the postwar agricultural depression began to affect northern and western grain producers. As grain prices plummeted, so did sales of farm implements, greatly troubling Peek and Johnson. Realizing that "you can't sell a plow to a busted farmer," the pair immediately went to work on a solution that would benefit America's farmers as well as those businesspeople whose livelihoods depended upon selling items to them.[31]

In 1922, Peek and Johnson began publicizing a plan that would eventually serve as the basis of the McNary-Haugen bills. "Equality for Agriculture" soon became the rallying cry for many suffering farmers. As cotton prices declined in 1926, many southern growers and their representatives in Congress also jumped on board.

Peek and Johnson's proposal used a combination of an agricultural tariff and a government-operated surplus-buying corporation to benefit producers of numerous farm commodities. The men suggested the enactment of a high agricultural tariff to block foreign competition, which would, in turn, raise domestic prices. A government corporation would buy surplus commodities not purchased on the domestic market and dump them overseas on the lower-priced world market. To prevent the government from taking any losses on its transactions, an "equalization fee" would be assessed on participating producers. Peek and Johnson anticipated that the increased income generated by domestic sales at the higher, protected prices would more than offset the expenditure of the equalization fee. Overall, the plan sought to boost prices for numerous farm commodities without reducing production. The desired domestic prices were labeled "parity prices"—prices that would give farmers purchasing power for industrial goods to prewar levels, when overproduction and underconsumption were not chronic problems.[32]

The sheer forcefulness of his will drove George Peek to seek acceptance of his plan wherever he could get a hearing—from farm groups, prominent agricultural leaders, and, especially, his many contacts within the halls of Congress. Peek eventually resigned from Moline and devoted all his energy to getting Congress to accept the equality-for-agriculture idea.[33]

Greatly aiding Peek's efforts in Washington was Chester C. Davis, a Montana newspaper editor and the state's agriculture commissioner. In addition to superior debating and lobbying skills, Davis possessed ability in the fine arts of publicity and propaganda that would make him an invaluable lieutenant for Peek in the coming campaign. In Congress, Peek and Davis acquired the key support of Sen. Charles McNary of Oregon and Rep. Gilbert Haugen of Iowa. Both agreed to introduce bills based on Peek's plan. Greatly aided by the endorsement of the American Farm Bureau Federation, the nation's largest farm organization, Peek and Davis next concentrated on getting the votes needed to pass the bills.[34]

Two versions of the McNary-Haugen bill eventually passed each house of Congress—in 1927 and 1928—but Republican president Calvin Coolidge vetoed both measures, citing several objections: that the bills were price-fixing schemes; that the equalization fee was an illegal tax; and that the bills would produce large, burdensome bureaucracies. Gilbert Fite posits, however, that Coolidge based his objections on the belief that the Peek plan would unnecessarily raise the cost of living and the price of raw materials for American industry.[35]

Despite the setbacks, George Peek remained a strong influence in the growing drive to aid American agriculture. Down but not out after President Coolidge's vetoes, Peek (a lifelong Republican) and Chester Davis strongly supported Democrat Al Smith's candidacy for president in 1928. Although Smith gave only tacit approval to the Equality for Agriculture movement's principles, Peek and Davis were determined to resist Republican nominee Herbert Hoover because of his steadfast opposition to the McNary-Haugen bills. Despite Peek's considerable efforts to lure rural Americans to the Democratic candidate, Hoover defeated Smith handily and soon introduced his own plan for improving the lives of American farmers.[36]

Contrary to his popular image, Herbert Hoover was not a rugged individualist unwilling in any way to use the government to aid citizens. Early in his administration, the new president sought to use government resources to help improve the economic position of American agricultural producers. Hoover's approach to the overall agricultural problem stressed cooperative marketing. A strong believer in voluntary cooperation, he wanted to use the federal government's financial resources to help producers form national marketing cooperatives. After establishing the cooperatives, Hoover proposed to reduce government intervention and allow farmers to help themselves through voluntary efforts.[37]

At Hoover's suggestion, Congress passed the Agricultural Marketing Act in June 1929. This measure created the Federal Farm Board, which was authorized to administer a government fund of $500 million, from which farm organizations might borrow for the purpose of supporting agricultural prices. Hoover hoped that cooperatives would aid producers by eliminating the numerous intermediaries from the marketing process who the president believed ate away at farmers' income. The Agricultural Marketing Act also empowered the Farm Board to set up special commodity corporations to help stabilize prices by purchasing and storing any unusual crop surpluses.[38]

With the coming of the Great Depression in late 1929, the Farm Board soon became overwhelmed by the sharp decline in prices and could never function as planned. It established national cooperatives for a host of agricultural commodities, including cotton, but these vehicles provided meager relief for farmers. In 1930, it also established cotton- and wheat-stabilization corporations in a desperate effort to control prices. Mass purchasing by the stabilization organizations succeeded in pegging cotton and wheat prices until 1931, when the corporations exhausted available funds. Prices plummeted again, with cotton soon reaching single digits per pound. After the Farm Board suspended stabilization efforts and began to liquidate some of its holdings, prices slid even further.[39]

The Farm Board's plea to growers to reduce cotton production voluntarily by plowing up every third row fell on deaf ears. Producers in the newer growing areas of Oklahoma and Texas continued to break new soil, as did farmers in the traditional cotton-producing areas of the South, though to a lesser extent. In a disruption of the conventional pattern, growers in the early Depression years added to their planted acreage, despite falling prices, in a desperate effort to make up lost income with increased volume. The result was more overproduction of cotton, decreasing prices, and additional misery for America's cotton farmers.[40]

With the Farm Board's failure and the Depression entering its second year, efforts to convince farmers to cut cotton production by reducing planted acreage resurfaced. The key stimulus came in August 1931, when the USDA's Crop Reporting Board released its forecast for the coming year. The board estimated that American cotton farmers would produce 15,584,000 bales in 1931, the third-largest crop ever. This huge harvest would add to the large carryover of 6,369,000 bales of unconsumed cotton. Panic seized many growers as they faced the prospect of a second consecutive year of single-digit prices.[41]

In response to the rapidly deteriorating economic situation, Huey Long, the bombastic governor of Louisiana, assumed leadership of a radical plan to eliminate the surplus and boost sagging cotton prices by simply ceasing *all* cotton planting in 1932. On August 16, 1931, Long sent telegrams to governors, lieutenant governors, and legislators of the cotton-producing states requesting attendance at a conference to be held in New Orleans on August 21 for the purpose of considering a "cotton holiday" for the next season.[42]

Outside Louisiana, Long's call initially received a cool reception. Only two governors accepted the invitation; the others sent only representatives. Texas governor Ross S. Sterling did not attend, claiming that the declaration of martial law in the oil fields of East Texas occupied all his attention. Sterling sent commissioner of agriculture J. E. McDonald as Texas' official representative.

At the conference, Long promised the delegates that if they supported the plan he would guarantee Louisiana would lead the way as the first state to pass a law prohibiting cotton planting in 1932. The conference overwhelmingly endorsed the Long plan, with an added proviso that any planting holiday law should be binding only when the states collectively producing at least 75 percent of the country's cotton passed similar legislation. The amendment clearly placed the ball in Texas' court. Because the Lone Star State produced one-third of the nation's cotton, all hope for the cotton holiday depended on its acceptance by the Texas State Legislature.[43]

After the Louisiana Legislature passed restrictive legislation, Governor Sterling received great pressure to call a special legislative session. Everyone interested knew that Sterling's actions in the coming days would prove decisive because of Texas' position in the American cotton market. The national press was also aware of the governor's importance, as evidenced by Sterling's appearance on the cover of the September 21, 1931, issue of *Time.* Underneath his portrait, the caption read: "Governor Ross Shaw Sterling: As Texas Goes, So Goes the South." The conservative Sterling believed that the people were "unduly excited" over the drop in cotton prices. Nevertheless, he eventually bowed to the pressure of several mass meetings and called a special session to convene on September 5.[44]

The Texas Legislature considered the proposed cotton holiday bill for ten days, while the impatient Long lobbed verbal assaults at Texas legislators for their deliberate action on the measure. Despite the best efforts of the holiday forces, the power of interested lobbyists and the inherent conservatism of Texas' legislators doomed Long's radical proposal. On September 16, the legislature killed the cotton holiday bill by a vote of 92–38. Less than a week later,

"Every Man Must Get into the Play." *Dallas Morning News* editorial cartoon, November 23, 1931. Reprinted with permission of the *Dallas Morning News*.

however, it passed a more moderate bill limiting cotton acreage in 1932. Known as the Texas Cotton Acreage Control Law, the legislation stated that no person could plant cotton in 1932 and 1933 that exceeded 30 percent of the acreage cultivated during the preceding year. The law also stipulated that farmers could not plant cotton two years in a row on the same acreage after 1933.[45]

As it turned out, the Cotton Acreage Control Law never had a chance to prove its worth as an alternative to Long's holiday plan. A state district judge voided the legislation, stating that the new law violated property rights, posed a threat to free government, and conflicted with the constitutions of Texas and the United States. The legislation died after an appeals court upheld the lower court's ruling. Dying rapidly along with the holiday plan and the Texas Cotton Acreage Control Law was the belief that any significant reduction in the cotton crop could be achieved by the voluntary efforts of farmers or by state government action alone.[46]

The failed efforts of the 1920s coupled with the ongoing depression lessened resistance to federal government intervention on behalf of American farmers. This new attitude led to eventual acceptance of an idea that would become the cornerstone of New Deal agricultural policy—the Voluntary Domestic Allotment Plan. W. J. Spillman, a USDA economist, developed an early version of this scheme during the early 1920s. Spillman intended to give farmers parity prices for the home market, much as the Equality for Agriculture movement had tried to do, but the means of achieving this objective differed sharply from George Peek's proposals. Under the economist's plan, first articulated in a small book published in 1927 entitled *Balancing the Farm Output,* participating producers would receive a "domestic allotment" from the federal government for the portion of their average past production consumed domestically. For their domestic allotment, farmers would receive the parity price through a series of debentures from the federal treasury. Growers would receive only the lower world market price for any crops produced over their allotment. For example, if Americans consumed 75 percent of American-grown cotton domestically, then a farmer who raised an average of 10 bales over a certain base period would be guaranteed the parity price for 7.5 bales but would have to accept the lower, unprotected world price on the remaining 2.5 bales. Although the plan set no production limits, Spillman believed that the lesser price for the nonallotted production would be enough incentive for many farmers to reduce their planted acreage for a variety of crops, including cotton.[47]

Despite Spillman's espousal of the domestic allotment idea, the concept did not gain popularity in agricultural circles until 1929, when Harvard economist John D. Black popularized a version of the plan in his book *Agricultural Reform in the United States.* In this influential work, Black analyzes the depressed agricultural situation and summarizes numerous proposals to solve the problem, including a modified version of Spillman's domestic allotment plan. Although similar in focus to Spillman's plan, Black's version contained a couple of key modifications, such as requiring agricultural processors to pay the guaranteed price for the allotted domestic production rather than using Spillman's treasury debenture system.[48]

Black's work, especially the chapter on Spillman's domestic allotment plan, caught the eye of Milburn Lincoln "M. L." Wilson, a Montana State College agricultural economics professor who was destined to become the guiding force in a national movement for acceptance of the allotment idea. Wilson was born and raised on an Iowa farm and studied farm management at Iowa State

M. L. Wilson—major advocate of the Voluntary Domestic Allotment Plan. USDA photo, National Archives II.

College. He later pursued graduate work at the University of Chicago, Cornell University, and the University of Wisconsin (where he received a master's degree in agricultural economics). After running commercial wheat-farming operations in Nebraska and Montana to test various farm-management theories, Wilson accepted a teaching job at Montana State. Amid the growing national agricultural problems of the mid-1920s, he agreed to head the Farm Management Division of the USDA's new Bureau of Agricultural Economics, responsible for researching and developing more efficient land-use techniques. In 1926, Wilson returned to his post at Montana State to teach and gained notoriety in the agricultural education community by directing a nonprofit educational institution's efforts to put into practice his methods for successful wheat farming.[49]

By the late 1920s, Wilson had begun to reevaluate his belief that efficient management practices were all that American farmers needed to succeed on the land. In 1929, he traveled to the Soviet Union to advise the Russian government on large-scale mechanized agricultural methods. The trip had a profound effect on the professor. He observed firsthand the tremendous potential of developing nations like the Soviet Union to utilize mechanization in

order to exploit huge expanses of land for wheat farming. Wilson returned
to Montana doubting the feasibility of such export-dumping proposals as
McNary-Haugen (which he had previously supported). He began to search
for ways that would enable American wheat growers to reduce production
profitably by concentrating on the domestic market until world trade conditions improved. While in this state of mind, Wilson read John Black's book
and became reacquainted with the domestic allotment idea. As the Depression worsened, Wilson became convinced that only some type of domestic allotment plan could aid American agriculture.[50]

Despite his conversion, Wilson still saw room for improvement of the
allotment idea. With the help of fellow agricultural economist Mordecai Ezekiel, Wilson sought to strengthen the plan's production-control aspects without resorting to coercive government controls. The economists searched for
mechanisms to make the administration of the plan bureaucratically efficient—not an easy task, considering how many Americans were engaged in
farming in the early 1930s.[51]

Wilson and Ezekiel eventually modified the domestic-allotment concept
in three important ways. First, envisioning a self-financing program, they sub-
stituted an excise tax on commodity processors for Spillman's complicated
series of debentures. Second, Wilson supported using referendums as an important means of inducing cooperation on production control while maintaining its voluntary features. Producers for each crop could simply vote on
whether they wanted a limitation program. Farmers who agreed to reduce
their planted acreage would receive benefit payments derived from the processor taxes for an amount geared toward achieving the parity price goal; growers not participating in the program would receive no benefits other than the
anticipated higher crop prices from the reduced supply. Finally, Wilson and
Ezekiel added an important new element regarding administration of the
program at the local level: committees elected by the growers would determine
acreage allotments for each producer at the community level after federal officials decided on total allotments for each county. These local committees
would also be responsible for enforcing adherence to the determined allotments.[52]

The last change reflected the economists' belief in cooperative action and
decentralized control—what Ellis Hawley labels "associationalism." Advocates of an associative state feared the growing impingement of bureaucratic
government on the liberties of Americans in the modern industrial age, yet
they acknowledged that intervention by the federal government might also be

necessary at times to preserve individual liberties. Wilson and Ezekiel believed that they had found a compromise for solving the problems of agriculture: allow the government to formulate a national plan of action, but allow the farmers to administer the plan at the local level. By working in this cooperative fashion with the government, farmers might improve their economic situation without government bureaucrats making direct decisions affecting their lives.

When Wilson and Ezekiel developed their ideas about the administration of the allotment plan, they were certainly thinking of the farming areas with which they were familiar—the relatively egalitarian and democratic corn-, hog-, and wheat-growing regions of the Midwest and the Dakotas—rather than the cotton-growing South. As will be shown in subsequent chapters, after the allotment plan became the basis of the New Deal's agriculture program, the lack of true democracy in the rural areas of Texas (and the South in general) during the 1930s became evident and showed the limitations of this type of administration south of the Mason-Dixon Line. Large landowners dominated the committees and worked consistently against tenant farmer and sharecropper interests in ways never imagined by the northern professors who formulated the plan.[53]

Wilson worked incessantly to promote the allotment plan, gaining converts along the way through correspondence with influential farm and business leaders, as well as politicians of both major parties. He spoke before farm gatherings and business groups and organized well-attended conferences dedicated to discussion of his ideas. In April 1932, he spoke before a large group of national business and farm leaders in Chicago. Although many present agreed with George Peek's negative appraisal and chose to adhere to the McNary-Haugen proposals, others, such as Chester Davis, slowly began to modify their views in favor of production control. Also in attendance was Henry Agard Wallace, editor of the influential farm journal *Wallace's Farmer*. Although a former supporter of the McNary-Haugen bill, Wallace had changed his allegiance to the concept of production control. His assistance would soon prove to be crucial in generating favorable public opinion and political support for acceptance of the production-control concept.[54]

Henry A. Wallace was a third-generation Iowa agriculturalist. His grandfather, the first Henry Wallace, was a legend in Iowa farm circles. The farmer-minister preached the gospel and scientific agricultural principles with equal fervor. His son, Henry Cantwell Wallace, became a professor of agriculture at Iowa State College and gained further notoriety for the family in 1895, when he founded the successful farm journal that would become *Wallace's Farmer*. Henry C. Wallace eventually served as Warren Harding's and Calvin Coolidge's secretary of agriculture and strongly opposed Coolidge's stand on the McNary-Haugen bills until Wallace's death in 1924.[55]

Henry A. Wallace grew up absorbing his father and grandfather's zeal for scientific agricultural practices along with their sense of duty about helping others, especially farmers. He early developed a wide interest in a myriad of agricultural fields, especially corn cultivation. As a student at Iowa State, the young Wallace excelled in agricultural genetics, economics, and statistics. On graduation in 1910, he joined *Wallace's Farmer* as a writer and editor and remained with the family's journal for the next twenty years.

Wallace became a staunch supporter of his father's positions on various issues, particularly the McNary-Haugen legislation. Despite being a lifelong Republican, displeasure with President Coolidge's vetoes led Wallace to join George Peek and other Republicans in supporting Democrat Al Smith for the presidency in 1928. He was never enamored of fellow Iowan Herbert Hoover or his Farm Board and eventually came to believe that only production control could help farmers out of their economic bind. Such thinking ultimately gravitated him toward M. L. Wilson. With Wallace's editorial support and enthusiastic speeches on behalf of the allotment plan, Wilson's drive for acceptance of the allotment idea would be a much easier task.[56]

Fortunately for M. L. Wilson, 1932 was a presidential election year, and the professor would do his best to pressure the nominees of both major parties to accept the allotment idea. In August, the Republicans renominated Herbert Hoover. The president disliked the whole idea of reduced production and refused to support Wilson's plan or anything resembling it. Wilson's only chance for acceptance of his plan would be with the Democrats and their presidential nominee, Franklin D. Roosevelt.[57]

Roosevelt discovered Wilson's Voluntary Domestic Allotment Plan (as the professor formally called his proposal) through Rexford Guy Tugwell, a member of his famous "Brain Trust" of intellectual political advisers. FDR called on Tugwell, a Columbia University economics professor with an interest in the farm problem, to devise a national agricultural program for the candidate. Knowing of the economist's influence with Roosevelt, Wilson invited Tugwell to another Chicago conference on the allotment plan, to be held in June. At the gathering, the brain truster met Wilson and Wallace for the first time. Tugwell soon accepted the plan and promised to arrange a meeting between Wilson and Roosevelt. After the interview, FDR, characteristically, refused to commit himself outright to the allotment plan, but the candidate liked what he heard and soon endorsed production control as a central component of his farm program. Roosevelt asked Wilson to provide a rough draft for a major speech on agriculture that he planned to deliver in the fall.[58]

After Roosevelt's victory in November, support for the allotment plan grew. Because of growing impatience and mounting discontent in the nation's agricultural areas, the president-elect asked Congress to work on a farm bill based on Wilson's allotment plan during its upcoming lame-duck session in January. If the bill failed because of Republican resistance, Roosevelt reasoned, the nation could at least observe the Democrats trying to work on a solution before assuming power in March. In December, following a series of conferences in Washington, several farm organizations, including the American Farm Bureau, sanctioned the allotment idea. With the support of these major farm groups, Marvin Jones (from Amarillo, Texas), the chairman of the House Committee on Agriculture, agreed to sponsor a bill embodying Wilson's ideas.[59]

Under the terms of the Jones bill, farmers of cotton, tobacco, and wheat who proved that they had reduced their acreage by 20 percent would receive "adjustment certificates" from local representatives of the USDA when they marketed their crops. The certificate value would equal the difference between the price being paid to producers at local markets and the prewar parity value of the commodity minus small administrative costs. These vouchers would cover only the portion of the commodity that the secretary of agriculture determined to be required for domestic consumption. Any exportable surplus would not be covered under the program, nor would any farmer receive any of the certificates (funded by a processor tax) if the grower did not signify agreement with the program by reducing planted acreage. The certificates could be redeemed at the United States Treasury or any fiscal agency designated by the secretary of the treasury. Chairman Jones was masterly as he steered the bill through committee hearings and spoke out passionately for the measure on the floor of the House. On January 12, 1933, the bill passed the House by a vote of 203–151, but the Republican-controlled Senate refused to pass any version.[60]

The failed Jones bill signaled the birth of New Deal agricultural policy while marking the emergence of Marvin Jones as an important player in future efforts to help American farmers. Although the measure died in the Senate, its defeat did not doom Wilson's domestic allotment idea. After months of anxious waiting by Texas growers, a bill containing the allotment plan would ultimately pass Congress. The passage of the Agricultural Adjustment

House Agriculture Committee chairman Marvin Jones conferring with President-elect Franklin Roosevelt on the rear platform of Roosevelt's private train, Washington, D.C., January 20, 1933. Marvin Jones Papers. Courtesy of Southwest Collection/Special Collections Library, Texas Tech University, Lubbock.

Act during the first hundred days of the Roosevelt administration culminated the decade-long agitation to boost sagging farm incomes. The only previous federal legislation designed to provide aid for farmers was Hoover's Agricultural Marketing Act, which failed dismally under the crushing weight of the Depression. In early 1933, as Franklin Roosevelt took office and supported a fresh plan for agriculture, no one knew whether the new president's program would suffer the same fate.

CHAPTER 2

CREATION OF THE AGRICULTURAL ADJUSTMENT ADMINISTRATION AND THE 1933 PROGRAM

On May 27, 1933, as the Roosevelt administration undertook its initial efforts to aid southern cotton farmers, the editors of the *Dallas Morning News* raised an important issue:

> One begins to wonder how acreage reduction would be brought about at this late day when the South's cotton crop, excepting the drought sections of the Southwest, is practically planted. . . . If reduction of acreage means plowing up of land already planted, and paying farmers actual cash to do so, such procedure would arouse much opposition, and justly so.

Although a majority of farm leaders and politicians agreed to pursue production control, two months transpired before Congress hammered out a farm bill. Meanwhile, most Texas cotton growers had planted their crops without knowing what the government planned to do for them; they knew only that officials were promising to do *something*. Many producers questioned whether too much time had passed for the Roosevelt administration to begin recovery operations during the current season. The economic and political ramifications would be great, however, if the government waited another full year to act.

Much to the chagrin of the *Morning News* editors, administration officials decided to achieve cotton reduction in 1933 by compensating farmers who agreed to plow up a portion of their crop. Because crop destruction would be completely voluntary, the cooperation of a majority of southern cotton farmers, especially Texas' large number of growers, was essential to the plan's success. The untested nature of the program, along with the great haste of its implementation, was very characteristic of the early New Deal.

Crafting the Farm Bill

President-elect Roosevelt's first action to aid growers was to select a strong secretary of agriculture to lobby for his farm bill and to oversee his administration's recovery efforts. As speculation abounded, three serious contenders emerged. The front-runner seemed to be George Peek. Despite his being highly respected in the agricultural community, Peek's conservative politics and his opposition to the concept of production control seriously handicapped his chances. Another strong candidate with much southern support was Cully Alton Cobb, the editor of *Progressive Farmer and Southern Ruralist*—the South's leading farm journal. Although he strongly supported production limits, the fact that Cobb was a southern Democrat weakened his prospects. Indeed, FDR's eventual choice—Henry Wallace—should be obvious to anyone even remotely trying to understand Franklin Roosevelt (and scholars have been attempting to do this for decades). As David M. Kennedy discerns in *Freedom from Fear,* because Wallace was a progressive Republican from the Midwest who strongly supported the Democratic nominee during the presidential campaign, the scales tilted in his favor. By choosing the Iowa native, Roosevelt was sending a message to traditional Republican growers in the midwestern Farm Belt that he wanted to include them in a new progressive coalition within the Democratic Party.[1]

Soon after his inauguration, the president called Congress into special session to deal quickly with the urgent banking crisis. Although FDR had planned to dismiss the members for several weeks before recalling them to deal with other pressing concerns, Wallace and Rexford Tugwell convinced him to hold Congress in session until it passed emergency farm legislation. Wallace and Tugwell invited agricultural leaders to Washington for an important March 10 conference to discuss the pending farm relief bill.

Because leaders had been debating the nation's agricultural difficulties for over a decade, the philosophical arguments over how to attack the farm problem had largely taken place. Thanks to M. L. Wilson's promotional efforts and the key endorsement of the American Farm Bureau Federation, production control was now the consensus choice for a majority of agricultural experts. Given the great variety of agricultural commodities to be covered under the farm bill, the toughest question before the conference was how the federal government could administer its production-control programs for so many different commodities. The conferees approved a report suggesting that the bill give the secretary of agriculture broad discretionary power to choose among alternative devices (including Wilson's allotment plan) for achieving production control for each commodity. After approving the report's contents, Roosevelt directed Henry Wallace to draft legislation that followed its guidelines.[2]

Over the next few days, administration lawyers quickly constructed the farm bill. Secretary Wallace, Rexford Tugwell, Mordecai Ezekiel (now serving as Wallace's economic adviser), and other administration personnel supervised the drafting. Several congressional leaders provided additional input, including Marvin Jones and Ellison D. Smith of South Carolina (chairman of the Senate Committee on Agriculture). Working around the clock, the lawyers completed the bill in time for Roosevelt to send it to Congress on March 16.

The proposed legislation borrowed from the concept of parity prices first conceived in the McNary-Haugen bills and later incorporated into the Voluntary Domestic Allotment Plan. It stated that the objective of the bill was to "establish and maintain such balance between the production and consumption of agricultural commodities . . . as will reestablish prices to farmers at a level that will give agricultural commodities a purchasing power with respect to articles that farmers buy, equivalent to the purchasing power of agricultural commodities in the base period." The bill specifically defined August 1909 to July 1914 as the base period. Many agricultural spokespersons had previously claimed that this pre–World War I interval was a time of fair exchange between farm products and industrial goods, hence its inclusion in the bill.[3]

The theoretical soul of the proposed legislation was the notion that increased purchasing power in the agricultural sector would be a vital element in producing overall economic recovery. Restoration of farmers' purchasing power, while providing imperative relief for those engaged in agricultural pursuits, would also provide an essential stimulus for industrial production. Thus, by increasing the income of America's agricultural producers, the legislation would be a key element in bringing about general recovery and become a major force in ending the economic depression.

The bill gave the secretary of agriculture wide latitude for achieving its objectives. The most important weapon with regard to cotton was the secretary's ability to enter into voluntary contracts with agricultural producers. These agreements would provide for the reduction of crop acreage and the volume of marketable agricultural goods, or both, for nine agricultural commodities: cotton, wheat, corn, rice, tobacco, cattle, hogs, sheep, and dairy products.[4] The government promised to compensate all cooperating producers who agreed to reduce output. It would fund the program with a tax on the first domestic processing of the enumerated commodities. Agricultural producers could agree not to join the various commodity programs, but they would receive no benefit or rental payments from the fund amassed by the processing taxes. Noncooperators would gain only from the expected increase in price due to the decreased supply caused by the cooperating producers' reduction in output.[5]

The farm bill included an important proviso authorizing the secretary of agriculture to establish producer committees to administer the programs. The bill's authors, borrowing directly from M. L. Wilson's allotment plan, sought to use these farmer committees to monitor compliance with the provisions of the legislation, thereby eliminating the need for a large new bureaucracy at the grass-roots level.

The legislation gave the secretary of agriculture an additional device for inducing cotton reduction during the first year: the so-called Smith Cotton Option Plan. The plan's sponsor was Ellison Smith. "Cotton Ed," as he was commonly known, was a mildly progressive yet thoroughly racist senator from South Carolina who "talked cotton, breathed cotton, and almost ate cotton," as Marvin Jones later recalled. Continuing his constant fight to aid southern cotton farmers, Smith had pushed for his own reduction scheme in the lame-duck Congress after the Jones bill failed.[6]

The option plan provided a means for the faltering Federal Farm Board to dispose of its large holdings of surplus cotton while inducing cotton farmers to restrict future production. Under the plan, the secretary of agriculture would acquire title to all government-controlled cotton and enter into voluntary agreements with growers to reduce their cotton acreage. In return, farmers could buy an amount of government cotton equivalent to the estimated reduced production at a low base price. Because the price was expected to rise as a result of decreased production, farmers could then sell their "option cotton" at the higher price and pocket the difference as compensation for reducing output.[7]

When Roosevelt sent the completed draft of the farm bill to Congress on March 16, he issued a statement urging quick passage: "Deep study and the joint counsel of many points of view have produced a measure which offers great promise of good results. I tell you frankly that it is a new and untrod path, but I tell you with equal frankness that an unprecedented condition calls for the trial of new means to rescue agriculture . . . The proposed legislation is necessary now for the simple reason that the spring crops will soon be planted and if we wait for another month or six weeks the effect on the prices of this year's crops will be wholly lost."[8]

The Farm Bill in Congress

Despite the president's wishes for quick action, Congress deliberated for two months. While House conservatives from both political parties provided boisterous opposition, they could not block its passage. Further delays occurred during Senate deliberations because many pro-farm advocates quibbled over technical details in the legislation. Throughout the lengthy debate, Texas' congressional delegation firmly supported the farm bill, and no Texan proved to be more important to its fate than the House Committee on Agriculture's chairman, Marvin Jones.

During his years in Congress, Jones had abhorred production control plans of any kind, and he felt no different about the proposed new farm measure. Despite growing up on a North-Central Texas farm, he had attended the University of Texas law school and considered himself a lawyer, not an agricultural expert. The congressman tutored himself in agricultural matters only after being appointed as a minority member to the House Committee on Agriculture in 1920. During the 1920s, Jones became an agrarian advocate and supported any measure that coincided with his belief that government could help American agriculture best by encouraging exports. A consistent opponent of high tariffs, he believed that taxing foreign goods entering the domestic market only encouraged retaliation by other nations, thus retarding potential American exports. Jones also opposed export-dumping proposals such as the McNary-Haugen bills, theorizing that they would have a similarly negative impact on foreign trade. Simply stated, in his mind, there was no overproduction problem for American agriculture, only a distribution problem. As long as the world contained hungry mouths to feed and bodies that needed clothing, there were potential markets for American agricultural surpluses.[9]

On receiving the new farm bill from the president, Jones immediately held committee hearings on the proposed legislation. Although he had sponsored a production-control measure during the lame-duck session, he had done so reluctantly, more out of party loyalty than conviction, and probably because he thought it would never pass. The chairman now had it within his power to block the current bill, but he refused.[10]

Jones allowed his committee to report the bill out favorably, despite his doubts about its feasibility. He objected to certain provisions so strongly, however, that he refused to sponsor the measure. He publicly stated his belief that many aspects of the bill were unconstitutional and that he continued to favor aiding farmers by reducing their taxes, lowering tariffs and freight rates, and providing mortgage relief. The debate in one hearing got so heated that he simply walked out on his committee. He then issued a statement to the press reiterating his view that the elements in the farm bill embracing the Voluntary Domestic Allotment Plan and the cotton option were unnecessary. Nevertheless, he felt compelled to make it clear that, despite his personal opinions, he would not block the bill. As the editors of the *Dallas Morning News* correctly determined, his actions were "less a revolt than a refusal to take responsibility." Sponsorship of the bill in the House fell to the committee's second-ranking Democrat, Rep. Hampton Fulmer of South Carolina.[11]

Although he disagreed with many parts of the legislation, Jones did more than simply let the farm bill out of committee. Acting again out of party loyalty, he decided to lead the members of the Texas delegation who supported the bill on the House floor. Most members of the Texas delegation who gave speeches on the measure (Richard M. Kleberg of Corpus Christi, W. D. McFarlane of Graham, Wright Patman of Texarkana, and Hatton Sumners of Dallas) stated that, despite having some reservations, they favored quick passage. In one speech, Jones remarked that in ordinary times he would not support a measure of the kind proposed in the farm bill. The worsening depression, however, convinced him that the president needed the support of Congress to end the economic paralysis. After a quick retelling of his personal preferences for an agricultural relief plan, Jones finally announced:

> That is my program, but I am only one out of 435 members. We have been discussing and trying to secure these things for ten years while agriculture has been languishing. We are in a desperate emergency . . . We are at war, and war is the grimmest business that ever engaged the attention of mankind. While this war is on, I am going to follow the man at the other end of the Avenue, who has the flag in his hand . . . I am in favor of giving these strong powers in this tremendous emer-

gency in accordance with the desires of the President of the United States, and I am going down the line on that, notwithstanding my personal views.[12]

Among the entire Texas House delegation, only at-large representative George B. Terrell of Alto spoke out against the farm bill. Terrell, a former Texas agriculture commissioner, vociferously attacked the measure, stating that "the strongest argument and the only argument that has weight in favor of this bill is the call to arms to follow our leader." Without President Roosevelt's leadership and prestige, the congressman proclaimed, "this bill could not command a corporal's guard." He also objected to the wide power given to the executive branch: "We should stop conferring dictatorial powers upon administrative officers, for when these powers are once conferred they are seldom withdrawn." Despite opposition from Terrell and other conservative representatives, mostly Republicans, the House quickly voted in favor of the farm bill.[13]

Both senators from Texas supported the farm bill. While vigorously supporting the measure, Tom Connally admitted that he did not know whether it would be a success. Nevertheless, he commended Roosevelt for trying something to address the problems of American agriculture. "President Roosevelt at least has offered a program," the senator noted in one speech, "and he is entitled to have that plan have its place in the sun." Morris Sheppard did not speak on the floor of the Senate in support of the legislation, but he joined Connally in voting for the measure. Six weeks after Roosevelt sent the farm bill to Congress, the Senate passed a version of the proposed legislation by a vote of 64–20. Both houses quickly voted in favor of a joint conference committee compromise version.[14]

On May 12, 1933, surrounded by a coterie of congressional and agricultural leaders, President Roosevelt affixed his signature to the farm relief bill, now known formally as the Agricultural Adjustment Act of 1933. In spite of Marvin Jones's refusal to sponsor the bill, FDR acknowledged the agriculture committee chairman's efforts on the House floor by presenting him with one of the pens used to sign the bill into law.[15]

Development of the 1933 Cotton Program

The lengthy congressional deliberations increased the burden on the administration to develop workable commodity programs for the current growing season. The farm act created a new agency within the USDA, the Agricultural

Adjustment Administration (commonly referred to as the AAA or the "Triple-A"), to manage the assorted commodity programs. In less than a month, Secretary Wallace and USDA officials organized the AAA bureaucracy, consulted with farm leaders and agribusiness representatives, and developed programs based on guidelines stated in the new law.

Wallace's first task was to staff the top levels of the AAA hierarchy. Although he was disappointed that FDR had not offered him the agriculture secretary post, George Peek agreed to serve as the AAA's first administrator. At first glance, Peek's appointment would seem to be something of an enigma since he was on record as being strongly opposed to production controls. In addition, his obstinate nature was well known. (Rexford Tugwell might have been too harsh when he wrote in his diary that Peek was "a little stupid but shrewd, like an English squire.") The new administrator continued to prefer the McNary-Haugen formula as the ultimate answer to the farmers' plight; nevertheless, because he was long identified with improving the lot of American agricultural producers, it was felt he could be useful to the administration. Peek could certainly add his prestige and his conservative reputation to the AAA in order to help placate businesspeople and nonprogressive politicians who disapproved of the new agency. FDR simply reasoned that it would be more politically prudent to have him on board as part of the team than as a potential enemy.[16]

Peek also became more acceptable after he began to show signs of accepting the notion that the economic emergency might warrant temporary production controls for some crops. As AAA administrator, however, he did not hesitate to promote another means of achieving parity allowed by the Agricultural Adjustment Act, namely, marketing agreements. Through this mechanism, Peek hoped to negotiate deals between processors and producers of agricultural goods whereby the former would agree to pay higher prices to farmers for goods without the latter having to restrict production (with the price increases being absorbed by consumers). In large part, Peek accepted his new position because he believed that he could convince FDR to focus on marketing agreements rather than production controls. In his tenure as administrator, however, Peek would be greatly disappointed, because Roosevelt and Wallace never saw the situation his way. Expansion of the marketing-agreement device was approved only for tobacco, dairy products, and a few minor commodities.[17]

Peek recruited Chester Davis to head the AAA's important Production Division, which was responsible for overseeing the planning and implemen-

Henry A. Wallace, M. L. Wilson, and Chester Davis confer in Washington. USDA photo, National Archives II.

tation of the agency's various production-control programs. Secretary Wallace heartily approved the choice. Although an ardent supporter of the equality-for-agriculture effort during the 1920s, Davis proved to be more flexible in his thinking than George Peek. Whereas his old mentor still believed in the McNary-Haugen panacea, Davis was now strongly in the production-control camp. To lead the important commodity sections within the Production Division, Peek made two notable selections: M. L. Wilson as head of the Wheat Section, and Cully Cobb as chief of the Cotton Section.[18]

Politically, Cully Cobb proved to be an excellent choice to head the section most important to southern farmers. He was raised on a poor family farm in rural Tennessee and grew up determined to get an education to better his status in life. On the advice of family members, Cobb enrolled in Mississippi A&M College and excelled in the study of agriculture. In 1910, Mississippi

A&M's president recommended Cobb, only two years after graduation, to lead the state's "corn clubs"—the first of many commodity groups for youths that were the forerunners of the modern 4-H clubs. For the next nine years, Cobb headed the corn clubs, developing methods of teaching Mississippi's rural youth proper corn-raising techniques and cost-efficient crop management. He eventually became the Extension Service leader for all rural youth clubs in Mississippi. He left the state in 1919 to serve as editor of the Georgia-based *Southern Ruralist*—a major southern farm journal. Beyond its much higher salary, Cobb saw his new job as an opportunity for greater service to the agricultural community through farm-related journalism.

Throughout the 1920s, Cobb became a well-known and highly respected farm editor. He geared his editorials in the *Southern Ruralist* (which became the *Progressive Farmer and Southern Ruralist* after the two major southern farm papers merged) toward the white small farm owner. Consistent with his Extension Service background, Cobb preached constantly about improving farming methods through scientific techniques. He was a militant supporter of McNary-Haugenism throughout the 1920s. By the early 1930s, however, Cobb had converted to the cause of voluntary acreage reduction. His support of production controls and strong political support in the South guaranteed that he would have an opportunity to serve in a high position within the AAA. Eager for added prestige and completely devoted to the mission of helping southern cotton producers, Cobb welcomed the chance to offer his services in Washington.[19]

To head the AAA's Finance Division, which had responsibility for supervising the financial operations of each commodity program, Peek turned to Oscar Goodbar Johnston, a southern plantation manager highly regarded as an expert in all facets of the cotton business. Johnston was the son of a small-town Mississippi Delta banker. He attended the University of Mississippi, earned a law degree, and returned to the Delta in 1901 to practice law and acquire wealth as a landlord on the region's rich cotton lands. In 1926, Johnston became general counsel for the Delta Pine and Land Company. The British-owned conglomerate operated one of the South's largest cotton plantations, which comprised tens of thousands of prime Delta acres. He soon became the company's president, in charge of managing its lands.

By all accounts, Johnston was a warm, personable gentleman who ran the plantation in an efficient yet paternalistic manner. He acquired a reputation in the southern business community for expertise in all aspects of the cotton business, from farm and labor management to legal and economic matters.

Peek had known Johnston for several years and could not think of anyone more qualified to handle the AAA's complex financial arrangements. Henry Wallace approved the choice because, like him, Johnston had once supported the McNary-Haugen bills but was now a firm believer in acreage reduction. It would be Johnston's responsibility to work out the financial details of a cotton acreage reduction plan based on general outlines provided by the Cotton Section.[20]

Cotton Section officials spent the month following the passage of the Agricultural Adjustment Act hurriedly developing a program for their commodity. Time was crucial, as many cotton farmers had already planted their crops for the year. In some sections of South Texas, such as the Lower Rio Grande Valley, harvest time would arrive in little more than a month.[21]

In the spring of 1933, American cotton farmers faced a truly critical situation. The carryover of unconsumed cotton had reached 12.5 million bales, more than the average annual world consumption of American cotton during the preceding three years. Thus, if cotton producers made even an average crop in 1933, they faced the prospect of record-low prices.[22]

On June 3, Cully Cobb chaired a cotton conference in Washington at which representatives of diverse agricultural interests gave advice to the AAA regarding the pros and cons of reducing cotton acreage in 1933. A majority of the farm organization spokesmen and members of Congress in attendance favored the idea of immediate acreage reduction, even if it meant plowing up growing cotton. Two prominent Texans from businesses geared toward high-volume cotton production—John C. Thompson, president of the Texas Cotton Ginners Association, and Will Clayton of Anderson, Clayton and Company—actively opposed any plan to reduce cotton production, however. Thompson implored the conference to remember those employed by the ginning industry and insisted that a reduction in volume would increase unemployment in the South. Clayton urged restraint regarding any hasty decision to employ "artificial means" to solve the cotton crisis. Reminding the conference that the large surplus of 1921 had dissipated within three years, Clayton concluded: "Those things have a way of settling themselves."[23]

The editors of leading Texas newspapers concurred with Clayton and Thompson's position against any plow-up of growing cotton. As the editors of the *Houston Post* opined:

To plow under a growing cotton crop is on par with "dumping" milk on the highways to create a shortage, and with destroying shipments of vegetables sent to market, in order to bolster prices, while people go hungry in the cities. These practices stand condemned by public sentiment. The popular reaction from plowing under cotton and paying farmers not to cultivate cotton lands, at a time when one-third of the people of the United States lack adequate clothing, and when perhaps more than one-half of the world's population is little less than naked, is certain to be unfavorable. The administration, if it allows the administrators of the farm relief emergency legislation to resort to that action, will invite deserved criticism of itself.[24]

When Will Clayton read this editorial and another from the same day in the *Dallas Morning News,* he telegraphed George Peek to relate that public sentiment in Texas was against a cotton plow-up. Clayton concluded his message by stating: "I am sure you and Secretary Wallace would want to be the last to fall in with an expedient plan of this kind if it is to bring discredit upon President Roosevelt's Administration." When Oscar Johnston read Clayton's telegram, he fired a memo to Peek: "The cotton grower is confronted by an emergency, heroic and extreme measures must be resorted to. There are many critics of any proposal, but few responsible persons willing to offer a solution." Peek replied to Clayton in a more diplomatic fashion, noting that he would appreciate further comments if Clayton, the *Dallas Morning News,* or the *Houston Post* could come up with any "constructive suggestions" for restoring parity prices for cotton.[25]

USDA and AAA officials had, in fact, determined before the first of June that there must be a plow-up of growing cotton. Nevertheless, it still took five weeks from the AAA's inception for Secretary Wallace to declare what the AAA intended to do for America's cotton farmers. On June 19, he finally announced that there would, indeed, be a plow-up campaign to reduce the size of the 1933 crop. Wallace called on farmers to destroy at least ten million acres of growing cotton. Producers who agreed to reduce their 1933 acreage by a minimum of 25 percent but not more than 40 percent (soon raised to 50 percent) would be eligible for government payments derived from excise taxes paid by the processors of cotton goods. Farmers were not under any compulsion to join the program, but noncooperators would benefit only from the expected increase in cotton prices. Growers could utilize land taken out of cotton production for the production of soil-improvement or erosion-preventing crops or food and feed crops for home use.[26]

Cooperating farmers could choose between two plans developed by Oscar Johnston. The "cash-only" plan offered growers cash payments based on a sliding scale corresponding to the average yield of their reduced acreage. Payments under this plan would range from seven dollars per acre (for land averaging at least 100 pounds per acre) to twenty dollars per acre (for land with an average yield of 275 pounds and above per acre).[27]

The Smith Cotton Option Plan provided the basis for the farmers' second choice. Under the "cash-and-option" plan, a grower would receive a cash payment based on the average yield of the reduced acreage, but less than under the cash-only plan (ranging from six dollars per acre to twelve dollars per acre). In addition to the cash payment, the producer would receive an option contract giving him title to a quantity of government-owned cotton equivalent to the amount he had plowed up, for six cents per pound. The secretary of agriculture would agree to sell the producer's option cotton at any time designated by the producer, if the price rose above six cents per pound, subject to certain limitations.[28]

Henry Wallace later wrote that the proposed plow-up was "a shocking commentary on our civilization. I could tolerate it only as a cleaning up of the wreckage from the old days of unbalanced production." Nevertheless, the AAA had finally developed a cotton-reduction plan. Although the plow-up was unprecedented and controversial, hopes were high that it would succeed if executed properly.[29]

The AAA Cotton Plow-up Campaign in Texas

The AAA faced numerous problems in 1933 because of the haste with which it was set up and the simple fact that those involved had no experience whatsoever in the work they were being asked to perform. The agency had to establish itself quickly at the grass-roots level, then educate over a million southern cotton farmers (including a quarter million Texas producers) about the details of the government's plan. The AAA relied strongly on the cooperation of a majority of Texas growers for success. Still, numerous logistical difficulties and the reluctance of some farmers to participate threatened the plow-up with failure. A look at the AAA plow-up campaign in Texas reveals how quickly many relief and recovery agencies during the early New Deal typically had to work and recaptures a pivotal moment in Texas history.

To oversee policy implementation, the AAA was fortunate that the Federal Extension Service already had agents in a majority of southern counties. The Extension Service is a USDA agency created at the turn of the twentieth century to spread information about scientific farming research conducted at the nation's land grant institutions, such as Texas A&M University. By 1933, many county agents had organized producers into local farm bureaus to ease the transfer of information via publications, press releases, mass meetings, and demonstration work.[30]

Cully Cobb wished to tap into this existing network in order to carry out the plow-up. He forcefully argued that the AAA had to use the Extension Service because there was simply no time to organize and train a new field force from scratch. Given many farmers' potential hesitancy, he firmly believed that government officials supervising the plow-up would have to be familiar to the local communities and be in good standing there. In Cobb's opinion, the extension agents met the criteria. He also had a long history of association with many Extension Service and land grant college officials and remained loyal to them. For all these reasons, Cobb did not wish to see a parallel federal organization rising up in the countryside to rival the Extension Service.[31]

Cobb had to overcome the opposition of many USDA officials, especially Rexford Tugwell, now assistant secretary of agriculture, who wanted a new federal field force created to run the plow-up. Tugwell simply did not trust the state extension directors or county agents to get the job done. On one occasion, he walked out of a meeting in Wallace's office after stating that he didn't have "a damned bit of confidence" in any of them. In the end, Tugwell's opinion failed to persuade Wallace. The secretary agreed with his Cotton Section chief that the AAA had to utilize the Extension Service as the field force to supervise the commodity programs, especially the cotton program. With Roosevelt's approval, Wallace drafted the Extension Service to oversee AAA work at the grass-roots level. State extension directors, or extension officials of their choosing, were to direct the AAA within their state while the county agents were placed in charge of operations within their respective county.[32]

Giving aid to southern cotton farmers in 1933 posed an enormous challenge for the Extension Service. Its agents had only a limited time to learn the program, explain it to the farmers, and illustrate its potential benefits for producers. The farmers also needed to be signed up very quickly: Wallace issued a July 8 deadline for ten million cotton acres to be pledged before he would authorize crop destruction to commence. Farms would then have to be inspected, yields estimated, and representative portions of fields selected for plowing. After the plow-up, farms would have to be reinspected to check for compliance before the AAA would approve the distribution of money.[33]

In 1933, Oscar Baker "O. B." Martin, a twenty-year extension work veteran from South Carolina, was serving as the director of the Texas State Extension Service. Martin was not too keen on using his beloved Extension Service to reduce cotton production. When Cobb invited him to a conference of state extension directors in Memphis to discuss the use of extension personnel in AAA activities, Martin replied: "I do not especially like the idea of being the party to carry out the purposes of the conference as stated in your telegram. I am afraid it would bring the Extension Service into ridicule if not disrepute. I regret that matters have taken this particular turn, but there is nothing for me to do except give you a frank expression."[34]

Despite his reluctance, Martin dutifully began to organize the impending campaign before placing his vice-director, Howard "H. H." Williamson, in charge of the actual plow-up campaign in Texas. Martin gave Williamson an extremely important responsibility—not just for the success of the cotton program in Texas, but for the entire South as well. Because Texas' cotton growers farmed two-fifths of all the cotton acreage in the United States, the AAA absolutely depended on a large enlistment of Texas producers, or there would be no cotton program.[35]

The AAA assigned each state a cotton-acreage quota, based on a 30 percent reduction from 1931 production figures. These quotas would serve as a working guide for the Extension forces during the sign-up. As Cobb reminded all state extension directors in a blanket wire, the quotas were "merely for guidance and . . . in no way to limit the campaign" to any minimum or maximum. He stressed that the campaign had to continue in each state until every farmer had the opportunity to join the movement. Based on a 30 percent reduction of the state's estimated 1931 acreage of 14,979,000, the AAA challenged Texas farmers to pledge destruction of 4,493,700 acres of growing cotton. All offers would be irrevocable until July 31. After that date, if the government had not yet accepted their pledges, the farmers could cancel their decision to plow up their cotton.[36]

Following instructions from Washington, H. H. Williamson called Extension Service district meetings to explain to Texas' county agents how the AAA expected them to conduct the cotton campaign. At these gatherings, district leaders informed the agents that they would not be acting alone in implementing the program; they would receive some aid from the vocational teachers who taught agricultural courses in local schools and conducted educational work for adult farmers. Moreover, counties with black county agents, located mainly in the eastern portion of the state, would utilize these extension employees' services to conduct the campaign for African American farmers. The AAA promised funding for temporary assistant county agents in heavy-cotton-production counties, and temporary emergency agents for any counties that did not currently have a county agent.[37]

Although agents were glad to receive reinforcements, major help would also come from control committees of local farmers and citizens. As Cully Cobb wished, district leaders instructed their agents to appoint "men of outstanding ability and integrity and in full sympathy with the program."[38] He expected these county committeemen to be well-known leaders in their respective counties. In fact, Cobb dictated that county agents should include bankers and merchants as well as farmers on the county committees.[39] The county committee's main task would be to assist separate "local committees" consisting of three to five farmers. The local committees would perform the basic tasks of enrolling producers, inspecting farms, and checking compliance.[40] The AAA expected the extension agents and county committeemen to do their best to complete paperwork correctly and to make reasonable estimates of producers' average yield.[41] Following the district meetings, the extension agents returned home to form their county committees. In most cases, the agents appointed willing farmers, but agents in three northwest Texas counties reported that farmers elected their local committees.[42]

The agents and committeemen had from June 26 to July 8 to sign up enough farmers to meet Texas' quota. With the help of the state and local press, the extension agents conducted a publicity barrage to kick off "Cotton Week," as the AAA dubbed the first week of the campaign's educational phase. Although the editors of the state's major newspapers, the *Dallas Morning News* and the *Houston Post,* expressed disapproval of the plow-up campaign, they reluctantly lent support after Cobb ventured to Dallas for a June 22 meeting with Texas and Oklahoma newspaper representatives. In editorials following the conference, the major dailies urged their readers to support the Roosevelt administration's efforts to promote agricultural recovery, no matter how impractical they appeared.[43]

The acreage-reduction program's educational phase focused on meetings of local farmers held in communities throughout southern cotton counties. At these assemblies, growers could learn about the government's offer firsthand and could question the extension agents, county committeemen, and any vocational teachers helping out.[44]

The Extension Service and its allies did their best to promote high attendance at the meetings. Texas extension agents placed news stories in local newspapers to publicize the gatherings. Agriculture commissioner J. E. Mc-

Plow-up campaign publicity. *Terry County Herald,* June 30, 1933.

Donald conducted a highly publicized speaking tour to encourage support for the cotton program.[45] On June 25, President Roosevelt issued a direct appeal to the country's cotton growers:

> The fate of any plan depends upon the support it is given by those who are asked to put it into operation. This program for the cotton producer essentially places the responsibility upon the individual farmer. He and he alone will, in the last analysis, determine whether it shall succeed. This plan offers the cotton producer a practical, definite means to put into immediate application the methods which Congress

has prescribed to improve his situation. I have every confidence that the cotton producer will face the facts and cooperate fully in the reasonable and practical plan that
is proposed.[46]

Because the local meetings were not to commence until June 26, a Mon-
day, many industrious agents apparently made an attempt to spread the AAA
"word" at Sunday religious services. A farm woman who lived in the Newburg
community of Comanche County in North-Central Texas recalled that the
first time she heard about the government's plan to plow up cotton was at
church. The Dallas County agent asked his county committeemen to enlist
the cooperation of pastors and Sunday school teachers to announce the local
meetings. The Negro county agent for Dallas County reported that he can-
vassed five black communities on Sunday, June 25, personally asking local
ministers to announce the educational meetings for the African American
public at church services that day.[47]

A large turnout characterized the local educational meetings throughout
the state. At a majority of these assemblies, few farmers voiced open opposition to the government's plan. Numerous meetings adopted resolutions
supporting the program in principle. But even though the plow-up received
majority approval at the local meetings, most growers did not sign up immediately. The meetings helped spread information about the program and generated publicity and favorable public opinion; however, local committeemen
soon realized that they would have to spend an inordinate amount of time visiting farms to personally invite growers to join the campaign. The sign-up
phase of the campaign proved to be no picnic for the local committeemen.

The county agents and local committeemen faced a number of logistical
problems in conducting the sign-up. Language barriers had to be overcome in
some regions of the state. Many producers had difficulty understanding English, not only Hispanic farmers (mainly in southern Texas), but also many
Czech-speaking growers (primarily in South-Central Texas). Agents served
their needs by selecting local committeemen with the ability to converse in
the farmers' native language. In Atascosa County, the extension agent reported that many of the educational meetings were held entirely in Czech or
Spanish.[48]

The poor roads and distant locations of many farms in the eastern portion
of the state hampered sign-up efforts there. The Freestone County agent, for
example, reported that roads were so bad in the eastern section of the county
that the committeemen had to leave their automobiles behind. They found

themselves riding horses to visit farms and secure contracts, which necessarily delayed their work.[49]

Committeemen working in counties with favorable terrain found themselves hampered by a chronic shortage of government contract forms from Washington. On the second day of the sign-up, H. H. Williamson wired Cobb: "Agents crying out for more contract blanks. What can we tell them?" By July 5, Williamson reported that the clamor for contracts from agents had dropped off, but many counties would not be able to finish inspections by the July 8 deadline due to the lack of adequate supplies of contracts. J. E. McDonald wired George Peek that "practically every section has been badly handicapped because of insufficient supply of contract blanks."[50]

Even while county agents and members of the local committees were overcoming various logistical problems, they faced resistance from many farmers who, for a multitude of reasons, delayed or refused to sign up. Some invoked religious reservations, insisting that to deliberately destroy a part of God's bounty would be a grave sin.[51] Others expressed doubts that the government's current plan, or any government plan, could do anything for them. As the Callahan County agent later reported: "Many men who did not sign up for cotton acreage reduction afterward acknowledged they did not co-operate because they did not believe the government would actually help the farmer. It had never seriously attempted to do so before, so it was no wonder there was a feeling of skepticism among a class of people so disheartened." Many producers even viewed the plow-up as some sort of government trick.[52]

Numerous Texas cotton farmers wished to implement the government's plan, but refused when they disagreed with their local committees on the estimated yield of the acreage they offered up for plowing. Several angered growers addressed complaints directly to officials in Washington. A Gonzales County farmer wrote to Secretary Wallace, charging that his local committeeman grossly underestimated the potential yield of his acreage to be destroyed: "I told him that I know every acker for about 35 years of its yeald, that with favorable weather, and no bolweevel this year, and maybe making cotton from 3 to 5 months to come, that it would be very reasonable for me to say, that I am entitled for 1/3 bale per acker. He wanted to allow me 124 lb. per acker . . . Meantime I have learned that the same man ofered 11 dollars per acker to a neighboring farm that did not everaged as good as mine, and it apeared to me that it was not fair."[53]

President Roosevelt received a letter from a producer accusing his local committee of giving a higher estimate to his neighbors even though the land produced less per acre. As the farmer attested: "Our estmater sure did not give us a fair deal. Mr. Montower is not a good praiser. He has pets. I am sure not sadfied a bit over this . . . If you will put the rit kind of a estermater down here we will all bee treated a like."[54]

Another major difficulty that the agents and committees had to overcome was a speculative rise in the price of cotton. On the day of FDR's inauguration, cotton hovered around six cents per pound, but it reached ten cents on July 1 and showed no signs of leveling off. This price increase certainly hampered the sign-up efforts of the local committees. It took a barrage of AAA publicity in the press and personal cajoling by agents and committeemen to convince many growers to view the price rise as a temporary aberration that would reverse itself if enough farmers did not sign up to permit the plow-up.[55]

At the end of each day during the sign-up, local committeemen delivered piles of completed contracts to the extension agents and the county committees. The agents and committeemen pored over the documents into the late hours, checking for errors and telephoning state extension headquarters at Texas A&M College in College Station to report the number of farmers signed up along with their proposed acreage. Extension personnel relayed this statistical information to the main AAA office in Washington. By July 7, the AAA had received word that southern producers had enrolled only 5,566,169 acres of cotton. It was clear that the July 8 deadline for ten million acres could not be met. Citing the delay in providing the needed forms plus the desire to reach all farmers before making a final decision, Secretary Wallace extended the sign-up period to July 12.[56]

After the second sign-up deadline passed, Cully Cobb reported to Secretary Wallace that the Cotton Section had received pledges to plow up 9 million acres and that he expected a final total of 9.5 million. Based on these results, Cobb recommended that the cotton program be declared operational. On July 14, Wallace announced that the AAA would adopt the cotton plan, but reminded growers that they must wait until they received approval of their contract before they destroyed their cotton.[57]

By July 14, Texas farmers had enrolled 4,190,208 acres of their 4,493,000-acre quota. Ultimately, 252,683 Texas growers pledged 4,350,565 acres for destruction, or 27.1 percent of their total cotton acreage. Although Texas failed to reach its assigned quota of 4,493,000 acres, the formerly skeptical O. B. Martin congratulated the county agents and committeemen on their successful efforts to sign up farmers above the average minimum of 25 percent. "When history assays this remarkable month's work," he noted in a press release, "I believe that the work of the local committeemen will stand out as one of its greatest features and will be used by generations to come to illustrate the practical working of local self-government when it is invoked in earnest to handle a situation." President Roosevelt had equal praise for America's cooperating cotton producers: "The whole hearted response of the cotton growers to the first test of the Administration's program for Agriculture is not only deeply gratifying but is also evidence of an intelligent determination on the part of farmers to take the necessary steps to improve the price and buying power of their products. I wish to offer the forces who are putting the cotton program into effect, my heartiest congratulations upon the initial success achieved and at the same time to urge the farmers that nothing be left undone to make the program completely successful."[58]

AAA officials initially intended to send out individual contract acceptances early enough to allow growers time to plow up their cotton and plant other crops for soil improvement or home use. Because of the delays in receiving the contract offers from the field, however, the original plan had to be changed. On July 18, after a series of meetings among high-level AAA officials, the Cotton Section announced a plan for farmers who wished to plant food or feed crops. These growers could immediately destroy their cotton if they completed special emergency permits provided by their county agents, assuming their county committee had no objection to the offer on their contracts.[59]

The rush of events in Washington that dogged other New Deal efforts in 1933 also created problems for the AAA when the agency experienced further delays in producing and distributing the special permits. In a memo to Chester Davis, Cully Cobb described how the Government Printing Office botched the Cotton Section's order of emergency permits by mailing triplicate forms one section at a time, leading to "utter confusion from one end of the Belt to the other." One week following announcement that emergency blanks would be immediately forthcoming, a number of agents still had not received any forms. As E. A. Miller, Cobb's assistant, explained to H. H. Williamson: "We are in the midst of another madhouse incident to getting forms to the county agents. The usual mix-up has taken place in the mailing room of the printing office and believe me we are hearing it from the country." By the end of July, scattered plowing up of cotton had begun where farmers were able to secure emergency permits from their agents.[60]

Continued favorable growing weather led Secretary Wallace to make another important change. Because of the important sign-up provision that contract pledges were irrevocable only until July 31, he began to fear that the prospects of high yields might convince farmers to change their minds and cancel their contracts. On July 29, in order to forestall the possibility that growers might sever their ties to the program, Wallace announced that the AAA would accept all offers approved by agents and the county committees, except for certain special cases, and authorized farmers to begin plowing up their cotton. On being informed of the blanket acceptance of most remaining contracts, many Texas county agents worked frantically into the early morning hours to ensure that their farmers received written notice by the next day to begin destroying their cotton. After receiving the notices from their county agents at the beginning of August, the majority of farmers throughout Texas undertook the task of burying the portion of their cotton promised in their sign-up contracts. The deadline for the plow-up was subsequently set at August 23.[61]

Most farmers buried their cotton in a timely fashion, but the actual plow-up portion of the campaign was not all smooth sailing. On the Texas-Louisiana border and along the Gulf Coast of Texas, plow-up efforts halted when a series of tropical storms inundated these areas, turning many cotton fields into swamps. H. H. Williamson asked Cully Cobb whether the AAA would make exceptions for flooded-out growers who failed to make the August 23 deadline. Cobb replied that reasonable extensions would be allowed for delays in acreage reduction "in cases of providential hindrance." Commenting on the effect of the Gulf storms on implementation of the plow-up, the county agent for Matagorda County noted: "It slowed up the campaign to such an extent that we were getting no cotton destroyed at all for a stretch of days and weeks, and many farmers finally decided that in order to destroy the cotton they would wade in there and pull it up."[62]

Concerned with the impact of the storms on producers in his border district, Rep. Martin Dies urged Secretary Wallace to allow some farmers to change their contracts so they could substitute hillside land for the more heavily flooded bottomland areas. Wallace informed Dies that it would be impossible to allow any changes to benefit the inundated growers in his district. As it turned out, storm damage in some areas caused many growers to lose all of their crop. Thus, the government plow-up check furnished the only money some two hundred Sabine County farmers received that year.[63]

In some parts of Texas, as apparently occurred in other sections of the South, many reports surfaced concerning delays caused by reluctant mules refusing to trample the cotton stalks. The mules had been conditioned over the years, often by the whip, to avoid what their owners were now asking them to do—pull a plow over the stalks of growing cotton. It took a great effort to coax these animals to believe that their owners would not punish them for changing their traditional practices. The reports of mules refusing to trample over growing cotton plants drew favorable comment from the editors of the *Dallas Morning News,* who had been critical of the plow-up since it began. The actions of the mules, the editors quipped, meant simply that they were "just showing ordinary horse sense."[64]

The campaign in Texas also came up against human hesitancy when some producers refused to plow up their cotton even though they had contracted to do so. Those declining to destroy cotton on their contracted acreage were served with a court order to bury their crop immediately. If they still refused to comply, as did one Panhandle farmer in Collingsworth County, the local sheriff sent a man with a tractor to destroy the cotton. The grower then had the expense of the plowing deducted from his check.[65]

After farmers completed their plow-up, local committees again took to the field, this time to inspect how well producers had complied with the crop-destruction instructions. Some growers had to plow their fields several times to satisfy local committeemen. Once their efforts were approved, farmers signed a compliance sheet, which local committees sent to the extension agent and county committee to be checked, signed, and forwarded to Washington. Then began what one agent described as the "long and weary, yet hopeful vigil" as growers waited for their plow-up checks to arrive.[66]

A long time passed before most Texas farmers received their payment. The delay, caused by the sheer volume of contracts (over one million) flooding Washington at the same time, made producers both anxious and angry. To a great extent, the AAA brought this wrath on itself. The growers were not being presumptuous in demanding prompt delivery of their checks; they had been told since the first day of the campaign that they would receive quick payment.

The AAA reinforced the expectation of speedy compensation by arranging an elaborate event when the first southern farmer, William E. Morris of Nueces County, Texas, received his cotton check. Morris, surrounded by Henry Wallace, Cully Cobb, Marvin Jones, Cotton Ed Smith, Cong. Richard Kleberg of Corpus Christi, and Texas Extension Service representative E. R. Eudaly, received his plow-up reimbursement from President Roosevelt at a White House ceremony on July 28, just as the cotton plow-up commenced in

President Franklin D. Roosevelt presenting the first AAA plow-up check to Texas grower William Morris, July 28, 1933. Behind Roosevelt and Morris *(from left to right):* House Agriculture Committee chairman Marvin Jones; AAA Cotton Division head Cully Cobb; Texas Agricultural Extension Service representative E. R. Eudaly; Texas representative Richard Kleberg; and Secretary of Agriculture Henry A. Wallace. Courtesy Franklin D. Roosevelt Presidential Library, Hyde Park, N.Y.

most parts of the South. At this same event, reporters quoted Cully Cobb as saying that plow-up checks would start going out to Texas growers early the following week.[67]

When farmers failed to receive swift compensation, many did not hesitate to contact their county agent to share their dissatisfaction. The extension agents' most common complaint regarding the plow-up program in their annual narrative reports is the length of time it took the government to send the checks and the fact that the agents had to take the heat for the delay.[68] The extension agent from Mason County made the most succinct appraisal of the correlation between the anger of farmers at the government delay and AAA publicity efforts when he complained that "[the farmers'] expectations are very much advanced by publicity appearing in the state papers far ahead of the actual doing of the things. This kind of publicity, and it only has done more to make the farmer lose faith with the program than anything else, would not be nearly so disappointing if the farmer were not made to believe through such publicity that he was to receive his compensation *immediately* after reading such statements in the papers. This idea alone does more to deceive the farmer than any other part of the A.A.A. program."[69]

Anxiety over delays in check disbursement multiplied when cotton prices began to plummet in early August, after a USDA crop forecast predicted that southern farmers, despite the plow-up, would harvest another huge crop (12.3 million bales) because of favorable growing weather. Although cotton prices remained higher on Texas spot markets than at the beginning of the growing season (near 8.25 cents per pound in mid-August as opposed to six cents in February), producers paid increasingly higher prices for factory items as a result of the National Recovery Administration's efforts to generate industrial recovery. Thus, growers were suffering from another price-cost squeeze that threatened to reduce their purchasing power greatly. A wave of protest rose up simultaneously in the countryside, especially in rural Texas, as farmers demanded action to stop the erosion of crop prices. Roosevelt's popularity in Texas began to plunge with the declining price of cotton. As Rep. Morgan Sanders confided to fellow Texas congressman Sam Rayburn: "With the price of everything that the farmer has to buy going up and his cotton coming down, you know the result. Sentiment down here is changing very rapidly and unless something is done in a few more days they will be hating [Roosevelt] as much as they loved him a few months ago. I have never seen sentiment change so fast against any one."[70]

The Roosevelt administration received tremendous pressure from Texans and their congressmen to support a myriad of proposals for increasing cotton prices. Some called for an additional 15 percent to 20 percent reduction of the current crop.[71] J. E. McDonald backed an effort to compel the War Department to purchase and stockpile two million bales as "war supplies" in order to keep the cotton off the market.[72] The Texas House of Representatives supported another McDonald request for the administration to mandate a minimum sixteen-cent price for cotton.[73] Some Texans even agreed with Alabama senator John H. Bankhead's proposal to restrict the amount of cotton that could be ginned.[74]

The movement for currency inflation, however, proved to be the proposal with the greatest support in Texas and the rest of the South. In mid-September, Cotton Ed Smith presided over a conference in Washington, D.C., attended by over two hundred farm leaders, local officials, and southern members of Congress united in their support for monetary expansion. After the assembly passed resolutions asking for currency inflation, Roosevelt agreed to meet with Senator Bankhead and other conference leaders to discuss the deteriorating cotton price situation.[75]

Before his meeting with the conference delegation, the president polled his advisers for alternatives to inflation as a means of halting the cotton price collapse. Oscar Johnston eventually sold him on a plan to have the federal government provide price-support loans to growers at a rate of ten cents per pound. Under his proposal, producers who agreed to sign up for the government's next cotton-reduction program (still under development) would receive loans to pay for storage of their cotton in government-approved warehouses. The advances would be "non-recourse loans," meaning that farmers could not lose even if prices remained below ten cents per pound. The grower would simply relinquish title to the cotton used as collateral and keep the money lent by the government. If prices rose above the loan rate, as Johnston assumed would happen, the farmer could then pay off the loan (with nominal interest) and pocket the difference. If successful, the plan would encourage cotton prices to rise by inducing many producers to hold their cotton off the market instead of selling their crop in a glutted market. At the very least, the plan would in effect set a minimum price for cotton at ten cents per pound since large numbers of growers would accept the government's offer rather than sell for less than the loan amount. It also served as a strong incentive for producers to pledge compliance with the government's next acreage-reduction efforts.[76]

On September 22, the day after meeting with Senator Bankhead and his entourage, Roosevelt announced that his administration would give growers an opportunity to secure an advance of ten cents per pound on their present crop without liability if they agreed to join the AAA's next acreage-reduction program. On October 16, the president created the Commodity Credit Corporation (CCC) by executive order to handle cotton loans and possible advances for other commodities.

The Texas press reacted favorably to Roosevelt's actions. A *Dallas Morning News* editorial appearing after the establishment of the CCC was typical: "This new policy is against the theory that Government should stay out of business as well as against the theory of good banking, but it is justified under the circumstances, nevertheless . . . The only criticism that can be made of the Government in the matter of the cotton loans is that action was not taken earlier." The presidential edict produced immediate results: cotton prices rose above ten cents per pound, the inflationary forces had the wind cut from their sails, and Roosevelt's growing reputation as a man of action continued.[77]

"Well, Well Stranger." *Dallas Morning News* editorial cartoon, July 23, 1933. Reprinted with permission of the *Dallas Morning News.*

FDR's popularity received a further boost when the long-awaited plow-up checks began to arrive at county agents' offices. Still, the checks did not come in fast enough for many farmers. Although the first payments began trickling in the first week of September, by the beginning of the fourth week of that month fewer than 9 percent of Texas producers had received their checks. By the second week of October, about 44 percent had been reimbursed. As late as the fourth week of October, the AAA had paid only 70 percent of Texas cotton growers. Feeling the heat from their constituents, Texas congressmen continued to bombard Secretary Wallace and Cotton Section officials with letters and telegrams urging swift delivery of checks. As Rep. Morgan Sanders reminded Wallace: "When the farmers of this country plowed up their cotton, they did so with the understanding that the government would pay them."[78] Despite congressional prodding, some growers did not get paid until November, December, or even the early months of 1934.[79]

Mixed Results

The 1933 cotton program produced both winners and losers. On the positive side, the plow-up clearly helped large numbers of Texas farmers, especially landowners. It maintained the price of cotton above ten cents per pound, and by the end of 1933, Texas producers had received $42,970,646.63 in cash for their destroyed cotton and 738,095 bales of option cotton.[80]

Although the plow-up money did not generate complete economic recovery, the additional cash did much to provide immediate relief to hundreds of thousands of Texas cotton growers and local merchants. For the first time in years, many farmers paid off debts and back taxes and purchased numerous other items that they had not been able to afford since the Depression began. Most of the extension agents elaborated on the many ways this money and the higher price of cotton made a real difference to cotton-growing families, not just economically, but psychologically as well. The money restored hope and produced in many farmers an improved attitude toward the government.[81]

The plow-up campaign was also a tremendous benefit for the Texas Extension Service, though the added duties and pressures of conducting the campaign, in addition to (or, as was often the case, instead of) performing normal extension work, rankled many agents. Indeed, in 1933, thirty-two county agents resigned or retired rather than oversee the campaign. In describing the heavy load that the remaining agents had to carry, O. B. Martin cited statistics in his annual report demonstrating that the Texas county agents who stayed on the job performed, on average, 300 farm visits, received 2,300 office calls, wrote 700 individual letters, issued 103 circulars, and wrote 30 publicity stories for local newspapers. Many agents put in eighteen-hour days and gave up their Sundays to perform AAA work. With this added burden, there should be no wonder that the vast majority of county agents reported that the cotton-reduction campaign took up most of their time, allowing very little for their normal extension duties.[82]

It would be a mistake, however, to conclude that most county agents viewed their added responsibilities as a burden devoid of any positive attributes. In fact, a great number of county agents actually viewed their AAA duties as something that could greatly aid their normal extension work. Numerous agents reported how the cotton-reduction campaign allowed them access to farmers who were formerly hard to reach. One agent frankly admitted that cotton meetings offered an ideal opportunity "to get in a wedge" to open up lines of communication regarding regular extension work.[83]

In the early years of the Depression, many counties, seeing the county agents as a frivolous expense in trying economic times, had begun to cut their funding. The county agents' work in the AAA cotton plow-up campaign, in addition to engendering pride in a job well done, helped restore the value of the Extension Service in the eyes of the public. As the agent for a county on the North-Central Texas plains wrote: "It has been a real source for reflection as far as the county agent is concerned. In addition to knowing that he has earned his salary, he feels that he is contributing something to the county and especially to the farming people of Baylor County. The experience gained by this agent cannot be measured in dollars and cents. It is hoped that this agent has established in no small measure in the minds of farmers and general public that the Extension Service of Texas and United States can measure up to any responsibility that is placed upon it."[84]

The plow-up campaign did have some losers. The most noticeable were a sizable number of tenant farmers and sharecroppers who received little reward from the program. Many tenants and croppers wrote to the AAA and their representatives to complain that even though they supported the government's plan, they could not sign up because of their landlord's stubbornness— either the proprietor would not let them destroy their cotton or the landlord demanded a larger portion of the benefits from the plow-up than the normal crop division. Although not against AAA regulations, the latter attempt by many landlords upset so many renters that they would not sign under those conditions.[85]

Many tenants and sharecroppers who did participate in the plow-up were outraged when the government checks arrived. Under terms of the cotton contract, the renter and the landlord were supposed to agree when they signed the plow-up pledges how they would divide the payment, though the AAA assumed that they would prorate the government funds on the basis of each party's interest in the crop. When the checks (made out jointly to producer and lienholder, in most cases) were delivered, however, many landlords forced their tenants and sharecroppers to sign over a portion or all of their proceeds.[86]

A. A. Allison, a special AAA inspector for Texas, received numerous complaints from tenants and sharecroppers wronged by their landlords, especially from the Brazos River bottomland area. Allison sent several reports to the Cotton Section in the latter part of 1933 to alert it to a "scandalous situation" existing in the Brazos Valley. He insisted that "something should be done to protect the weak and ignorant from the greed and imposition of stronger and cunning fellows."[87]

In one report, Allison forwarded a letter originally addressed to Gov. Miriam Ferguson from a Mexican tenant farmer. The inspector scribbled a note to Cully Cobb in the margin of the accompanying letter from the governor's secretary: "Mr. Cobb. I have gotten many of such complaints from the Brazos Bottom plantation area, where a near-peonage condition exists. It is lamentable. Something ought to be done to see that cotton benefits reach them."[88]

In another report written in response to a letter addressed to the governor by an anonymous tenant, Allison cited the case as just another example of a larger problem. "Unless some action is taken by the department to expose and correct the situation," the inspector noted, "gross injustice will continue . . . It is the duty of the department to see that monies it pays reaches those it designates as rightly entitled to it." The response to Allison's report, penned by Cobb's assistant, E. A. Miller, gives a very telling summation of the AAA's overall response to the division-of-payments problem: "We realize that in some instances avaricious landlords may be taking advantage of ignorant tenants. You know that it is the desire of the Department of Agriculture that an equitable distribution of the benefit checks be made to all interested persons. We regret that there is no signature in the case of the letter enclosed. If you will be kind enough to give us a list of the Counties in the Brazos Valley in which injustice is probably being done, *we should be glad to take the matter up with the local authorities* and use our good offices in every way possible to bring about a fair treatment to all concerned."[89]

In other words, if any help arrived for wronged tenant farmers, it would come from such local officials as the county agents and committees. The problem for the tenants was that the appeals process involved county committeemen, who often sided with the landlords (many times, the committeemen were landlords themselves), and, as Allison noted, "big operators" often had county agents "afraid to advise tenants on their rights" regarding the distribution of payments. As will be seen, failure to be duly compensated in the plow-up was just the beginning of the problems that many tenants and croppers would experience under the AAA cotton programs.[90]

Despite the inadequacies noted above, the 1933 AAA plow-up campaign and the entire cotton program were truly landmark accomplishments in the grand scheme of Texas and American agricultural history. Before the New Deal, numerous efforts to improve the economic conditions of America's cotton producers, with or without the intervention of the federal government, had been found wanting. These plans failed either because they neglected to address the necessity of decreasing production, or, if reductions were considered, they did not recognize the caveat of crop controls under the auspices of federal government supervision. Before the creation of the Agricultural Adjustment Administration, American growers were unable to unite as a group on a grand scale to cooperate with the federal government to improve their condition. The overall positive results of the AAA's inaugural season inspired great optimism among a large number of Texans. Many began to believe that the new Roosevelt administration, with the assistance of the farmers themselves, could help free the state's growers from the demoralizing grip of the Great Depression.

CHAPTER 3

THE RISE OF COMPULSORY CONTROL, 1934–35

The 1934–35 period was crucial for the AAA cotton programs in Texas. Of immediate importance, the AAA faced increasing pressure from cotton farmers wishing to change the voluntary nature of the programs by punishing noncooperating producers. A growing number of cooperators in Texas and other southern states complained that noncooperators were able to plant all the acreage they wished under the current system. This allowed those who refused to collaborate to earn more from increased cotton prices than those who received government checks to grow less. Many participating growers hoped that the government would somehow force cooperation with the 1934 program. As the extension agent for Comal County, Texas, commented: "There is a concerted demand among our farmers that some means be formulated by which those who cooperate in this campaign will have some definite and tangible advantage in the market next year over those who refuse to do so, and by staying out take undue advantage of their neighbors and fellow farmers." Such thinking, however, was counter to the desires of most Roosevelt administration officials, who believed strongly in maintaining the principle of voluntary participation. Nevertheless, the sentiment for compulsory participation was building, and FDR had already showed adeptness at changing positions on issues if the political rewards merited a switch.[1]

The AAA also had to contend with processors and handlers of agricultural products who, through the federal court system, sought to end the AAA experiment completely. Most Texas producers resisted volume-oriented businesses' efforts to end the commodity programs. Many even joined a spirited farmers' march on Washington, D.C., that was organized in Texas during the spring of 1935 to show continued support for the AAA. At the end of the 1935 growing season, Texans anxiously waited for a critical Supreme Court decision on the constitutionality of the Agricultural Adjustment Act. If the Court ruled against the AAA, many producers wondered what else the New Deal could do to rescue them from the chaos of the Great Depression.

Plans for 1934

Despite growing producer outcry for compulsory participation, the Roosevelt administration planned to keep the cotton program voluntary for the 1934 season. In August 1933, Oscar Johnston crafted a preliminary outline for a new cotton-reduction plan that Henry Wallace and AAA officials accepted after consultation with state Extension Service directors. In order to gauge the reaction of the public involved in agriculture, the AAA announced three regional meetings to be held simultaneously in Atlanta, Dallas, and Memphis in early September.[2]

On September 5, over six hundred farmers, members of Congress, state commissioners of agriculture, ginners, handlers, processors, county committeemen, and county agents from Arkansas, Louisiana, Oklahoma, and Texas packed the Crystal Ballroom of the Baker Hotel in Dallas to hear Cully Cobb describe the proposed cotton plan for 1934. Texas agriculture commissioner J. E. McDonald opened the meeting by introducing Cobb, who began his remarks by praising the county agents in attendance for their services in the ongoing plow-up campaign. After reviewing the cotton situation before the AAA and lauding the Roosevelt administration's efforts to aid cotton farmers, he proceeded to outline the principles of the Cotton Section's tentative plan.[3]

Cobb proposed a two-year program. Rather than paying farmers to plow up growing cotton, the government would now rent land from producers before they planted and continue to compensate them through a tax on processors. For 1934, the AAA asked growers to reduce their acreage by 40 percent from their average planted acreage over the 1928–32 base period. For 1935, the AAA requested only a 25 percent acreage cut. Each state and county were to receive an acreage allotment based on its base-period average, further subdivided for individual producers. The AAA planned to retain the committee system. The county committees would determine each farmer's individual share of the county allotment and estimate each grower's average yield. Producers were to receive rental payments in three installments for the acreage they took out of production, timed to provide aid at planting time, picking time, and during the winter season. In addition, those who signed contracts were to receive an unspecified bonus "parity payment" for the amount of their crop consumed in the domestic market. After lengthy discussion, those in attendance at the Dallas meeting accepted the plan and passed resolutions urging its adoption by the AAA. The conferees at the Atlanta and Memphis meetings also endorsed the government's proposal.[4]

Cobb returned to Washington and reported the favorable response to Henry Wallace and Chester Davis. The Cotton Section soon began work on a draft of the new contract, with attorney Alger Hiss of the AAA Legal Division providing legal counsel and Oscar Johnston acting as general adviser.[5]

On November 29, the AAA finally announced the official 1934-35 cotton program. Rental payments were to be made at a flat rate of 3.5 cents per pound for all estimated yields greater than one hundred pounds per acre, up to a maximum of $18 per acre. To qualify for the subsidies, farmers were to reduce their planted acreage by 35 percent to 45 percent of the average planted acreage during the base period. The AAA simplified distribution of the rental payments to two equal installments, with the first premium to arrive between March 1 and April 30, and the second disbursement between August 1 and September 30. The bonus parity payment, set at one cent per pound on each farmer's "domestic allotment" (defined for 1934 as 40 percent of the farmer's average yield), would come in December. On the rented acreage, farmers could produce food or feed crops for home use only.[6]

Landlords were to receive the bulk of the government money under the new plan. Although they and their tenants and sharecroppers had divided payments during the emergency plow-up according to their relative interest in the crop, Cobb and Johnston altered the arrangement for the 1934–35 program in two major ways. First, only landowners, cash tenants, and "managing share tenants" (the latter category to be determined by the county committees) could sign a cotton contract for the 1934–35 growing season. Second, landowners and cash renters were to receive all rental benefits; managing share tenants were to receive half of that amount. Sharecroppers and farmers identified by county committees as "non-managing share tenants" were to receive no rental benefits and only a portion of the parity payments equal to their interest in the crop.[7]

Cobb and Johnston used two interesting premises to justify the new, unbalanced payment schedule. First, both men firmly believed that the bulk of the payments should go with the land. They felt, reasonably enough, that land-owners suffered tax burdens and upkeep costs unknown to tenants and share-croppers, thus the additional money would help relieve their extra hardship.

Their second assumption merits reevaluation. Both felt strongly that the AAA needed solid landlord support for the new program to be successful. If landlords refused to sign up because they disagreed with the division-of-payment provisions, there would be no program. This was all true enough, but the thought of observing the issue from the opposite perspective, by dic-tating to the landlords a cotton contract with a more equitable payment schedule and forcing them to "take it or leave it," was never seriously consid-ered. Not only would such an action have been a bad move politically, but it also would have been very much against the ingrained prolandlord bias of both men. Cobb, raised in the rural South to respect local elites, possessed this trait from an early age; Johnston *was* a landlord. The background of both men and their conservative nature invariably led them to analyze matters through the landlord's prism.[8]

Although scholars who disparage the AAA often cite the inequitable bal-ance of payments of the 1934–35 cotton program, some have noted that share-croppers and nonmanaging share tenants could gain financially from the new plan. For example, David Conrad, while strongly criticizing the cotton pro-gram's division of payments in his acclaimed book *The Forgotten Farmers,* nev-ertheless concedes that sharecroppers and nonmanaging share tenants who remained on the land and were dealt with fairly by their landlords were helped by the program, albeit nominally. Due to the sizable increase in cotton prices caused by the decreased supply, tenants and croppers still earned more cash than if there had been no government program.[9]

Some Texas tenants and sharecroppers desiring to keep the equitable divi-sion of payments they had enjoyed under the plow-up petitioned the admin-istration for changes in the contract. One Dawson County tenant group, or-ganized "to secure justice," demanded that the new contract contain the same division of payments as during the plow-up, so they could receive "the usual division of all moneys derived from the leasing of cotton acreage taken out of production." Cully Cobb responded to the petition by insisting that the ten-ant received ample consideration during contract deliberations, certainly a questionable assertion. He concluded by reaffirming the program's monetary benefits for tenants: "We believe that when you have had opportunity of read-ing the 1934–35 contract you will agree that it gives generous financial benefits to both landlord and tenant, and that the tenant is given ample protection."[10]

The word "protection" in Cobb's statement refers to the AAA's ability to ensure that landlords did not evict unneeded tenants and sharecroppers in order to acquire all of the government payments. In hindsight, his promise was a highly debatable claim. Historians have long noted and criticized the following provision of the 1934–35 cotton contract designed to prevent the widespread displacement of farm laborers:

> The producer shall endeavor in good faith to bring about a reduction of acreage contemplated in this contract in such a manner as to cause the least possible amount of labor, economic, and social disturbance, and to this end, *insofar as possible,* he shall effect the acreage reduction as nearly ratable as practicable among the tenants on this farm; shall, *insofar as possible,* maintain on this farm the normal number of tenants and other employees; shall permit all tenants to continue in the occupancy of their houses on this farm, rent free, for the years 1934 and 1935, respectively (*unless any such tenant shall so conduct himself as to become a nuisance or menace to the welfare of the producer*).[11]

This flimsy proviso elicits a stern but accurate judgment from David Conrad: "The paragraph was full of good wishes for the tenants, but it was purposely made unenforceable by qualifying provisions." Cobb and Johnston instructed Alger Hiss (over his objections) to formulate the provision in such a way as to place a *moral responsibility* on the landlords, but certainly in no way to make it a *legal obligation.* The phrasing reflected a combination of paternalism and wishful thinking by Cobb and Johnston. As they believed about the division-of-payments provision, the two officials were convinced that landlords would not sign a contract that dictated any aspect of landlord-tenant relations. The thought of including such terms did not garner serious attention. The failure of the AAA to enforce the "protective provisions" of the cotton contracts regarding evictions would contribute greatly to widespread tenant and sharecropper displacement in the South, especially Texas, during the 1930s.[12]

Tenants were not the only class of farmers initially critical of the new program. Secretary Wallace and the AAA received numerous complaints from Texas farm owners, many of whom displayed dissatisfaction with the projected five-year base period (1928–32). They warned that a base period would result in penalizing farmers who either voluntarily reduced their cotton acreage during the base period or suffered from harsh weather sometime during that period. AAA officials responded by stating that they had tested various combinations to determine the base period and had concluded that the

1928–32 interval was the fairest to most individual farmers and to most sections of the Cotton Belt, though it would not be equitable in many cases.[13]

Before the 1934 program got under way, the AAA experienced an important reorganization when George Peek resigned as head administrator. Never an advocate of production controls, Peek clashed constantly with Secretary Wallace throughout 1933 over policy and authority issues. FDR created the position of special adviser on foreign trade for Peek and urged him to accept it. In his new position, Peek was charged with the responsibility of collecting trade data and helping American businesses export their products abroad. Production Division chief Chester Davis succeeded Peek as the AAA's head administrator on December 15. Davis's first official duty was to announce that the sign-up campaign for the new cotton program would begin January 1, 1934. The goal for Texas committeemen and the Extension Service was 6.42 million cotton acres by the January 31 deadline.[14]

For the 1934–35 program, the AAA attempted to solidify the organizational system at the local level. Officials considered it advisable to retain a large number of experienced committeemen while working gradually toward the election of all committee members. Beginning in 1934, the AAA instructed extension agents to assemble "production control associations" from among contract signers in each county. These associations were designated as the agency in charge of carrying out the provisions of the Agricultural Adjustment Act locally. The AAA further directed county agents to appoint as "charter members" those producers who had served as committeemen during the plow-up and had signed a 1934–35 contract. Charter members were to elect the new county committees from their own number. The AAA advised extension agents and the county committees to divide their counties into areas of approximately three hundred farmers each and to appoint three charter members to serve on each local committee. Only charter members could vote to fill vacancies on the county committees, but all farmers in the production associations could now elect local committee replacements. Although the revised framework represented a slight democratization of the committee system, the changes did little to remove power from the hands of elites, who maintained control of the cotton program at the local level.[15]

Texas county agents generally followed the committee-selection procedure laid down by the AAA, but some noted deviations in their annual reports. The Duval County agent reported that he personally selected all the county committeemen, while agents from Cameron, Hockley, Jones, and Lubbock counties noted that farmers elected all the members of their local committees.

Meanwhile, the agents of both Howard and Scurry counties reported that they appointed all county and local committeemen to start the new campaign, then allowed the producers to elect new local committee members after completion of the sign-up.[16]

A group of South Texas farmers residing in Jim Wells County, none of whom were charter members, voiced their displeasure with the AAA for not allowing them to choose their own committeemen. This group of forty-four Orange Grove producers wrote the Cotton Section to request permission to choose their own county committeemen. One of the farmers attached a letter to the petition expressing his view that the growers were "entitled to such representation as will assure us that our interests and rights will be protected from biased and faulty decisions." The farmer reminded the Cotton Section that the AAA allowed other commodity producers to select members of their county committees: "You gave it to the wheat farmers so why can't you give it to us?" He also criticized his local county agent: "You must realize that from among a group of some 150 county agents in this state that some are inclined to be bigoted, selfish and politically enwrapped and what recourse has the participant in a cotton acreage reduction contract?" E. A. Miller, assistant to Cully Cobb, replied by merely reviewing the procedure laid down by the Cotton Section and stating that the county agent appeared to have followed his instructions in setting up the county organizational structure.[17]

Soon after extension agents organized the producer associations and committees, Texas county and local committeemen attended educational meetings to learn the procedure for implementing the new government program. After receiving their own crash course, local committees held educational meetings for growers in their communities, much as they had done for the plow-up during the previous year, and then solicited farmers to sign the cotton contracts.[18]

The 1934 Sign-up Campaign

Early in the new year's sign-up campaign, H. H. Williamson wrote Cully Cobb to express his opinion that the task of enlisting farmers would present no trouble for the AAA. He stated confidently: "The program will go over in Texas if it goes over anywhere." As the campaign commenced, however, two major problems developed to hinder progress in Texas. These difficulties derived from points of contention in the cotton contract over definition of the phrase "managing share tenant," as well as the minimum-yield requirement of one hundred pounds per acre for all potential contract signers.[19]

Tenants in many parts of Texas argued that they qualified as "managing share tenants." The cotton contract loosely defined managing share tenants as those who provided all the work stock, equipment, and labor necessary to produce the crop, and who also "managed" operations on their farms. This last caveat created the difficulty. Many tenants believed they qualified as managing tenants and thus deserved to sign the cotton contract and receive one-half of the rental payments. But Cotton Section officials, who considered committeemen to be the best judges of local conditions, deferred to them. The committee members, in turn, often sided with landowners, who insisted that their tenants were nonmanagers. As a result, many tenants initially refused to cooperate with their landlords in arranging to put out a new crop. Sensing potential danger to the sign-up, the editors of the *Dallas Morning News* implored both the landlords and their tenants "not to jeopardize the interests of 6,000,000 cotton farmers because of selfish motives . . . No time should be lost for landlords and tenant farmers to reach an understanding for their own and the State's welfare."[20]

The minimum acceptable yield provision of one hundred pounds per acre caused even more concern in Texas because it restricted the ability of tens of thousands of willing farmers to sign a cotton contract.[21] Throughout January, Texans barraged the AAA with requests to lower the minimum permissible yield. Many growers organized meetings then fired off petitions to their congressmen and the AAA calling for reductions in the minimum-yield limit. A local committee from Wolfe City urged Rep. Sam Rayburn to push for a reduction in the minimum yield to fifty pounds per acre. J. E. McDonald went even further, suggesting to Secretary Wallace that the AAA drop the minimum to ten pounds per acre, thus ensuring that every American farmer wishing to cooperate had the opportunity to do so. O. B. Martin also pleaded the case of willing growers who could not secure a contract: "I earnestly hope," he wrote Cully Cobb in late January, "that a modification of the regulations can be made at once so that these farmers who really want to cooperate may be allowed to do so."[22]

As the sign-up deadline approached, Williamson wired Cobb requesting that the Cotton Section chief call a meeting of state extension directors to find ways of "injecting new life" into the campaign. Cobb replied that the Texas vice-director's telegram signaled the only indication of failure in any state: "Reports from all other states give assurance of great victory. Can't you put on pres-

"Let's Have Cooperation." *Dallas Morning News* editorial cartoon, January 18, 1934. Reprinted with permission of the *Dallas Morning News.*

sure?" On January 27, with some reports indicating that not more than one-eighth of Texas cotton farmers had signed up, Cobb told reporters that the delayed sign-up was cause for some concern, but he reiterated his belief that the situation was not yet alarming and boldly stated: "We have no fear of Texas."[23]

On January 30, the AAA responded to the Texas sign-up problems in two major ways: first, by extending the deadline to February 15; second, and most important, by lowering the minimum acceptable average yield during the base period to seventy-five pounds per acre. This double move had the desired effect, as over the next two weeks a flood of signed contracts inundated Texas county agent offices. On February 15, Cobb reported to Chester Davis that enough southern producers had signed up for him to recommend that the program be declared effective. Acting Secretary of Agriculture Rexford Tugwell announced success to the public later that day. Eventually, 81.8 percent of

Texas cotton producers signed 235,183 contracts, agreeing to retire 5,322,365 acres, or 37.7 percent of the state's acreage, during the 1928–32 base period.[24]

Implementation of the 1934 Reduction Program in Texas

The 1934 cotton program in Texas began much less hurriedly than it had the previous year. The county agents and committeemen had a year's experience under their belts. In addition, their main task in the field would be to check for correctly planted acreage rather than to police growers to ensure proper crop destruction. As more farmers pushed for compulsory controls, however, the AAA received a jolt that threw out all notions that the 1934 program would be a smoothly run operation.

Beginning in March, county committees assembled the cotton contracts passed on from the local committees, checked the documents for errors and blatant yield overestimations, and tabulated data summaries. County committeemen did not send the 1934–35 contracts immediately to Washington, unlike the procedure during the plow-up. The AAA instructed the Extension Service to set up special "State Boards of Review" in every cotton-growing state to provide more bureaucratic efficiency during the contract-review phase. The review boards were responsible for ensuring that farmers provided data that added up to the official government state and countywide figures. Texas provided a special case in that committeemen sent county summaries to one of nine district boards of review before they were sent to the State Board of Review in College Station. The creation of special district boards was the result of requests initiated by H. H. Williamson, who feared that the crush of work by one review board responsible for a state the size of Texas would result in endless delays.[25]

With few exceptions, the county summaries submitted to the district review boards contained overestimates in base acreage and production when compared with government figures. Undoubtedly, deliberate padding by producers caused some inflated assessments. Nevertheless, many farmers (who usually had few written records to fall back on) and local committeemen probably did the best job they could, but still overcalculated average acreage and crop yields for the base period. Regardless of the cause, on determination of countywide overestimation, the district review boards sent the summaries back to the county agents and committeemen, instructing them to revise the individual claims until they correlated with government figures.[26]

County committees revised the overestimates, as high as 33 percent in some counties, through different means. In some locales, such as Lubbock and Victoria counties, the county and local committeemen went over each producer's contract and reduced figures. A majority of agents, such as those in Bell, Duval, and Hopkins counties, reported that their committeemen had instituted blanket percentage cuts on all contracts, which hurt those farmers who turned in honest and accurate production figures. Other committees, such as those in Henderson, Lamb, and Nueces counties, combined both approaches. These committees first instituted individual contract reductions "to squeeze all the water possible out of the contracts" before finally resorting to blanket cuts.[27]

According to AAA regulations, county committees needed farmers' approval for all changes in the original contracts. When word reached growers about the necessity for cuts, "a mighty howl" arose in numerous counties. Some angry farmers canceled their contracts rather than accept any cuts. A majority of producers simply grumbled, but accepted their committee's explanation and approved the revisions. Nevertheless, many growers wrote their representatives to decry perceived injustices laid on them by the apparent arbitrariness of the reductions. Some farmers even demanded investigation of their committeemen.[28]

Despite the protests, the county committees made the required cuts and sent the revised county summaries to College Station for consideration by the state review board. The committees forwarded the approved cotton contracts to Washington. The AAA had promised originally that the first rental payments would arrive between March and April. No county agent, however, reported any checks arriving in their counties until early June. Some counties experienced prolonged delays in receiving the first rental checks. The Trinity County agent, for example, reported that the first rental check did not come into his county until August 3. With the exception of the delays in payment, however, all seemed to be working well.[29]

The Push for Compulsory Crop Control

Had there been no push for compulsory controls, the 1934 cotton program would probably have been a simple and straightforward operation. The immediate desire among a majority of participating growers for restrictions on noncooperators, however, ensured that the 1934 cotton season would be just as frenzied as the previous year's.

One of the prevalent structural problems of the 1933 cotton program was the lack of guarantees that growers who refused to cooperate with the government's efforts would profit less than the cooperators. Indeed, as one contemporary report concluded, even though nonparticipants received no government money during the plow-up, they benefited enough from increased cotton prices to make a larger profit on average than those farmers who reduced production. In early 1933, Mordecai Ezekiel projected greater benefits for noncooperators. In June, the economist wrote Secretary Wallace with suggestions for the upcoming plow-up. Ezekiel ended his memo with a warning: *"The men who cooperate should receive a larger share of the benefits than those who do not.* Under the present schedule of payments, non-cooperators will, on the average, receive the most benefit if cotton sells next fall at 8 cents or higher."[30]

Many farmers realized that noncooperators seemed to profit at their expense. Throughout the plow-up, the Roosevelt administration received a large volume of correspondence from southern cotton producers demanding that the government prescribe various types of penalties for noncooperators during the next program.[31]

The desire of many cotton producers for action against noncooperating farmers did not escape the attention of Alabama senator John H. Bankhead, Jr. The legislator believed that cotton grown by noncooperators greatly contributed to the continuing large carryover of cotton—a key hindrance to the long-term success of the government's price-raising efforts. Beginning in August 1933, Bankhead entered the agricultural policy debate by lobbying President Roosevelt and Secretary Wallace to put all ginners under a license and to limit the amount of cotton that any producer could gin to 50 percent of the amount produced in 1931. Both Roosevelt and Wallace replied that the administration had studied the matter of baleage control, but had found such an option to be impractical, possibly unconstitutional, and potentially harmful to the producers it was intended to help. Wallace in particular stressed his desire to keep the government's cotton-reduction efforts completely voluntary. Undaunted by these rebukes, Bankhead still worked to persuade Roosevelt and Wallace to accept his position.[32]

John Bankhead, motivated by a combination of politics and paternalism, emerged in 1933 as a strong advocate for southern cotton farmers. Although formerly a lawyer for Birmingham steel corporations and president of his family's coal company, he began his efforts to aid cotton growers when he was elected to the U.S. Senate in 1930. Although Ellison Smith served as chair of the Senate Committee on Agriculture when the New Deal began, his gradual estrangement from the Roosevelt administration allowed Bankhead (also a member of the agriculture committee) to emerge as a leading administration spokesman in the Senate on agricultural matters. It would be a give-and-take relationship, with Bankhead never acting as FDR's puppet. The president grew to respect the senator and valued his advice, even though the men disagreed occasionally on agricultural policy.[33]

On the first day of the new session of Congress in 1934, Bankhead pushed his plan for compulsory cotton control by introducing a bill in the Senate imposing strict controls on ginning. Under the senator's plan, the government would assign a quota to each state and individual grower based on a percentage of past production. No one would be allowed to gin any cotton over the assigned quota. On the same day, Bankhead's brother, Rep. William Bankhead of Alabama, introduced a similar bill in the House.[34]

The editors of the *Dallas Morning News* immediately assaulted the Bankhead measure as a blatant attack on property rights and personal liberty: "What does title to property mean without the liberty to direct one's production efforts according to one's own ideas of economic self interest, excepting moral restraint?" Seeing the senator's proposal as an unreasonably radical measure, the editors warned: "The American people have accepted extreme measures as a way out of the depression, but they are not yet willing to see individual economic enterprise become the vassal of bureaucracy." Bankhead replied to the editors' spirited defense of individual rights two weeks later in a lengthy open letter to the editors. In his response, the senator defended his bill and questioned the editors' reasoning, given the situation southern farmers faced. He stated at one point: "Your insistence upon the rights of individualism among farmers is in line with the condition which has always prevented any effective agreement among cotton farmers to adjust the supply of cotton to meet the market demands."[35]

Bankhead's efforts found support in Texas. Before the Senate Committee on Agriculture conducted hearings in mid-January, representatives, senators, and administration officials began receiving letters from farmers endorsing the Bankhead bill or some other form of compulsory control. "I warn you now," wrote one Plainview farmer to Secretary Wallace, "if there isn't something done to curb the large [noncooperating] cotton raiser . . . I fear we will not have the reduction desired. Please put some restraint on them."[36]

Under pressure from the grass roots, the Cotton Section undertook a study of two possible forms of compulsory cotton control. Cotton Section analysts compared the Bankhead measure with a rival plan based on placing a heavy tax on cotton over a fixed amount and found the taxing method much more appealing. The tax plan would eliminate numerous headaches foreseen in the stricter Bankhead bill, such as storage problems for surplus seed cotton, bootlegging of illegally ginned cotton, and numerous political consequences that might result from farmers being unable to sell any unintended surplus crops.[37]

The day after a January 26 meeting with the Bankhead brothers, Roosevelt informed reporters at a news conference that he believed some form of compulsory control was necessary. The president stated that he favored the Cotton Section's plan to place a prohibitive tax on all cotton ginned over a specific allotment assigned to individual farmers. He expressed his belief that the taxation method, from a legal point of view, would stand up better in the courts than the pending Bankhead bill. The president also stated that he thought Senator Bankhead would be willing to accept the prohibitive tax method to help control excess production. Roosevelt made clear, however, that if his administration decided to adopt such a policy, it would first seek the approval of the cotton growers.[38]

The administration's attempt to gauge growers' opinions of compulsory legislation materialized in the form of a questionnaire mailed by Secretary Wallace on January 26. The ostensible purpose of the poll was to ascertain grower sentiment, but the limited number and reach of the questionnaires leaves that premise much in doubt. Wallace mailed only fifty thousand survey forms, including thirty thousand addressed to USDA crop reporters, approximately six thousand to local committeemen, and another one thousand to county agents. The questionnaires asked about the individual's position on a plan of compulsory cotton control and the percentage of cotton farmers in the community who favored such an obligation. The results indicated that 95 percent of the respondents favored some form of compulsory control, while community support ranged from 70 percent to 90 percent, depending on the state (with 82 percent support in Texas). Although the administration acted disingenuously when it implied that the surveys went out to a representative group of cotton farmers, there could be little doubt that a majority of southern growers favored compulsory control.[39]

Grass-roots pressure provided the main impetus for administration approval of compulsory cotton-crop control. The conversion demonstrates the adept political maneuvering of Franklin Roosevelt. The president, sensing which direction the political winds were blowing, decided to commit his administration to the ginning tax. Although Secretary Wallace opposed compulsory control, he reluctantly announced on February 7 that he would follow the will of producers, who displayed overwhelming support for it, as evidenced by the results of the survey. The administration began to work with Senator Bankhead, who agreed to support the ginning tax and abandon his proposal for a strict limit on the amount of ginned cotton. At Bankhead's request, the Senate Committee on Agriculture altered his bill to emphasize the prohibitive tax feature.[40]

In February, Marvin Jones held hearings on the Bankhead bill in the House Committee on Agriculture. The chairman believed that the proposal was unconstitutional and hoped to preserve the voluntary crop-reduction principle. He grudgingly changed his mind, however, after Roosevelt wrote him to express his approval of the revised Bankhead measure. In similar letters to Jones and Ellison Smith, Roosevelt cited his belief that the great majority of cotton farmers agreed with the idea of compulsory control. The president concluded both letters with the statement: "My study of the various methods suggested leads me to believe that the Bankhead bills in principle best cover the situation. I hope in the continuing emergency your Committee can take action."[41]

Despite his apprehension, Jones refused to block the Bankhead bill. As he had done with the 1933 farm bill, the chairman allowed legislation that contained features he disliked to pass through his committee out of party loyalty and support for President Roosevelt. In addition, he planned to speak on behalf of the Bankhead legislation during the coming debate on the House floor.[42]

Although party loyalty may have been important to Marvin Jones, it meant much less to George B. Terrell. The at-large Democrat from Alto, Texas, was the only representative from a cotton-growing state to speak out against the Bankhead bill on the House floor. Speaking for many of the bill's conservative opponents, Terrell attacked the compulsory tax as "a subterfuge and a scheme to get around the plain letter of the Constitution." He took solace in his belief that if Congress ever enacted the Bankhead law, the Supreme Court would intervene and strike it down. Terrell concluded his lengthy denunciation by announcing: "Before we adopt this Soviet system of government and Russianize this country, we should submit an amendment to the Constitution and permit the people to change our Government from a republic to a despotism, where no personal liberty or property rights are safe."[43]

During his major speech supporting the Bankhead bill, as well as in answers to questions during debate on the House floor, Marvin Jones often returned to the theme of personal liberty, arguing that the proposed measure's compulsory features were not antithetical to the concept of freedom. In response to the attacks made earlier by George Terrell, but more specifically to a speech made by New York representative James W. Wadsworth, Jones retorted: "He [Wadsworth] discussed liberty, the finest word in the language of man, a word that means more, perhaps, to Americans than any other word, a word we all love, and, therefore, a word that should be used carefully and accurately. He talked as though the proposed measure would take away all the liberties of men who are engaged in the cotton business. Exactly the contrary is true. We are undertaking to adjust it to the welfare of all. That is the very essence of organized government."[44]

Jones, citing the results of Wallace's questionnaires, hammered away at the opposition by emphasizing the principle of majority rule. Why should the activities of a small minority of noncooperating cotton growers be allowed to affect prices to the detriment of their neighbors' income? What kind of liberty would that be? "I ask you if it is liberty, and what kind of liberty it is if 5 percent are able to dictate to the other 95 percent? Was not that just the kind of liberty that Al Capone wanted? Was not that the kind of liberty that for a time he exercised? Why, liberty is not worth much unless it is ordered liberty. I have a right to swing my hands around as I please in any direction, but when I swing my hand in such a way that I hit this man's nose, my liberties end where his rights begin. Order was Heaven's first law. In other words, a liberty that is not organized is a savage liberty."[45]

"Ordered liberty." With that one phrase, Jones summarized an argument in favor of the Bankhead bill that one could extend to defend the entire AAA experiment and perhaps even much of the New Deal itself. By asserting the bill's compatibility with established American values and ideals, he strongly questioned the efficacy of another traditional American value—laissez-faire individualism. The Bankhead bill, like the AAA, was just another step in America's transition into the modern age.

Jones concluded his remarks with an eloquent reiteration of his belief that the Bankhead legislation, like the agricultural adjustment bill a year before, provided a means by which the government could intervene to protect its citizens. Such an action, he believed, was an obligation. By stepping in, the government could actually foster liberty, not destroy it:

> When a man assumes that liberty means a license to do as he pleases, without regard to his neighbor's rights, he abuses the term. A civilized nation defines the rights of its citizens in order to promote real liberty. The very organization of government means that if it means anything. Those who would construe it otherwise would

adopt a policy that would permit the financial wizard to enslave his fellowman, indulge in all kinds of abuses, and produce ultimate chaos. "O Liberty, how many crimes have been committed in thy name!"

Let us have an ordered liberty that protects the rights of all and assures equal rights to all. Equality and liberty should go hand in hand. That is liberty in its finest form.[46]

On March 19, the House passed a version of the Bankhead bill by a 251–115 margin. The Senate passed its own version on March 29. After a conference committee ironed out differences, the House and the Senate quickly passed the compromise measure. Both Texas senators voted for the bill and all Texas representatives, except lone standout George Terrell, joined to vote for passage. President Roosevelt signed the Bankhead Cotton Control Act into law on April 21, 1934.[47]

The final version of the Bankhead Act established a national quota of 10,460,251 bales of cotton to be marketed tax-free during the 1934 crop year. Among other major provisions of the law, it required the AAA to assign each grower a maximum production quota based, in a majority of cases, on his average yield during the 1928–32 base period. The AAA would issue tax-exemption certificates to both cooperators and noncooperators in the acreage-reduction program sufficient to cover individual quotas. Cotton ginned over an individual's allocation would require payment of a ginning tax equal to 50 percent of the average price of seven-eighths-inch middling cotton on ten specified spot markets.[48] Growers with surplus certificates could transfer them to other growers who had a certificate deficit, but these transfers were subject to regulations to be laid down at a later date by the secretary of agriculture. Farmers could retain the Bankhead Act provisions into the next year if at least two-thirds of the producers voted for continuation during an end-of-season referendum.[49]

Implementation of the Bankhead Act, 1934

Now that the government had committed itself to compulsory control, the AAA had to implement the policy by melding the Bankhead Act's provisions and the existing acreage-reduction program. This course of action, as the Texas experience demonstrates, further complicated the government's efforts to aid southern cotton farmers.

The AAA assigned the Cotton Section to administer the provisions of the Bankhead Act. In the spring of 1934, the section's first major task was to determine tax-exemption certificate quotas for every cotton-growing county in the nation. It was instructed to prorate the national allotment to the cotton-producing states according to average annual production during the 1928–32 base period. Each county was then assigned a "regular allotment," determined by prorating 90 percent of each state's total quota according to each county's average annual production during the base period (excluding certain years in which counties experienced abnormally low average yields). The regular allotment was apportioned to individual farmers who signed a 1934–35 acreage reduction contract proportional to their average annual production, as stated in their contracts. Local committees assigned individual quotas for noncooperators with the acreage-reduction program. These quotas were determined by multiplying their estimated yield during the base period by the average percentage of base acreage that contract signers in the county were permitted to plant.[50] The law also provided for a "state reserve," derived from the remaining 10 percent of a state's quota, to be distributed to farmers under special circumstances. This reserve was created to offset criticism of possible injustices resulting from use of the 1928–32 base period.[51]

The Cotton Section took so long to determine county quotas (an entire month after the signing of the Bankhead Act) that it did not complete the job before growers had planted all of their crops for the coming year. An infuriated John Bankhead fired off an angry letter to Chester Davis, blaming "hostile influences" within the Cotton Section for the delay. "Please be assured," the senator warned, "that I will take whatever action it seems to me best to prevent the destruction by maladministration of my Cotton Control Law." Despite Bankhead's irate message, the sheer magnitude of the task involved prevented the AAA from releasing the county quotas until June 21.[52]

Although the Cotton Section had already assigned Texas a state quota of 3,237,530 bales, a real furor arose in some counties when the AAA announced the regular county allotments. In most cases, criticism came from localities that had greatly increased their cotton acreage since the 1928–32 base period, such as those counties in the Lower Rio Grande Valley. Numerous Texas congressmen and county committees urged the AAA to reconsider the county production quotas, but officials resisted making any changes, mainly because they believed that the Cotton Section had done the best job possible. In addition, balancing the state quotas required that any increase in one county's quota of tax-exemption certificates would necessarily result in a subsequent decrease in another county's allotment. There would be no end to the turmoil if the agency started shuffling county quotas in order to satisfy complaints. AAA officials replied to the protesters by merely citing the procedure that the Cotton Section used to determine the quotas and how that process followed the provisions set down in the Bankhead Act, and reminding them that their areas should soon qualify for a portion of the state reserve.[53]

To implement the provisions of the Bankhead Act in the field, the AAA again called on the network of county agents and committeemen, who were carrying out the 1934 acreage-reduction program. Because of the additional work required to implement the Cotton Control Act and the necessarily short turnaround for administering its provisions, the AAA provided so-called emergency adjustment assistants for each major cotton county. These assistants helped with record keeping and any other Bankhead-related functions. During the first week of July, county agents and their adjustment assistants attended district meetings to learn the details of their new responsibilities. These officials then returned home to hold instructional meetings for their committees and local farmers, as had been done for the acreage-reduction campaign. While simultaneously performing compliance-checking duties for the acreage-reduction program, county agents and committeemen now shouldered the added burden of securing farmers' signatures on applications for their individual tax-exemption quota certificates.[54]

Extension agents and county committeemen pored over the Bankhead applications, checking for errors and cross-matching the information on the applications of contract signers with the data from their acreage-reduction contracts. Instead of sending the applications to Washington, county agents directed them to the State Allotment Board in College Station. The board, consisting of two extension officials and three farmers appointed by O. B. Martin, received the Bankhead applications, computed individual allotments, and issued all tax-exemption certificates for Texas.[55]

Because the totals on the applications from most counties were higher than the county's assigned quota, the Allotment Board sent word that claims would have to be revised in order to comply. Already swamped by their duties, county committees applied blanket cuts to make their figures adhere to their county's quota. Many of these cuts were mild (less than 10 percent), but some were quite severe, such as occurred in Castro and Cochran counties, where the Allotment Board instructed committees to institute 45 percent and 46 percent cuts, respectively.[56]

Although the additional Bankhead reductions were moderate in a majority of Texas counties, the cumulative impact of all the AAA reductions proved to be too much for N. T. Lawler, a farmer from Hunt County. In a candid letter to Rep. Sam Rayburn, the grower reaffirmed his support of the government's efforts to help the nation's cotton producers, but expressed his disappointment with the AAA's administration of its programs. He wrote that in 1934 he had an average of 150 cotton acres over the base period amount. After initially reducing his acreage 40 percent under the 1934–35 contract, the county committee reduced his acreage another 16.6 percent under a county-wide blanket cut. This initial reduction did not anger the farmer because "the 3 1/2 cent per pound [rental payment] was quite liberal," and Lawler understood "the difficulties under which the administration was laboring." In making out the application for Bankhead certificates, however, the county agent for some reason told the farmer that his allotment would not be reduced any further because Lawler had kept all his past production records to prove his claims. When the same agent told him later that he would indeed have to take a 7.5 percent production cut, the frustrated farmer decided to write Rayburn. "Instead of a 40 percent cut as I had expected and prepared for, I now have a 64.1 percent cut [the math is fuzzy here], which you will readily understand is intolerable." The grower felt especially exasperated with the AAA's administration of the farm acts, because the agency did not do enough to stop producers who submitted incorrect claims. In Lawler's opinion, the agency simply conducted "a public policy of placing a penalty on honesty and a bonus on cheating." Given the rush in which the AAA had to carry out the Bankhead provisions, however, there was little else the Cotton Section could do except use the data obtained during the acreage-reduction campaign, as inflated and inaccurate as many of the figures may have been.[57]

The situation in the Lower Rio Grande Valley produced other problems. By the time farmers in this region discovered in late June that the AAA had assigned them low county allotments, it was almost cotton-picking time. In July, cotton that could not be ginned tax free began piling up at the gins as county agents and committeemen worked frantically to get farmers to sign Bankhead application forms. To make matters worse, a late-July hurricane inundated the region, degrading exposed cotton with water, mud, and debris. Needless to say, the low county quotas followed by the administrative delays combined to make the Lower Rio Grande Valley a leading anti-Bankhead area in Texas.[58]

Although the remainder of the state had more lead time than the Lower Rio Grande Valley farmers did, other Texas cotton producers soon found themselves facing the prospect of having to pick cotton before the Allotment Board had issued their tax-exemption certificates. Cotton piled up at gins before the certificates arrived. Farmers and congressmen again wrote to administration officials in order to apply the whip and expedite matters.[59]

The AAA responded to the requests for action by authorizing county agents to issue "interim certificates" for up to 50 percent of a grower's individual quota. The issuance of interim certificates placed yet another burden on the overworked county agents as they struggled with their meager resources to accommodate their farmers. The Nueces County agent reported a great deal of confusion and dissatisfaction among the growers who came into his office. "The county agent's office was in an uproar from early morn to dewy eve," the agent noted, with as many as three hundred farmers in line at one time awaiting interim certificates. Most agents reported that it was not until late September that regular tax-exemption certificates began to arrive for distribution.[60]

As events turned out, a majority of Texas farmers ended up with a large surplus of Bankhead certificates because most of the state suffered from a punishing drought in 1934. The only Texas regions that experienced good growing weather were the Lower Rio Grande Valley and the El Paso area. The remainder of the state received so little moisture that growers produced only 2.4 million bales, or just slightly more than half the normal harvest. Many areas produced yields only one-fourth of their regional average.[61]

While Texas and other southwestern producers endured a terrible drought, most farmers in the southeastern portion of the Cotton Belt experienced relatively good growing conditions and produced above their quotas; thus, they found themselves with a corresponding deficit of Bankhead certificates. As previously noted, the Cotton Control Act contained provisions allowing the transfer of certificates from one farmer to another, but left the logistics of the transfer up to the secretary of agriculture. In early August, members of Congress, county agents, and committeemen began to write Secretary Wallace to offer suggestions and ask how the AAA planned to facilitate the transfer of certificates.[62]

The Cotton Section soon provided certificate transfer instructions. To eliminate speculation and fraud, the county agent was to facilitate all certificate transfers in his office, with the price of all surplus certificates set at four cents per pound. For the relatively small number of transfers within counties, buyers and sellers could simply come into the county agent's office, fill out appropriate paperwork, and make the deal. For the larger number of inter-county exchanges, the AAA set up a national pool whereby farmers could surrender their certificates in the hopes that growers in certificate-deficit areas would buy them. Through the device of the national pool, as a biographer of John Bankhead has noted, "Texas farmers were given cash for cotton that they had not harvested to allow Carolina planters to market a product which they should not have grown."[63]

The Move for Suspension

As the 1934 season continued, rumors began to swirl that President Roosevelt might invoke a provision of the Bankhead Act allowing for suspension of the legislation by executive decree. The administration began to receive letters calling for its termination. Many argued that the legislation was no longer necessary because the drought in Texas and other southwestern states had already reduced total production far below the national quota. When Senator Bankhead caught wind of the rumors, he wired Cully Cobb to warn him that the agitation for suspension of his law came from noncooperators, big shippers, and ginners from Texas. The senator implored Cobb to fight within the administration for retention the Bankhead Act and for maintenance of the tax-exemption certificates: "Why take this property right away from them simply to aid producers who refused to participate in the reduction plan of the administration? . . . If the act is suspended, cooperators will be discouraged next year . . . Please record my vigorous opposition to the suspension of any part of the Cotton Control Act."[64]

Despite Bankhead's seeming commitment to all the provisions and spirit of his compulsory control law, steadily mounting protests led him to support compromise efforts to appease the small producers from his home state of Alabama and other states east of the Mississippi River. In those areas, growers had produced more than their individual allotments, and many could not afford the four cents per pound price of the transferable tax-exemption certificates, nor could they afford to store their unmarketed cotton until prices rose. Bankhead sensed the scorn many Alabama farmers felt toward his law and also began to fear the impact this criticism might have on his brother William's re-election campaign.[65]

Other representatives from southeastern states, most notably Cotton Ed

Smith, wished to cancel the Cotton Control Act outright. Bankhead hoped that less-drastic measures might be used to address the criticisms developing in his section of the Cotton Belt. President Roosevelt chose to stay out of the growing debate and used Bankhead as an intermediary between him and the increasingly troublesome Smith. "I hesitate to ask Ed Smith to see me," FDR wrote Bankhead in a "private and confidential" letter, "because he either orates or talks from all four directions at the same time. Use your discretion but do not bring me into it!"[66]

Bankhead decided to call on Henry Wallace to suggest a meeting between the secretary and a delegation of southeastern senators and congressmen to allow the representatives to express their concerns over the cotton situation in their states. Wallace agreed, arranging a meeting for September 22.[67]

Before the meeting began, Bankhead sent a telegram to President Roosevelt describing the cotton situation in Alabama. The senator explained that less than one-half of the tax-exemption certificates had been issued in Alabama, causing much irritation. Small farmers criticized the allotment basis because they believed it punished those who had previously reduced their production voluntarily (the 10 percent state reserve had not yet been released to aid in such cases). Bankhead then made a startling suggestion, given his authorship of the control law and his previous message to Cully Cobb: "In order to relieve the tension I recommend that the allotments be increased so as to exempt all cotton harvested this year. The crop will be a million bales under the limit of the act. By increasing the allotments rather than eliminating the tax, farmers who have underproduced this year will be protected by using *next year* the carryover exemption certificates for cotton in addition to next year's regular allotments."[68]

As the meeting approached, word spread in the press regarding the intentions of Senator Bankhead and the other southeastern representatives. Most Texas producers strongly supported continuance of the Cotton Control Act provisions, if for no other reason than to ensure redemption of their unused Bankhead certificates. Marvin Jones conferred with Secretary Wallace and Chester Davis to lay down his forceful objection to any changes in the law or suspension of the act unless the administration promised full and immediate protection for the holders of surplus certificates. Jones accepted Bankhead's invitation to participate in the conference with Wallace on September 22.[69]

Strong grass-roots support for the Bankhead Act surged in Texas as the meeting approached. Texas senators, congressmen, committeemen, and farmers bombarded administration officials with letters and telegrams beseeching

"Will He Be Left Holding the Bag?" *Dallas Morning News* editorial cartoon, September 22, 1934. Reprinted with permission of the *Dallas Morning News.*

them to continue the law in its existing form. One of the more succinct and expressive messages supporting the Bankhead Act came from the chairman of a southeast Texas county committee. He sent the letter to Rep. J. J. Mansfield, who forwarded it to Cully Cobb:

> Farmer committeemen of Lavaca County resent the fact that the author of the Bankhead bill would use his effort and influence to defeat the Bankhead bill for purely selfish and sectional [reasons] regardless of the disastrous effect it would have on Texas farmers who through act of Providence have failed to make their allotments and have looked upon their surplus certificates as a form of farm insurance.
>
> Farmers are just beginning to believe that the Agricultural Adjustment Admin-

istration through its Congress intends to be sincere. If Representative Bankhead causes the Bankhead Act to be invalidated now, these same farmers will lose all the confidence that they have ever had in their government and the sincerity of its purpose in bringing relief to farmers.[70]

At the Washington conference, Henry Wallace, Chester Davis, and Cully Cobb met with John Bankhead and members of Congress from the southeastern states, as well as with Marvin Jones and Texas congressmen Wright Patman and Milton West. After the meeting, Wallace announced to the press that the Bankhead Act provisions would continue without modification. In press statements and subsequent letters to congressmen, the secretary specifically cited the avalanche of correspondence that the administration had received from all over the Cotton Belt, but especially Texas, as clear evidence that a large majority of farmers preferred continuance, hence the decision to stay the course. If those seeking repeal of the Cotton Control Act wanted to have their way, they would have to convince the farmers themselves to defeat the law in the required referendum in December.[71]

The 1934 Bankhead Referendum

Under the terms of the Bankhead Act, the administration could continue the provisions of the legislation into the next year if at least two-thirds of the cotton producers voted to do so in a referendum. AAA officials decided to hold the vote on December 14 and allowed all farmers who planned to produce cotton during the 1935 season to voice their opinion.[72]

During the weeks leading up to the referendum, Texas' state and local newspapers published a lively debate on the continuation of the law. The *Dallas Morning News* ran numerous stories and editorials arguing against retention of the Bankhead Act on grounds that reduced cotton production contributed to the loss of foreign markets. Many pro-Bankhead farmers grew angry at the barrage of editorials and articles attacking the Cotton Control Act. One Mineola, Texas, grower presented the prevailing view of the law's supporters in a letter to the editors of the *Morning News*. Claiming to speak for "the average farmer," he asked: "Where is the logic in raising four bales of cotton at five cents a pound when experience has taught him that by reducing his crop to domestic needs he can get as much or more for two bales of cotton?" The farmer went on to praise the Roosevelt administration's efforts to support the growers and concluded with a statement capturing the general mood of the majority of Texas cotton producers at the time: "I don't know whether the Bankhead bill is the best we can get or not, but I have nothing to substitute for it, and none of the farmers upstairs has offered anything to take its place. So I'm willing to go along and try it out. But one thing the farmer wants, and that is Government control over cotton acreage to reduce the surplus. I'm for cotton reduction to our domestic needs, for Roosevelt, and the new deal."[73]

On December 14, Texas' cotton farmers went to polls set up at schools, churches, barber shops, general stores, and other meeting places and voted overwhelmingly with a majority of American cotton producers for retention of the Bankhead Act. Texas growers led the way by voting 241,018–51,051, or 82.5 percent, in favor of continuation. Collectively, American cotton farmers gave 89.4 percent approval for retention of the law.[74]

Some Texas counties voted against retention of the Bankhead Act. Farmers in some counties, such as those in the Lower Rio Grande Valley and Cochran County on the southern High Plains, were upset because they received low regular allotments due to production increases made after the 1928–32 base period. Other dissenting counties, such as Stephens in the North-Central Texas Cross Timbers and Tyler in the eastern Piney Woods near the Louisiana border, had mostly small cotton growers who felt especially restricted by the limits placed on production. Still other dissenting counties in the Hill Country of Central Texas, such as Gillespie, were home to German American farmers, who tended to vote Republican and generally opposed all crop-restriction measures offered by the Roosevelt administration.[75]

The cumulative impact of negative votes from some Texas counties was limited because they were largely minor cotton-producing areas. The farmers from prolific cotton-growing areas voted overwhelmingly for continuance of the Cotton Control Act. Texas producers supported the Bankhead provisions because they wanted to ensure their ability to receive compensation for surplus certificates, and, despite the frustrating cuts and delays that characterized implementation of the law, the AAA appeared to be helping relieve the farmers' burdens.[76]

In 1934, the cotton acreage–reduction program, the compulsory control law, and a new price-support loan combined with the drought to bring prices above twelve cents per pound. Although the average price fell short of the parity objective (15.9 cents per pound in 1934), Texas' cotton farmers in 1934 got a boost toward that goal with an aggregate total of $34,498,256 in rental and benefit payments. With such results, farmers could easily ignore the minority of ginners and handlers who decried the loss of volume and foreign markets. To further their interests and help promote general recovery in the national economy, Texas growers joined their brethren in other states to continue the application of the Bankhead Act provisions and forced their neighbors to comply with compulsory control measures for another year.[77]

The 1935 Program

For the first time since the AAA had instituted the cotton programs, county agents and committeemen in 1935 implemented a program essentially identical to the plan executed during the previous year. Consequently, most county agents reported in their annual narrative reports that such AAA functions as the educational meetings, the signing of new contracts and Bankhead applications, the adjusting of the old agreements, and the issuance of compliance checks flowed much more smoothly than in the preceding years.[78]

The 1935 program did differ in notable ways from the previous year's procedure, however. One basic modification involved the amount of permitted acreage reduction. The original two-year agreement required farmers to reduce their cotton acreage by 25 percent in 1935. As the 1935 crop season approached, however, John Bankhead began writing to Henry Wallace and Cully Cobb to express his belief that a 25 percent reduction would be insufficient to reduce the surplus and raise cotton prices. The senator called for a straight 40 percent cut in acreage for all producers, but later reduced his request to a more moderate voluntary 15 percent additional cut for all growers wishing to further reduce their acreage.[79]

After meeting with administration officials in the fall of 1934, Bankhead succeeded in persuading the AAA to modify the acceptable percentage for 1935 acreage reduction. On November 28, Wallace announced that the AAA would still require cotton farmers to reduce their acreage by a minimum of 25 percent, but growers could reduce their plantings by an additional 5 percent if they so desired. (The secretary also announced an increase in the parity payment to 1.25 cents per pound for 1935 and that the AAA would offer one-year contracts for the 1935 crop season to producers who wished to join the cotton program, but had failed to do so the previous year.) On January 17, he increased the amount of additional reduction by another 5 percent, thus permitting a maximum allowable reduction of 35 percent for 1935.[80]

On March 1, Wallace announced the 1935 national and state Bankhead allotments. The AAA assigned a countrywide tax-free quota of 10,983,264 bales (500-pound gross weight). Texas cotton producers received a quota of 3,406,117 bales.[81]

The cotton programs in Texas experienced, in addition to contractual alterations and modifications in the allotted Bankhead quotas, administrative changes in 1935. First, on June 30, O. B. Martin died of a stroke. H. H. Williamson soon succeeded him as the new director of the Texas Extension Service. Second, the AAA took further steps to democratize the selection process for the local and county committees. Senator Bankhead wanted cooperating producers to elect the local committees, and Cotton Section officials agreed. County production association members thereafter voted for all local committeemen, who then elected the county committeemen, though two members of the county committees from the 1934 operations were retained in each county to guide the 1935 program. Despite these changes, power remained in the hands of the larger farmers, who were consistently reelected to these positions.[82]

In 1935, the Roosevelt administration resisted offering another price-support loan of twelve cents per pound. The 1934 CCC loan had proved to be too high, as southern growers stored over 40 percent of the crop in warehouses, thus keeping the fiber from domestic and foreign trade channels until January 1936, when the loans matured. Plus, most AAA officials did not view commodity loans and artificial price supports as a permanent feature of the cotton programs.

Nevertheless, many powerful interests continued to lobby Roosevelt to offer another high loan in 1935. The president decided to accept a compromise plan formulated by Oscar Johnston that called for a below-market loan (eventually set at 10 cents per pound) supplemented by a direct government subsidy that would guarantee producers 12 cents per pound when they marketed their crop. Because the average price for cotton in 1935 (11.1 cents per pound) stood below the loan rate, very few growers accepted CCC loans. Most of the 1935 crop went directly into trade channels, as farmers accepted the per pound price of 12 cents. Without the encumbrance of widespread drought, Texas growers in 1935 produced 2,956,000 bales on 10,657,000 acres and received an estimated value of $162 million. In addition, they received an additional $39,547,226 in AAA rental and parity payments.[83]

The AAA under Attack

Attacks on the constitutionality of all the New Deal commodity programs increased substantially during 1935. Millers despised paying the processing tax required to finance the AAA cotton program (though in practice they passed the tax burden on to consumers), arguing that the tax placed cotton at a competitive disadvantage with synthetic fibers such as rayon. Ginners and handlers objected to the limits of tax-free cotton allowed under the Bankhead Act, because they reduced the volume of cotton. During 1935, processors, ginners, and handlers initiated litigation to have the Agricultural Adjustment Act and the Cotton Control Act repealed.[84]

In the spring of 1935, as opposition to the AAA mounted, Cully Cobb devised a plan for a farmers' march on Washington. From the beginning, Texans were at the center of the action. Cobb's plan called for growers to demand nothing new, just to maintain the status quo. He believed that such a display of rural support would impress government officials by showing the gratitude of the nation's farmers and their desire to keep the commodity programs intact. After a series of phone conversations about his proposal, Cobb eventually converted his old friend H. H. Williamson to the idea.[85]

Cobb and Williamson, who wanted to make the march appear to be a spontaneous event rising from the grass roots, arranged for Clifford H. Day, a Plainview, Texas, cotton farmer, to act as the front man for a group of fellow growers to Washington. On April 18, Day announced to reporters that he planned to recruit Texas dirt farmers to join him on a May trip to Washington to show support for the AAA. Meanwhile, Cobb and Williamson made final arrangements. Because President Roosevelt intended to be in the capital around May 15, they initially chose that date for the march, hoping that the president might agree to visit with the delegation.[86]

Although the Extension Service and the AAA did not sponsor the movement, the idea behind the march definitely originated with Cobb and Williamson. Nevertheless, Day did his best to portray the trek as being inspired by "a bunch of fellows sitting around talking" in Hale County, Texas. Supposedly, Day and his neighbors decided that the AAA was doing its best to help growers and must be continued. What the agency needed, presumably, was a reaffirmation of support from the producers. Day continued to stress throughout the preparation period that the growing movement was simply an impulsive reflection of gratitude on the part of average dirt farmers for all the AAA had done for them.[87]

Word of the farmers' march spread rapidly throughout the country, possibly with AAA encouragement. What began as a small publicity-seeking jaunt by a trainload of North Texas growers soon swelled into a sizable gathering of close to five thousand farmers coming by train, bus, and automobile from various parts of Texas, the South, and the Midwest. Day and Williamson moved the march date to May 14, arranging the highlight of the event to be a mass meeting at Independence Hall. On the morning of that day, the excited farmers assembled to hear speeches by Henry Wallace, Chester Davis, Marvin Jones, and Cotton Ed Smith, among others. The farmers had hoped that the president would also attend the assembly. Roosevelt did not show up, but the growers were electrified to hear that they had all been invited to the south lawn of the White House later that afternoon.[88]

The president did not disappoint the assembled farmers, as he entertained the crowd with a grand performance. Speaking forcefully from the south portico of the White House, FDR delivered what many contemporary observers believed to be the first speech of the 1936 presidential campaign. Using much of the anti–big business rhetoric that characterized the 1936 campaign and the so-called Second New Deal, Roosevelt repeatedly attacked and mocked "the high and mighty people" who wished to bring down the AAA for their own selfish gain. By all accounts, the farmers loved every minute of it.[89]

Just two weeks after the farmers' march, the U.S. Supreme Court fired warning shots at the AAA. On May 27, the High Court handed down the *Schechter* decision, invalidating the National Recovery Administration on the grounds that the NRA system of industrial codes was an unlawful delegation of power by Congress to the executive branch. Those in agricultural circles feared that the Court might use a similar argument to throw out the AAA processing taxes, because Congress had delegated to the secretary of agriculture the discretionary ability to set them. The House and Senate Committees on Agriculture hurried to change the Agricultural Adjustment Act, primarily through a series of amendments that included the grant of legal sanction by Congress to all previous processing taxes levied by the agriculture secretary and a firm procedure by which the secretary could collect future processing taxes. The law also extended the provisions of the Bankhead Act for another year. Roosevelt signed the so-called AAA Amendment Act containing the new modifications on August 24, 1935.[90]

Before the president signed the AAA Amendment Act into law, however, the U.S. Court of Appeals for the First Circuit in Boston ruled (on July 16) in the case of *Franklin Process Company v. Hoosac Mills* that the AAA processing taxes were, indeed, unconstitutional. Using language similar to that of the Supreme Court justices in the *Schechter* decision, the appeals court judges found that the processing taxes were illegal on the grounds that they had been instituted by an unconstitutional delegation of power by Congress to the executive branch. "The power to impose a tax and to determine what property to bear the tax," the judges noted, "can only be determined by the legislative department of the government." The court also added a surprise when it further determined that Congress had no right to control or regulate the production of agricultural products before those commodities were placed in interstate commerce. The administration wasted no time in appealing the decision to the Supreme Court, which agreed on October 14 to hear the case.[91]

On October 9, the High Court began hearing oral arguments in the *Hoosac Mills* case. As the decision on the AAA's fate loomed, Cully Cobb, Chester Davis, Henry Wallace, and other government representatives spoke out to reassure farmers. No matter how the Court ruled, the growers had no reason to fear—the government would not abandon them. If an adverse decision was handed down, the officials vowed to try other methods to ensure that the main AAA goal of raising farm prices by adjusting agricultural production to consumption would continue. Only by doing so, New Dealers believed, could the government promote the "ordered liberty" and economic prosperity that Marvin Jones and other agrarian advocates desired so strongly for the farmers of Texas and the entire nation.[92]

CHAPTER 4

TREADING WATER WITH THE SOIL CONSERVATION AND DOMESTIC ALLOTMENT ACT, 1936–37

On January 6, 1936, the United States Supreme Court relieved the mounting tension over the fate of the Agricultural Adjustment Act. In a 6–3 decision, the Court ruled in the *Hoosac Mills* case not only against the constitutionality of the processing taxes used to finance the AAA programs, but also against the AAA's regulation of agricultural production through production-control contracts. Writing for the majority, Justice Owen Roberts stated that the processing taxes were unconstitutional "exactions" appropriated from one group for the benefit of another. Further, Roberts declared, agricultural production was a local affair under the sole jurisdiction of the states. In a vehement dissenting opinion, Justice Harlan Stone noted that the majority avoided important issues, especially the fact that most agricultural commodities went into interstate commerce after harvest. In Stone's appraisal, the majority justices were relying on a "tortured construction of the Constitution" to justify their ruling.[1]

The Supreme Court's decision in effect killed the Agricultural Adjustment Act of 1933. After sharply criticizing the decision, the administration went back to the drawing board to create a replacement program without processing taxes, production-control contracts, or compulsory controls. Working with leaders from Congress and major farm organizations, the administration developed a temporary expedient combining voluntary crop reduction with soil-conservation practices. While Texas producers reverted to voluntary cotton control, New Dealers would be treading water for the next two years as they worked to establish a long-term plan for the nation's farmers.

Reaction to the *Hoosac Mills* Decision

When the Supreme Court announced its decision, Franklin Roosevelt was conversing with Henry Wallace and Marvin Jones at the White House. The president immediately invited the men to return later in the day to join him in a meeting with John Bankhead, Chester Davis, and Attorney General Homer Cummings. During the afternoon meeting, Roosevelt reviewed the High Court's decision, whereupon the conferees proceeded to fill the room with biting comments about the majority justices' reasoning. Although some suggested offering a constitutional amendment to allow direct agricultural production control by the federal government, Roosevelt quickly deflected such proposals. Instead, he asked the men to draft a new law that would achieve the AAA's goals within the limits imposed by the Court's verdict.[2]

In the days following the *Hoosac Mills* decision, administration officials, pro-AAA congressmen and senators, and agricultural leaders heaped venomous criticism on the Court. John Bankhead took his complaints to the floor of the Senate, where he responded point by point to Justice Roberts's opinion. In a press release, Marvin Jones stated that he could not comprehend how the Court had determined that a national tariff was legal, but not a national farm program that attempted to restore the price balance between agricultural and industrial products. Nevertheless, the Texan remained hopeful, stating that he was certain that lawmakers and the administration could find a constitutional method to help farmers. Meanwhile, Rep. O. H. Cross of Waco, Texas, held a meeting with a small bloc of angry House members to discuss the decision. Afterward, the congressman told reporters that he planned to introduce a bill that forbade inferior federal courts from ruling on the constitutionality of congressional acts and barred the Supreme Court from ruling on the constitutionality of laws in cases reaching it on appeal.[3]

Perhaps no AAA supporter reacted as angrily to the Court's decision as Henry Wallace. In a radio address delivered a few days after the decision, the secretary openly criticized the ruling and warned his listeners that, unless the government instituted a new farm program soon, the Court's decision would lead to "a repetition of 1932."

"Must Be Rebuilt to Withstand Cyclones." *Dallas Morning News* editorial cartoon, January 14, 1936. Reprinted with permission of the *Dallas Morning News.*

The *Hoosac Mills* decision so annoyed Wallace that he decided to write a book defending the constitutionality of the Agricultural Adjustment Act. In *Whose Constitution,* Wallace defended the AAA's crop-restriction policy as a government action, justified by the general welfare clause, to better society and to promote liberty. He also attacked the majority justices' seeming equation of liberty with property rights. At one point, Wallace, using language similar to Marvin Jones's earlier spirited defense of the Bankhead bill, challenged the Court's perceived reliance on laissez-faire individualism: "Society must ever be alert to renew economic liberty on a broader pattern, for if left too long uncontrolled, economic liberty becomes economic autocracy."[4]

Franklin Roosevelt abstained from making public comments on the *Hoo-*

sac Mills case, preferring to let subordinates and farm organization officials attack the Court's decision. At the annual Jackson Day dinner, held two days after the decision was handed down, the president emphasized: "It is enough to say that the attainment of justice and prosperity for American agriculture remains an immediate constant objective of my administration."[5]

Privately, FDR left a revealing note for posterity regarding his personal view of the Supreme Court's judgment. In a January 24 memorandum for his personal files, he recorded:

> It has been well said by a prominent historian that fifty years from now the Supreme Court's decision will, in all probability, be described somewhat as follows:
>
> (1) The decision virtually prohibits the President and the Congress from the right, under modern conditions, to intervene in the regulation of nation-wide commerce and nation-wide agriculture.
>
> (2) The Supreme Court arrived at this result by selecting from several possible techniques of constitutional interpretation a special technique. The objective of the Court's purpose was to make reasonableness in passing legislation a matter to be settled not by the views of the elected Senate and House of Representatives and not by the views of an elected President but rather by the private, social philosophy of a majority of nine appointed members of the Supreme Court itself.[6]

In February, Congress took action to further dismantle the farm program. Responding to a written request from President Roosevelt, both houses pre-empted the Supreme Court by repealing the Bankhead Cotton Control Act. A case brought by Texas ginners had just reached the High Court. The president and members of Congress, predicting an outcome similar to that in the *Hoosac Mills* case, decided to forgo useless litigation.

The main result of the repeal was the immediate devaluation of all unsold Bankhead certificates. The national surplus-certificate pool had sold 17.5 percent of the 1935 certificates before it closed; thus, producers who transferred their Bankhead certificates to the pool received only the fixed four cents per pound price on 17.5 percent of their transferred certificates. Over the next three years, many Texas farmers and their congressmen continued to protest, requesting government redemption of the remaining certificates. AAA officials responded by stating that the agency could do nothing legally to restore even part of the value of the old certificates.[7]

Development of the Soil Conservation and Domestic Allotment Act

One day after the Court's ruling, Henry Wallace and Chester Davis met with farm organization officials to discuss the decision. Wallace subsequently called farm leaders from every section of the country to come to Washington in order to consider possible courses of action.[8]

Although the *Hoosac Mills* ruling genuinely surprised many administration officials, the decision did not catch the AAA without a plan to propose to the Washington conferees. The Court's ruling actually accelerated efforts developed by the AAA's Program Planning Division under Howard Ross Tolley to shift the emphasis of the farm programs away from simple crop reduction to programs that rewarded farmers for promoting soil conservation and employing superior farm management techniques.[9]

Tolley took an unusual route to becoming an agricultural New Dealer. He was born and raised on an Indiana farm, but he sought to leave farm life and pursue an urban occupation. After studying mathematics at Indiana University, he taught school for several years before William J. Spillman recruited him in 1915 to work for the USDA's Office of Farm Management. Under Spillman's tutelage, Tolley's expertise and interest in agricultural problems grew. In 1922, he became head of the Division of Farm Management within the USDA's Bureau of Agricultural Economics, working alongside his good friend M. L. Wilson. Tolley left the USDA during the Hoover administration to become director of the Giannini Foundation, which supported research in agricultural economics at the University of California. He returned to Washington in late 1933 to head the AAA's Program Planning Division, concentrating his energies on developing methods to promote efficient land use and soil conservation.[10]

Beginning in late 1934, Tolley worked with M. L. Wilson (now serving as assistant secretary of agriculture) to organize a series of regional conferences to discuss their ideas with farmers, representatives from agricultural colleges, and extension workers. After the meetings, Tolley devised a program that would pay farmers to reduce production of cash crops harmful to the soil while encouraging growers to plant soil-conserving crops such as grasses and legumes. In addition, under the new plan, the AAA would reward producers with additional payments if they agreed to adopt soil-conservation practices, such as contour plowing and terracing. The plan promised to serve the dual purpose of achieving production control of cash crops while simultaneously promoting soil conservation.[11]

The soil-conservation issue certainly occupied the minds of many Americans in 1935, a notable year in American environmental history due to the incredible dust storms blowing out of the Great Plains, especially from the infamous Dust Bowl region centered in the Texas-Oklahoma panhandles. Many of the storms, shooting thousands of feet into the air and encompassing several square miles, spread far beyond their place of origin, even reaching the East Coast. One storm that originated in New Mexico traveled to Washington, D.C., just as Hugh Hammond Bennett, the director of the Soil Erosion Service (a temporary agency placed within the Interior Department) was testifying before a Senate committee. At the time, the committee was considering a bill authored by Marvin Jones that would establish a permanent Soil Conservation Service (SCS) to promote soil conservation throughout the country. With a progressive's zeal, Bennett had worked tirelessly since the turn of the century to preach efficient soil-conservation methods. As the dust storm hit and darkened the sky above the nation's capital, he seized the opportunity to lecture the senators: "This, gentlemen, is what I have been talking about!" Needless to say, Congress soon unanimously passed the Jones bill, with Bennett serving as the SCS's first director.[12]

Despite the great publicity for the cause of soil conservation generated by the dust storms, the AAA failed to enact Howard Tolley's recommendations in 1935. Convinced that AAA officials were dragging their feet and were content with paying farmers for production control, Tolley returned to the Giannini Foundation in mid-1935. He remained at his post until the *Hoosac Mills* decision, when Chester Davis recalled him to Washington to help develop a new AAA program based on his previous work with the Planning Division. As Richard Kirkendall has noted: "The Supreme Court . . . accomplished what Tolley could not." In the wake of *Hoosac Mills,* the Roosevelt administration chose to experiment with the economist's proposals. The administration's counterattack on the Court's ruling began with the efforts of Henry Wallace and Chester Davis to use the Washington conference to promote Tolley's program.[13]

On January 10, Davis opened the two-day conference by outlining the main features of six proposals then condemning each plan on grounds of impracticality or unconstitutionality. The AAA chief proceeded to tell the assembled farm leaders that the only pragmatic course was to institute a new plan that would pay farmers subsidies directly out of the federal treasury (rather than from processing taxes) as inducements to shift production from soil-depleting cash crops to soil-conserving cover crops. The government would also agree to pay growers who performed accepted soil-conservation practices. Instead of using formal contracts, farmers were to submit soil-conservation adjustment plans. Producers would receive payment when they presented proof that they had performed the work pledged in their plans. On the final day of the gathering, the farm leaders unanimously endorsed an executive committee report calling for a program based on Davis's outline.[14]

At a January 16 White House meeting, Marvin Jones, John Bankhead, Cotton Ed Smith, and other congressional leaders promised President Roosevelt and Secretary Wallace speedy passage of a bill based on the farm leaders' report. The representatives agreed to pass the new proposal as a temporary measure pending development of a permanent agricultural program. Draftsmen for the House and Senate Committees on Agriculture immediately went to work drawing up appropriate legislation.[15]

On January 22, Bankhead and Jones introduced bills as proposed amendments to the Soil Erosion Act to operate for a two-year duration. Both the House and the Senate acted quickly. On February 16, the Senate passed its version by a 56–20 vote, with Texas senators Tom Connally and Morris Sheppard voting for the measure. A week later, the House voted 267–97 in favor of its version, with all Texas representatives voting for passage (George Terrell had since retired). On February 27, a conference committee quickly adopted the House version, which both chambers affirmed by voice vote later that evening. Roosevelt signed the bill into law on February 29.[16]

The new farm measure, known formally as the Soil Conservation and Domestic Allotment Act, directed the secretary of agriculture to disburse payments up to $500 million per year to farmers in return for various soil-conservation practices. The law gave the secretary of agriculture power to decide the details regarding allocation of payments.[17]

Under the terms of the SCDAA, the AAA would pay farmers to grow approved soil-building crops and employ accepted erosion-prevention methods. Because farming conditions, topography, and soil composition varied so greatly throughout the United States, Secretary Wallace knew that it would be impossible to devise a blanket conservation program that would be fair and equitable to all sections of the country. To cope with such difficulties, he decided to schedule four large regional conferences. Farm leaders from each section would meet with AAA officials in order to discuss proper conservation practices and appropriate payments for performing such practices in

"At Last a New Deal for the Soil!" *Dallas Morning News* editorial cartoon, March 3, 1936. Reprinted with permission of the *Dallas Morning News.*

their region. These meetings occurred simultaneously from March 5 to 7. The southern conference took place in Memphis, Tennessee.[18]

At the Memphis meeting, delegates used an outline provided by the AAA to discuss details of the cotton program. Eventually, the conferees approved a set of recommendations. The delegates called for individual shifts of cotton acreage to a host of soil-conserving grasses and legumes in return for payments at a rate of five cents per pound based on a farmer's estimated average yield. As further inducement to join the program, they agreed that producers who planted soil-building crops or performed soil-conserving practices should receive payments up to one dollar per acre.[19]

Before releasing the final details of the new soil-conservation program, the Roosevelt administration announced some important organizational modifications to the SCDAA. The changes began when Chester Davis, wishing to take a break from his exhausting administrative duties, took a leave of absence in mid-March to travel to Europe, ostensibly to study foreign trade issues. He never returned to the AAA. In June, he decided to accept a position as agricultural representative on the Board of Governors of the Federal Reserve System. On Davis's recommendation, Secretary Wallace chose Howard Tolley to be the new AAA administrator.[20]

In March, soon after becoming acting administrator, Tolley announced major changes to streamline the AAA bureaucracy. First, five regional divisions were created to replace the commodity sections. Cully Cobb, who had led the Cotton Section, now led the new Southern Division, with jurisdiction over nine states, including Texas. Second, the AAA made a major attempt to further decentralize its administration. While maintaining regional headquarters in Washington, much of the administrative work, such as examination of grant applications and disbursement of payments, would now be performed in the states under the guidance of state conservation committees. These new state committees consisted of five farmers appointed by the secretary of agriculture on the recommendation of the Southern Division's director. The main tasks of the state committees involved advising the division chief on general policy within their states and hearing any appeals relayed by the county committees. County and local committees under the general leadership of the Extension Service continued to administer the new program at the grass-roots level.[21]

On March 20, Secretary Wallace announced the rather intricate details of the new program. For 1936, AAA officials hoped farmers would divert thirty million acres of commercial cropland to soil-conserving crops. The estimated cost to the federal treasury would be $470 million. Producers could qualify to receive three types of payment: first, a "soil-conserving" payment, for soil-depleting acreage diverted to the planting of cover crops; second, a smaller "soil-building" payment, up to one dollar per acre, for planting specified grasses and legumes on soil not typically dedicated to the production of soil-depleting crops, with the exact amount to be determined by Wallace on recommendations from the state conservation committees; finally, a payment to growers who adopted approved soil-conserving practices, with the exact rate of payment to be determined by Wallace. Although the AAA agreed to pay farmers for performing each soil-protecting procedure, farmers did not have to employ all three techniques in order to receive payment.

For cotton, Wallace set the soil-conserving payment rate at five cents per pound for the average yield per acre as determined by the local committees. The AAA would make no payments unless the individual grower reduced cotton acreage by a minimum of 20 percent from the farmer's base acreage (the same base used during the 1935 program), up to a maximum reduction of 35 percent. For reasons of fairness to other counties and budgetary concerns, however, the AAA did not allow any individual county to reduce its cotton acreage more than 25 percent.

To illustrate how the AAA would compensate farmers under the SCDAA, the following example may be helpful. Assume we have a farm owner who planted an average of one hundred acres of cotton per year with a yield of two hundred pounds per acre. The producer also typically planted twenty acres of alfalfa per year. The grower now wished to plant only seventy acres of cotton, shifting thirty acres to cowpeas while continuing to plant his normal twenty acres of alfalfa. Under the new plan, the farmer would receive a soil-conservation payment for the thirty diverted acres equal to five cents per pound times his average yield of two hundred pounds per acre, for a total of three hundred dollars. He would also receive a soil-building payment equal to one dollar per acre on his thirty acres of cowpeas and his twenty acres of alfalfa, for a total of fifty dollars. In addition, the farmer would be eligible to receive a payment for conducting any approved soil-conserving practice he wished to perform on his land.

In cotton-growing areas, the AAA established the division of payments between landlords, tenants, and sharecroppers. For soil-building and soil-conservation practices, each party would divide the money based on the contribution to the expense of carrying out the procedure. For the larger soil-conserving payment, the landowner received 37.5 percent of the payment, 12.5 percent went to whoever furnished the work stock and equipment, and the landowner and his tenant or sharecropper split the remaining 50 percent according to how each party divided the proceeds of the crop.[22]

The 1936 Cotton Program

For the third time in four years, the AAA in 1936 presented a fresh program to southern cotton growers. As during the 1933 program, novel and untried provisions combined with late passage of the farm act to produce haste and confusion during implementation of the cotton program. Once the growing season was under way, however, producers found that the stifling Texas heat and lack of rain would be more effective in reducing the cotton crop than the provisions of the SCDAA.

From late March to mid-April, a series of educational meetings took place throughout Texas to promote the new program. Although the plan involved new procedures, the decision to continue the grass-roots network of extension agents and committeemen prevented further problems that could have developed from creating a new, inexperienced administrative force. As in the earlier programs, Extension Service district personnel began the educational phase by explaining the new plan to county agents. The extension agents, in turn, held community meetings to relay the details to members of the local farmers' associations, now called "agricultural conservation associations." In 1936, the farmers at these community assemblies chose their new local committeemen. The county agents chaired another meeting with the local committee, which proceeded to elect members of the new county committee from its ranks.[23]

In a majority of cases, local committeemen did not canvass their communities to persuade producers to sign the worksheets signifying participation in the new program. Most Texas county agents reported that local committeemen stationed themselves at accessible locations within the community, including the county agent's office, and awaited the arrival of farmers. When growers appeared, the committeemen advised them on how properly to complete the worksheets containing their voluntary conservation pledges. Sign-ups continued until the June 15 deadline.[24]

One of the major sign-up problems cited by Texas county agents in their annual narrative reports involved the inherent confusion in implementing yet another new program. Many farmers had difficulty forgetting the details of the old crop-reduction plans. The new system of payments, with its large list of acceptable conservation crops and practices, proved vastly more complicated than the previous disbursement methods. Exasperated by trying to explain the new program in his county, the Bell County agent concluded his discussion on the topic with a succinct statement: "It is hoped that in the future the program may be simplified to the extent that it may be understandable to the average farmer."[25]

Another problem in the Texas sign-up effort came from the lateness of getting the program under way. Because many growers had planted their crops before the AAA presented the opportunity to enlist, thousands of farmers who wished to cooperate in the new government effort were unable to take full advantage of the program.[26]

"His Old Teacher Used to Solve the Problems." *Dallas Morning News* editorial cartoon, April 8, 1936. Reprinted with permission of the *Dallas Morning News*.

Even before committees completed the sign-up, producers were experiencing the effects of a second statewide drought in three years. In response to the worsening conditions throughout Texas and much of the South, AAA officials designed changes to allow growers to take full advantage of crop insurance provisions available under the SCDAA. On June 13, just before the sign-up deadline, Secretary Wallace announced his approval of two changes for the farm program in the Southern Region. First, small producers with a base acreage of five cotton acres or fewer could receive full payment for diverting up to two acres of cotton to grasses or legumes. Second, Wallace changed the provision that total payments to a county's producers could not exceed 25 percent of the county's total base; for 1936, farmers could shift up to 35 percent of their individual base acreage without any restriction.[27]

After checking for errors on the worksheets, county committees mailed completed forms to the State Conservation Committee in College Station for tabulation and analysis. In most cases, the state board returned the worksheets for final adjustments so that county figures complied with government data.[28]

Beginning in late August, the county committees started to verify compliance with the worksheets in two ways. The main procedure utilized the services of local committeemen and assistants who had passed a special examination. As in previous programs, these individuals measured land with tapes and chains. Close to twenty Texas counties, however, took part in a novel approach pushed by Cully Cobb. The AAA experimented with an accurate, low-cost alternative using aerial photographs to check compliance. After aerial surveying's initial use in Franklin County, the local extension agent noted that it reduced the cost of land measurement to two cents per acre, compared to the 1935 cost of three cents per acre using traditional tape-and-chain methods. The success of the Texas trials led to expansion of this practice to other parts of the Cotton Belt in future years.[29]

Because farmers performed many soil-conservation practices, such as terracing and planting of legumes during the early winter months, most committees did not submit applications for payment until December. The State Conservation Committee in College Station then relayed approved applications to the disbursement office of the United States Treasury in Dallas. The office mailed checks to county agents for distribution. As a result of this time-consuming process, most Texas farmers did not see any government money until March 1937.[30]

Government figures show that Texas cotton growers eventually received $34,799,112 for participation in the 1936 Agricultural Conservation Program. The AAA paid Texas farmers for diverting 3,077,833 cotton acres and conducting approved soil-conserving practices, most often listing and terracing. Texans signed 198,430 worksheets in 1936, covering 66.6 percent of their cropland (the average was 69.4 percent for all Southern Division states). As occurred during prior programs, however, numerous tenants and sharecroppers continued to report that their landlords either withheld or improperly divided government payments.[31]

As a crop-reduction measure, the 1936 agricultural conservation program did not perform as well as the drought. Texas growers planted one million more acres than in 1935, but statewide cotton production plummeted to 2,933,000 bales on 11,597,000 harvested acres (52 percent of the normal yield). Nevertheless, with an average price of 12.3 cents per pound, Texas farmers received $173 million for the 1936 crop.[32]

The 1937 Program and the Failure of the SCDAA

The inadequacies of the SCDAA's reliance on strictly voluntary cooperation for crop reduction became painfully apparent in 1937. Higher crop prices, smaller payments under the SCDAA than the rental and parity payments under the Agricultural Adjustment Act, and the absence of strict production controls led to more planted cotton acreage than in the early programs. In 1936, poor growing conditions in Texas and other growing areas obscured potential problems with the SCDAA. In 1937, however, the return of good weather plus the human factors mentioned above combined to produce the largest cotton crop in American history—18,946,000 bales—despite southern producers' diverting 8.9 million acres to soil-building crops. Texas cotton farmers contributed greatly to this glut, harvesting 5,154,000 bales on 12,539,000 acres, for the third-largest crop in the history of the Lone Star State. (Texas production increased 75 percent from 1936, while non-Texas production increased 45 percent.) The repercussions of this development would reverberate before the crop was even harvested.[33]

The 1937 program began simply enough. The AAA made an early effort to educate producers about the plan by announcing its details in December 1936. The new program possessed essentially the same features as the 1936 program, except for the deduction of county administrative expenses from the farmers' checks rather than from general administrative funds, as had been done in previous years.[34]

Educational meetings in mid-February inaugurated the 1937 agricultural conservation program. The early start enabled extension agents and committeemen to disseminate information on the 1937 plan before most farmers planted their crops. As a result, farmers participated in the program on a larger scale than during the 1936 campaign. Although much confusion over the various aspects of the program continued, Texas growers signed a total of 241,766 worksheets and secured $30,626,239 in performance payments while diverting 2,762,000 cotton acres to soil-building crops.[35]

Cully Cobb decided to make 1937 his last year as head of the Southern Division. At the end of July, he informed Howard Tolley that he would soon resign in order to return to private business. Fully satisfied that he had helped successfully launch the government commodity programs, Cobb felt ready for new challenges. To succeed him, Cobb recommended Ivy W. Duggan, a former Georgia extension agent and vocational agriculture professor from Clemson College. Duggan had joined the AAA in 1934 as the principal agricultural economist of the Cotton Section. After a long selection process, Tolley chose Duggan to replace Cobb at the end of the 1937 season.[36]

As early as March 1937, Cobb spotted signs of another cotton crisis on the horizon. After reviewing crop forecasts, he wrote H. H. Williamson to express fears that rising prices were causing southern farmers "to forget the situation which brought about 5-cent cotton." He stated that the AAA needed to make a special effort at the start of the coming season to educate farmers about the potential dangers of a sizable increase in cotton acreage. "Unless farmers help themselves," Cobb concluded, "there is nothing the Government can do to maintain the balanced production necessary to obtain reasonable prices." In order to keep farmers from deserting the crop-reduction aspects of the government program, he instructed Williamson to have Texas county agents distribute pamphlets reiterating the negative consequences of enlarged cotton acreage. Despite these and other educational efforts, Texans joined their southern brethren and increased cotton acreage to the highest level since the Hoover administration, resulting in the return of single-digit-per-pound prices in 1937.[37]

Throughout 1937, Henry Wallace urged members of Congress to pass a new, long-term agricultural program. The fierce battle between FDR and Congress over the president's controversial judiciary reform, or "court-packing" plan, however, prevented congressional action as long as no emergency existed. The huge 1937 cotton crop proved to be the needed stimulus for many Southern members of Congress to seek action. Nevertheless, the return of a large carryover and low crop prices did not automatically lead to congressional acceptance of a new farm measure. The president and Secretary Wallace discovered that in the tumult of Roosevelt's second term, nothing could be taken for granted.

Formulation of the Ever-Normal Granary Plan

In January 1937, the impetus toward formulation of a new farm plan commenced with a series of meetings between Secretary Wallace and the executive committee of the American Farm Bureau Federation, the most influential farm organization in the nation. Both Wallace and the Farm Bureau desired a long-term program for agriculture, but disagreed on many details. Farm Bureau leaders argued strongly for strict production-control measures and par-

Secretary of Agriculture Henry A. Wallace, promoter of the ever-normal granary. USDA photo, National Archives II.

ity prices, while Wallace lobbied hard for his Ever-Normal Granary Plan—a farm-price and income-stabilization scheme to supplement the SCDAA with moderate production-control measures involving price-support loans and marketing quotas when commodity supplies reached specified overproduction levels. The plan promised to insulate agricultural producers and consumers from excessively high or depressed prices while ensuring adequate supplies of the major farm commodities at all times. Wallace found his plan to be a tough sell, not just to the major farm organizations, but also to a Congress increasingly hostile to the Roosevelt administration because of the president's efforts to reform the Supreme Court. In 1937, the secretary found congressional allies such as Marvin Jones not nearly as amicable as in previous years.[38]

Wallace had been thinking about the basic outline of the Ever-Normal Granary Plan since the 1910s and wrote often about the idea in *Wallace's Farmer*. The Iowan certainly did not invent the concept of storing surpluses for lean growing years. Still, the plan reflected diverse influences on his eclectic mind: the biblical story of Joseph storing food in Egypt for use during famine; a system used by the ancient Chinese; even, to a certain extent, Herbert Hoover's Federal Farm Board. The secretary's contribution to the idea was to synthesize the combined AAA experience of the previous four years in order to develop the complex machinery needed to implement the plan and publicize it as a rational long-term national policy.[39]

Wallace and Farm Bureau leaders struck a compromise on the major elements of a new farm bill. The Farm Bureau endorsed the ever-normal granary concept in return for the secretary's support of strong production controls. Following the January meetings, Wallace called for another farm leaders' conference in Washington to take place in February. In addition to fifty chosen farm organization representatives, he also invited Marvin Jones and Cotton Ed Smith to participate in the proceedings.[40]

On the first day of the Washington conference, Wallace explained his intricate plan during an address to the assembled delegates. Noting that the existing soil-conservation program had merit as "a step in the right direction," he urged its continuance while at the same time arguing that the SCDAA did not offer long-term stabilization. The nation needed a superior mechanism to protect the principal farm commodities' supplies and prices from drastic fluctuations.

Wallace presented commodity loans as the next phase. Whenever agricultural supplies became excessive, Commodity Credit Corporation loans could serve the dual purpose of providing support for farm prices while diverting excess production to storage in the nation's granaries and warehouses. The government would use a standard to determine the normal supply for each commodity covered under the plan. Whenever the supply of any crop became larger than normal, the CCC would offer nonrecourse loans to producers in exchange for storage of their excess production, thus precluding the sale of commodities below the loan rate. In lean years, when prices rose higher, farmers could sell their crops for a reasonable profit and repay their loans.

If either a succession of favorable growing seasons or an unusual decline in demand occurred (causing "the granary to overflow"), the secretary stated that it would be unwise to continue offering loans without seeking definite reductions in production. Thus, in order to avoid repeating the mistakes of the Farm Board, whenever the supply of any commodity reached a threshold 10 percent or 15 percent above normal, the plan called for "storage in the soil" rather than "storage in the bin." By this method, the government would simply offer another voluntary inducement by paying additional subsidies for increased diversion of land from cash crops to soil-building crops.

Wallace noted that, in most instances, the control machinery of loans and increased conservation payments would be enough to contain large surpluses. Nevertheless, he acknowledged that a succession of exceedingly favorable growing seasons could make these additional steps insufficient to prevent the accumulation of excessive supplies. In cases of extreme surplus, strict production-control measures would have to be employed, most likely in the form of marketing quotas following the example of those provided for in the Bankhead Act. Wallace specified that the AAA would consult producers and their representatives to determine each commodity program's parameters. A formal referendum would be used for all "questions of major importance."[41]

In their final report, the conferees endorsed the general principles of the Ever-Normal Granary Plan. They established the Drafting and Steering Committee, composed of farm organization leaders, to draft a bill based on the plan's principles and to fight for its enactment.

Although the plan was too complex for most laymen to understand immediately, the editors of the *Dallas Morning News* did not hesitate to show their lack of enthusiasm for it. They protested Wallace's eagerness "to give the Government full power to tell farmers what and how much they should produce." Noting perceived dangers in the new plan, the editors warned: "It is high time for farmers to consider long and well whether they are willing to have a bureau in Washington to control their activities as if they were school children."[42]

Overall, the secretary's plan was an audacious strike at the Supreme Court, because his proposal continued to advocate federal government intervention. The plan's boldness came in part from a hope that the High Court would reverse itself, but it also showed a confidence that the Court would have more pro–New Deal members by the time any challenge reached the justices.

By May, Farm Bureau staff and USDA experts had completed a draft of a farm bill along the lines outlined in the Washington conference report. Despite the unified front presented at the meeting, however, few major farm organizations other than the Farm Bureau endorsed the legislation. Many smaller organizations followed the lead of the important National Grange, which opposed the bill, in part, because it was so visibly connected with the rival Farm Bureau. Most of the Grange's dissent, however, derived from the group's basic opposition to mandatory crop controls of any kind.[43]

The Farm Bureau measure faced immediate opposition from perturbed members of Congress. Some of the resistance originated in the bill's provisions, but more of the antagonism derived from the congressional environment. In February, Roosevelt stunned Congress and the nation with a surprise plan to reorganize the judicial branch of the federal government, especially the Supreme Court. Through legislation aimed at increasing the number of pro–New Deal justices, Roosevelt intended to address the problem of judicial constraints on New Deal initiatives at its source. In the attempt, the president paid a heavy price, as the administration immediately faced opposition from large numbers of Republican and Democratic members of Congress who were unwilling to tamper with the traditional system of checks and balances. As a result, senators and representatives began to stall most administration-sponsored bills.[44]

In the Senate, Cotton Ed Smith sounded his declaration of independence before the farm bill even reached his committee. In late April, he served notice that his committee intended to play an autonomous role in the formulation of agricultural legislation. Another, unnamed, committee member relayed to the press that others on the committee were "rather tired" of being considered "rubber stamps" for the administration. Smith reported that, henceforth, the committee would refuse to bow to the "dominance" of the Department of Agriculture.[45]

In the House, Marvin Jones showed little enthusiasm for the Farm Bureau bill during hearings on the proposed legislation. Never a strong advocate of compulsory measures, the Texan held to his belief that the voluntary features of the SCDAA worked quite smoothly and did not need amending. "We've got a good farm adjustment bill as it is," the chairman commented after the first committee hearing on the bill. Displaying continued skepticism and lacking any sense of urgency, Jones stated that any new farm law would require lengthy analysis before any alteration of the current farm program. His belief that President Roosevelt had failed to strongly support the new farm measure during the current congressional session also lessened pressure for action during the early spring months. Although FDR stated that he supported the Farm Bureau legislation "in principle," as yet, he was unwilling to insist on the bill's passage.[46]

Despite the farm bill's cool reception, Henry Wallace pressed for congressional acceptance during hearings before the House and Senate Committees on Agriculture. In late May, FDR finally gave his public endorsement to the legislation when he expressed his "hope" that Congress would adopt the bill during the current session. The president's open support for the measures failed to move Congress, however, as the legislation continued to languish in both agriculture committees. In the House, Chairman Jones slowed deliberations to a crawl; in the Senate, Smith openly challenged Wallace's assessment that the country faced a "very disquieting" agricultural situation if Congress failed to pass new farm legislation quickly. Smith declared his belief that administration officials "exaggerated" the seriousness of the farm situation and insisted that "unless we are all blind," little chance existed for a recurrence of the 1932 economic collapse.[47]

By mid-June, the Farm Bureau bill seemed almost doomed. After a disheartening meeting with congressional leaders, Wallace all but agreed to abandon serious efforts to get a new farm law during the current session in exchange for a promise that Congress would reintroduce the farm measure, hold extensive hearings, and prepare the legislation for passage in early 1938. Although he was discouraged, the secretary refused to give up all hope that the bill could be passed during the current session. Then suddenly, two weeks later, at the end of June, the White House issued an announcement stating that the president wished to press for passage during the current session. The growing realization among administration officials that the 1937 growing season looked to produce bumper crops in a wide range of commodities best explains FDR's unanticipated policy shift.[48]

On July 12, Roosevelt sent open letters to Marvin Jones and Ellison Smith. In the correspondence, the president reminded the chairmen that the government had not yet solved the farm problem. Although he believed that "the situation of the moment is excellent," he informed them that the "warning signals are already in sight" in the form of huge agricultural surpluses for the coming year. Roosevelt stated that no better time existed than the present to act on a long-term plan to stabilize agricultural income: "It is my philosophy that the time to repair a leaky roof is when the sun is shining." After summarizing the basic principles of the Ever-Normal Granary Plan and reiterating his support for the scheme, the president implored them to act decisively in the coming weeks: "The vital interests of the Nation demand that sooner or later protective measures of this type be placed in effect. If we wait until next year the ultimate objective will be the same but we may be faced with emergency conditions which would make the legislative and administrative problem more difficult because of the very fact of moving hurriedly under the fire of an emergency."[49]

Roosevelt's appeals failed to move either chairman. Smith decided to delay matters further by conducting hearings throughout the country with ordinary farmers before approving any permanent farm program. "We are only going to listen to one-gallus men. Anybody with a white collar on won't be admitted to these hearings," Cotton Ed bellowed. One week after receiving the president's letter, Jones responded by introducing his own farm bill. The Jones bill included the ever-normal granary method, but preserved the voluntary nature of the farm program by excluding marketing quotas for production beyond established individual allotments. Instead of the rigid tax penalties envisioned under the Farm Bureau plan, overproducing growers could be punished only by the government's refusal to make soil-conservation payments or offer commodity loans. By late July, Jones had not progressed very far with his legislation before the House and Senate Committees on Agriculture agreed to postpone deliberations on farm legislation for the remainder of the year. Thus, until 1938 at the earliest, any movement on a long-term farm bill appeared hopeless.[50]

The alienation of Congress caused by the court-packing plan, the complexity of the proposed agricultural programs, the lack of a clear consensus among major farm groups, and the reluctance of Marvin Jones and Ellison Smith all combined to block administration efforts for the Ever-Normal Granary Plan. In late 1937, however, as Secretary Wallace's predictions of tremendous surpluses and low farm prices were becoming a reality, senators and representatives found themselves scurrying for solutions. Representatives from the farm states who had been looking forward to adjournment now began to panic as they considered the prospect of returning home to face the wrath of angry constituents. From the White House, Franklin Roosevelt sensed this turn of events and planned to capitalize on the mounting discord by demanding passage of the long-term farm measure that had eluded him during what would turn out to be the most antagonistic congressional session he ever experienced as president.[51]

CHAPTER 5

EMERGENCE OF THE EVER-NORMAL
GRANARY, 1937–39

Before the USDA released its first official estimate of the 1937 crop, reports of record-high production began to appear in southern newspapers. In early August, Rep. Nat Patton of Crockett, Texas, wired President Roosevelt after reading press reports of the likelihood of a huge cotton harvest. The congressman pleaded with Roosevelt to peg prices between twelve and fifteen cents per pound through CCC price-support loans: "Why not act now and save our southern farmers and all from utter ruin and beggary conditions?" Patton refused to blame the president for the imminent crisis, however, preferring to place fault with his colleagues: "Crop control legislation should have been enacted long ago. We in Congress in a measure are to blame. We should have foreseen this impending disaster and acted accordingly."[1]

A shock wave hit the South on August 9, after the USDA Crop Reporting Board released its first official cotton forecast of the season. The board estimated the 1937 crop at 15,593,000 bales—over a half-million bales more than the average of most respected private estimates. This appraisal, which made the 1937 crop the largest since 1931, spurred a sharp decline in cotton prices on all major exchanges. As near-perfect growing conditions continued in Texas and elsewhere in the South, the Crop Reporting Board continued to revise its crop estimates upward until it became apparent that southern producers would harvest a record crop in 1937. Widespread anxiety permeated the Cotton Belt, resulting in pressure on the president to provide immediate relief. Despite the worsening situation, FDR probably could not resist a sly smile while watching Congress fidget. He would take advantage of its procrastination by using the price decline to push for immediate acceptance of Henry Wallace's Ever-Normal Granary Plan.[2]

Impact of the 1937 Crop Forecast

The cotton forecast, coupled with the release of the extremely high corn and wheat estimates the following day, fueled a commotion in Congress. Numerous Texas congressmen joined other representatives in immediately calling for a commodity loan program to protect cotton growers from declining prices. Prominent among those seeking price-support loans was Ellison Smith, who had discounted earlier estimates that predicted even smaller crops than the August report did. In an effort to solicit Roosevelt's approval for commodity loans, Smith's committee pledged to report a general farm bill within a week after Congress reconvened in January.[3]

Sensing a shift in the mood of Congress, Roosevelt decided to gamble. Banking on the members' reluctance to return home amid plummeting cotton prices, the president resisted the issuance of an immediate executive order authorizing CCC commodity loans. Instead, as a condition for establishing price-support loans for the 1937 cotton crop, he insisted that Congress pass a crop-reduction measure that included the ever-normal granary concept during the *current* session.[4]

Roosevelt's assertive tactics only succeeded in antagonizing southern members of Congress. Representatives from cotton states on the House Rules Committee retaliated by blocking floor consideration of the administration-supported minimum wage–maximum hours legislation. Even Marvin Jones turned against the administration, delivering a floor speech that garnered a standing ovation from the assembled House members as he reprimanded the president for his "whip and spur" tactics.[5]

The squabbling between Congress and the White House over price-support loans lasted only two days. The feud ended when the president and congressional negotiators struck a deal. In exchange for a resolution stating that passage of a farm bill would be the first order of business in the next session of Congress, Roosevelt agreed to issue an executive order mandating a loan-and-subsidy plan (similar to the 1935 price-support effort). The order guaranteed twelve-cent cotton in 1937 for farmers who promised to participate in a new crop-reduction program. Although he did not get his way entirely, FDR surely benefited from the turn of events. At the same time that he received accolades from grateful southern cotton farmers for providing the loan-and-subsidy package, the president also achieved his coveted goal of a congressional promise for action on the long-term farm bill.[6]

The 1937 Special Session of Congress

Exactly when Congress would next convene, either in a November special session or the regular January meeting, depended on Franklin Roosevelt. The president, though eager to pass a host of legislation, including a long-term agricultural measure, was leery of agitating Congress and proceeded cautiously. He was torn between the idea of giving the representatives some cooling-off time and the desire to press forward with an extra session. Thus he held a series of meetings with Marvin Jones, Tom Connally, and other congressional leaders to learn their opinions. By mid-October, Roosevelt decided to call Congress into special session for the first time since March 1933.[7]

At an October 12 press conference, FDR issued the call for a special session to begin on November 15. That evening, Roosevelt followed the announcement with one of his famous "fireside chats," in which he touched on the five-point agenda that he wished Congress to consider during the special term, including farm and wages-and-hours legislation. After the radio address, John Bankhead sent the president congratulations on the inspiring talk and reassured him that he had the support of southern farmers: "Their faith in you is unbounded. They do not look to their Senators and Representatives, or to Henry Wallace. President Roosevelt is their Moses."[8]

A week after delivering his address, Roosevelt sent identical letters to Marvin Jones and Ellison Smith. In the letters, he recalled his deal with Congress at the end of the previous session and stated that the "pressing nature" of the emergency dictated action as soon as possible. The president also asked the chairmen for help in passing farm legislation containing the Ever-Normal Granary Plan, an "effective provision" for surplus-crop control, and the continuation of local administration "in the farmer's hands."[9]

Jones continued to push his voluntary-control bill. The Texan persisted in his belief that commodity distribution, rather than excess production, was the main problem for growers. Thus, he continued to prefer legislation that promoted surplus exportation as the remedy for American farmers. Jones also had to answer to his constituents. Many farmers in his district opposed any controls based on past production. The reason for their opposition was similar to that of growers in the Rio Grande Valley—they felt that because they farmed a relatively new cotton-growing region, quotas or allotments based on past production discriminated against them and served only the interests of the older cotton regions. Jones had acquiesced to the administration's previous programs because of the economic crisis and out of party loyalty. With the immediate emergency over and strained party relations caused by the Court battle, however, he tried to stake his own ground and fight for a plan based on his principles and consistent with the views of voters back home.[10]

Soon after the president's special session call, Jones delivered a speech before fellow representatives Lyndon Johnson, Richard Kleberg, W. R. Poage, Nat Patton, and over fifteen hundred farmers at a meeting held in Taylor, Texas. The congressman outlined his measure before the assembled crowd, then stated that his committee would quickly deliver to the House floor a program based on the principles of that plan. He noted that, despite some differences, both Wallace's plan and his agreed on the principle that the government should directly aid Texas farmers. At one point, Jones reiterated his belief that unrestrained individualism in American agriculture was near an end and boldly proclaimed: "The man who says it's my land and I'll do what I please with it regardless of my neighbor and my children's heritage is as bad as a Communist."[11]

Members of the House Committee on Agriculture met in late October, before the special session began, and immediately split over the control provisions of the Jones bill. This set the stage for a drawn-out debate in Congress over production control that would carry over into the regular session in 1938. A majority of the committee members supported Jones's voluntary enforcement methods of reducing or withdrawing conservation payments in addition to making noncompliers ineligible for commodity loans. A sizable minority, however, agreed with John Bankhead, the major Senate supporter of strict crop controls, that the AAA should assess stiff overmarketing penalties.[12]

Senator Bankhead believed that Jones's bill was completely inadequate as a means of reducing surpluses. "There is no control in the bill," Bankhead complained to President Roosevelt. "No effort is made to restrict production." In his opinion, Jones's bill was unacceptable because it simply would not induce enough growers to cooperate to ensure the program's success. "There is no penalty for violation, except that the violator is declared to be a noncooperator and cannot receive payments the following year under the Soil Conservation Act." Referring to a prominent Texas cotton shipper, the senator believed such thinking was simply "the Will Clayton doctrine."

Bankhead also included in his letter to FDR an incorrect view of the attitudes of Texas cotton growers toward production control: "Marvin has always had the *Texas* viewpoint on production control." Although many business leaders (such as Will Clayton) and many of Texas' political leaders (such as Marvin Jones) preferred policies that promoted foreign trade over highly restrictive production measures potentially harmful to foreign markets, it should be noted that this preference was more representative of Texas agribusiness than of the "average" Texas grower. Most producers probably had no ideological foundation for their support of the AAA cotton programs other than a desire for higher cotton prices. But, as I demonstrated in the discussion on the first Bankhead Act referendum, numerous Texas growers explicitly rejected the emphasis on foreign markets, favoring production controls because they believed that rigid crop control was the best way to raise the domestic price. During the debate on the referendum, farmers also openly expressed their belief that a lack of controls favored intermediaries in the cotton trade at the producers' expense.[13]

After long, heated sessions, the House Committee on Agriculture compromised and agreed to add marketing quotas with moderate penalties (two cents per pound for cotton) whenever supplies reached prescribed levels. The Senate's farm bill, endorsed by the Farm Bureau and forcefully supported by John Bankhead, placed much stronger penalties on commodities marketed above set quotas—75 percent of the sale price in the case of cotton. Although a majority on the committee supported the bill, Cotton Ed Smith did not. Nevertheless, the senator, facing reelection in 1938, bowed to pressure from the administration, members of his committee, and his constituents to end his obstruction.[14]

On December 10, after a long debate on the degree of compulsion, the House passed the Jones bill by a 267–130 vote. The Senate also experienced a tough debate over production controls before finally passing its version of the farm bill by a 59–29 unrecorded vote on December 17.[15]

Marvin Jones, John Bankhead, Cotton Ed Smith, and other congressional leaders deliberated for a month over the rival farm bills in a conference committee. The conferees debated into the early days of the regular session in 1938 before coming to an agreement. They took a moderate stance on the crucial issue of compulsory controls. In the case of cotton, farmers who excessively marketed their cotton when quotas were in effect were to receive reduced soil-conservation payments, lose eligibility for parity payments, receive worse terms for CCC loans, and pay a penalty of two cents per pound on all over-marketed cotton in 1938 and three cents per pound thereafter.[16]

On February 9, by a 263–135 vote, the House passed the compromise bill, with all Texas representatives voting in favor of the measure except Richard Kleberg of Corpus Christi, Albert Thomas of Houston, and Milton West of Brownsville. The Senate passed the compromise bill on February 14 by a 56–31 vote, with Tom Connally and Morris Sheppard voting in favor. On February 16, President Roosevelt signed the bill, known formally as the Agricultural Adjustment Act of 1938. While noting that the bill was not perfect, the president stated that it did represent "the winning of one more battle for an underlying farm policy that will endure."[17]

Cotton Provisions of the Agricultural Adjustment Act of 1938

The new farm act contained all the major aspects of the long-term farm program sought by Henry Wallace. Although the new price- and income-stabilization measures applied only to five major agricultural products (cotton, corn, wheat, rice, and tobacco), payments continued to producers of all commodities who cooperated with the soil-conservation program. The cotton provisions of the new law were incredibly more complex than those of the Agricultural Adjustment Act of 1933. Anyone who has problems understanding the following details should try to imagine what the average Texas cotton farmer went through.

With regard to production control, the secretary of agriculture could call a marketing quota referendum in any year that the total cotton supply exceeded the normal supply by more that 7 percent. Since this was the situation in 1938, an initial referendum would be held within thirty days of the farm act's promulgation. For subsequent seasons, the plebiscite was to be held no later than December 15. Because the law dictated a two-thirds majority for passage, Texas' approval would once again be essential to the program's success.

If farmers approved marketing quotas for the season, the government would apportion the national cotton allotment, in bales, among the states on the basis of production during the preceding five years. State acreage allotments were to be determined by calculating the number of acres required, at average state yields, to produce the baleage allotment for each state. State acreage allotments were then prorated among the counties on the basis of the acreage planted to cotton during the previous five years.

County committees, with the assistance of local committeemen, determined the acreage allotments for individual farms. Each cotton farm was to be assigned an allotment that was a percentage of its tilled or regularly rotated acreage. This percentage was the same for all cotton farms in a county, with certain exceptions made for small farmers, and equaled the county's cotton acreage allotment divided by the total tilled acreage of cotton farms in the county. No producer was to receive an individual allotment less than 50 percent of his 1937 planted and diverted cotton acreage.

In order to avoid the complex system of using Bankhead certificates to determine exactly how much cotton a farmer could market legally (as was done in the 1934–35 programs), the new law simplified the process by allowing the sale of *all* cotton produced within a farmer's acreage allotment without penalty. If a grower exceeded his allotted acreage while a marketing quota was in effect, he could still sell as much cotton as he produced on his allotment without restriction, even more if his actual production (plus any cotton stored from previous seasons) was less than the average yield from his allotment. Beyond this permitted amount, however, the farmer would have to pay the marketing penalty. The penalty did not apply to cotton produced on any farm with an acreage allotment if total production was less than two bales.

The AAA developed a new way to calculate soil-conservation payments. Farmers would now receive maximum soil-conservation payments for planting within their acreage allotments. For 1938, these payments equaled 2.4 cents per pound on the normal yield of the farm's allotted acreage. Payments to landlords, tenants, and sharecroppers were to be made in the same proportion as their interest in the crop. Farmers who overplanted their crops would receive reduced conservation payments (at the rate of 5 cents per pound on the normal yield of excess cotton acreage), in addition to losing eligibility for price-adjustment parity payments (whenever appropriated by Congress) and best terms for commodity loans. The AAA would continue to compensate growers for completing specified soil-building practices as under the previous program.[18]

During years when the price of cotton fell below 52 percent of parity, or when the August crop estimate indicated that a cotton crop would be larger than needed for domestic consumption and exports, the CCC would offer loans to cooperating growers at rates ranging from 52 percent to 75 percent of the parity price. Noncooperators could also receive loans, but only at 60 percent of the rate that cooperators received. The CCC would not offer loans, however, during any marketing year in which the supply of cotton reached levels that triggered a marketing quota and cotton growers failed to approve the quotas in a referendum.

The AAA continued the practice of using producer committees to administer the cotton program at the local level. Extension Service agents, however, played a lesser role in carrying out provisions of the farm programs. County agents were to be *ex officio* members of the county committees, unless elected to serve as committee secretaries. Otherwise, the agents would dedicate more time to their normal extension duties and allow the producers on the county committees to have greater autonomy. As during the previous two years, state committees of three to five farmers appointed by the secretary of agriculture would hear appeals from county committees and recommend to the AAA program changes relevant to their state.[19]

The editors of the *Dallas Morning News* did not approve of the cotton provisions of the new farm act. In an editorial appearing the day Roosevelt signed the bill into law, the editors decried the anticipated drastic reduction in Texas' cotton acreage. They also expressed fears that the new legislation would result only in the loss of foreign markets and reduced income for Texas growers.[20]

Marvin Jones wrote the editors to correct factual errors and to explain his belief that the federal government had intervened in a positive way to aid America's cotton farmers. He stated that without a new program, the 1937 and 1938 cotton crops would sell at four or five cents per pound. In Jones's opinion, this would have meant "utter ruin" for the South by "putting the cotton farmer in rags" and practically destroying southern business and industry. The congressman maintained his strong belief in expanding the American cotton trade, but not at the expense of ruining growers through low prices:

> I believe that every effort should be made to broaden and expand our foreign markets and to widen distribution at home. The restrictions on marketing in the new bill are much milder than many wished them to be. I was not willing, and many others were not willing, for control of marketing to go to the degree of temporarily jacking the price of cotton entirely out of the price picture at a sacrifice of the long range cotton interests. On the other hand, there is no profit, either to the cotton farmer or to business and industry, in growing cotton at four or five cents per pound to sell either at home or abroad.[21]

Jones admitted to the editors that the farm bill was imperfect. He noted that there would certainly have to be future improvements. Nevertheless, he stated his belief that the law was a "step in the right direction" and urged the editors to support the act and the government's efforts to aid America's farmers: "The farm movement is the most tremendous one in America. Its purpose is to place the farmer on an equality of income with other business. Whether the new Act will succeed can only be told by experience; but if it does not succeed, a new program must be adopted that will succeed. So long as we have a tariff, the farmer is entitled to a tariff equivalent. The movement must go on."[22]

Implementation of the New Farm Act

The intricacy of the new program caused massive problems for Texas committeemen and extension agents trying to implement it. Many producers were frustrated with the program's details. The Brazos county agent summed up the situation: "1938 reached a high-water mark of complaint, or 'bellyache' about the AAA and its vacillating rules and regulations."[23]

In early March, the AAA launched the 1938 cotton program. Farmers elected their committeemen, then attended educational meetings to hear not only explanations of the new plan's provisions but also sales pitches pushing for acceptance of marketing quotas in the coming referendum. The March 12 plebiscite was the first test for the AAA's new program. Because the world supply of American cotton for the marketing year beginning on August 1, 1937, was approximately 24.5 million bales (far greater than the 7 percent surplus threshold), quotas, unless rejected by the growers, were to be imposed immediately. Farmers conducted their referendum before being informed of their county and individual allotments. Secretary Wallace was able to announce only a 10 million–bale national quota, translated into a national allotment of 28,285,572 acres, with Texas receiving a state allotment of 10,429,865 acres. Before the vote, no marked opposition to the quotas appeared in Texas.

Despite the lack of knowledge concerning their allotments, Texans joined other producers and endorsed marketing quotas by a huge margin. Texas' farmers heartily approved the quotas by a vote of 217,425–28,666, or 88.4 percent. (The national vote in favor of the quotas was 1,406,088–120,940, or 92.1 percent.) In only three Texas counties did a majority of growers vote against the quotas. Cameron and Willacy counties, in the Lower Rio Grande Valley, were in an area whose producers had been against the concept of production limits based on past production figures ever since its bad experience with the Bankhead quotas during the 1934–35 program.[24]

Despite its success in convincing cotton growers to accept marketing quotas, the AAA had a much harder job explaining all the facets of the new program. From the beginning, the complexity of the new plan overwhelmed all but the most informed committeemen, agents, and producers. As the Lavaca County agent complained: "One thing that can be said about the 1938 AAA Program. It was long on work but short on information."[25]

In 1938, the AAA conducted farmer interviews throughout the Cotton Belt to ascertain the degree of producer knowledge about the program. Survey results bore out the agents' contentions. From March to December, the AAA interviewed 952 cotton farmers. The inquiry showed that only 52 percent had a "minimum understanding" of the mechanics of the new farm program, defined as a farmer knowing his crop limits and having some definite notion of how the AAA determined his payment. Only 28 percent had "partial understanding" of these criteria; 20 percent had absolutely "no understanding" of the new cotton plan.[26]

The distribution of allotments also upset Texas growers. The main sources of contention were low county allotments, the delay in determining individual allotments, and perceived injustice when many growers received their individual allotments. Complaints to the AAA forced the agency to push Congress for amendments to the 1938 farm act in order to pacify the irate growers.

Soon after the AAA announced the county allotments in mid-March, numerous Texas farmers and committeemen filed protests with senators, representatives, and the AAA over their counties' low allotments.[27] As occurred during the 1934–35 period under the Bankhead Act, counties that had recently expanded cotton production received low allotments because the 1938 farm act based the county quotas on previous years' production figures. Bailey and Cochran counties in the southern High Plains were two such counties. The AAA distributed an allotment to Cochran County that equaled only 40 percent of its 1937 cotton acreage. This resulted in a strong protest from an irate farmer to Rep. George Mahon: "Our county is young, but we want justice!" Members of the Cochran County committee wrote Mahon to express their great fear that producers in their county would be "definitely sunk" unless the AAA allocated additional acreage.[28]

In response to the clamor by producers from around the Cotton Belt, Congress passed amendments to the Agricultural Adjustment Act of 1938, which

President Roosevelt signed on April 7. The most important amendment pertaining to cotton allowed for a 4 percent increase in state acreage allotments. This supplemental acreage would provide direct relief for producers in counties that had received abnormally low allotments.[29]

Another major source of dissatisfaction with the new program was the long delay before farmers received their individual allotment. Numerous county agents reported that farmers had already planted their crops by the time Congress passed the new law in late February. The late arrival of individual allotments caused considerable consternation among growers, especially those in the Lower Rio Grande Valley, who did not obtain their allotments until almost picking time.[30]

Many farmers also grew upset when they finally learned the amount of their allotments. Low county-reduction factors, applied equally to every producer in a county (after exceptions were made for small growers), drove many Texas farmers to write their representatives, senators, and the AAA in protest. Most claimed that their allotments were insufficient to take care of their needs.[31]

On receiving their allotments and discovering that they had overplanted, several Texas farmers complained to Tom Connally. The senator passed on the complaints to Secretary Wallace, suggesting that penalties be radically reduced in 1938 for accidental overplanting of cotton "in cases where farmers acted in good faith and were earnestly endeavoring to comply with the program." Wallace expressed regret for the delay in issuing allotments and the problems it caused, especially the reduction in soil-conservation payments. Nevertheless, he refused to recommend any changes in AAA policy with regard to overplanting penalties. Diplomatically, the secretary described reduced soil-conservation payments as merely "deductions" from maximum payments and claimed they "should not be regarded as penalties." He concluded by stating: "The principle of reducing payments when there is failure to effect full compliance with the program is sound . . . The deduction rates for overplanting should be maintained in the interest of the large majority of farmers throughout the nation."[32]

The clamor from growers who were assigned low allotments proved to be so strong that Congress passed further revisions to the 1938 farm act to allow for additional increases in individual allotments. On May 31, Roosevelt signed amendments that allowed for the redistribution of so-called frozen acreage, or that portion of the 1938 individual allotments that farmers had not planted. The reallocated cotton acreage was determined by means of questionnaires sent by county committees to growers. In a signed statement returned to the county agent's office, each farmer was to state how much of his cotton allotment remained unplanted. The unused portion would then be deducted from the grower's allotment for redistribution. The unused acreage figures from each county were sent to the state AAA office in College Station. The State Board reallocated the frozen acreage on an equitable basis to farmers whose original 1938 cotton acreage allotments were low and who did not expand their 1937 cotton acreage above normal. Farms that received minimum allotments (50 percent of their 1937 cotton acreage) and farms within the same county as the released frozen acreage received first consideration for additional allotments. The editors of the *Dallas Morning News* stated the obvious when they noted that it would have eliminated numerous complaints over low allotments in Texas had these adjustments been made earlier. They were also certainly correct when they stated that "considerably more experience" would be required before the AAA perfected a "reasonably satisfactory acreage plan."[33]

By June, compliance checking had begun in most areas of Texas. First, the local committees measured farms to determine whether growers had overplanted their allotments. Next, the committees issued special marketing cards developed by the AAA for producers to present at each sale. A farmer who planted within his allotment received a white card, indicating that he could sell without penalty all the cotton produced on his farm in 1938, or stored from a previous season if his yield did not reach his quota. Producers found to have overplanted (and who did not plow up their excess) received a red card that indicated the amount of cotton produced in 1938, or held from a previous year, that farmers could sell without penalty. The AAA required buyers to keep records of each cotton purchase, collect penalties on the excess cotton, transfer these funds to the United States Treasury, and send copies of each record to the county committees.[34]

A majority of Texas extension agents who commented on the subject of marketing cards reported that the number of red marketing cards they issued was low (fewer than ten), because farmers either planted within their limits or plowed up the excess after overplanting. Some agents, however, reported that growers in their counties received large numbers of red marketing cards. The Austin County agent, for example, reported that 875 producers were issued red marketing cards in his county. In Lavaca County, over 1,800 farmers received red marketing cards.[35]

Under the 1938 program, Texas cotton growers harvested 8,784,000 acres—

one-third less than in 1937 and the lowest harvested acreage in Texas since 1905. The yield was 3,086,000 bales. Farmers received an average price of only 8.3 cents per pound, due in large part to the huge carryover from the previous year's record crop. The total value of the 1938 Texas crop was $127 million, but this amount was supplemented with $34 million from the 1937 cotton subsidy (paid out September through November 1938) and $36 million in soil-conservation payments (paid out January through March 1939).[36]

The term of the 1938 cotton program was one of the busiest times for county agents and committeemen. Not only did they have to contend with the soil-conservation program, but they also had to finish disbursing the checks from the 1937 program, distribute and collect applications for the 1937 subsidy payments, explain and administer the allotments for the 1938 program, supervise the cotton-loan aspects of the 1938 program, implement the marketing-quota provisions of the new program, oversee two referendums, and initiate the 1939 program. The Hockley County agent believed that carrying out the provisions of the second Agricultural Adjustment Act took three times as much work as was needed under the SCDAA.[37]

Despite the work and problems involved in launching the new cotton program, most county agents remained hopeful that the 1939 program would run more smoothly. With an earlier start and a year's experience under their belts, the extension agents believed that the new long-term farm plan would do much to benefit cotton growers. John Bankhead agreed. In an October 1938 letter to Roosevelt, the senator stated: "In my opinion we have the best farm law ever enacted by Congress." To Bankhead, the main problems seemed to be administrative in nature and could be eliminated over time.[38]

The 1939 Program

The AAA extinguished a key source of discontent by allocating the 1939 allotments in November 1938, long before planting time. Texas congressman Sam Rayburn was correct about the previous year when he noted in a mid-September 1938 letter to Ivy Duggan that "the thing that makes the program most unpopular is that farmers are compelled to sign up so long before they know what the program is." He believed that the extension agents and committeemen were doing the best job they could under the circumstances, but wanted Duggan to know that "there has been a slowness about the whole program that has done the whole set-up a great harm." Duggan replied by stating that the AAA was exerting every effort to ensure that growers received their allotments before planting time in the coming year. "It will be inexcusable," he assured Rayburn, "if they do not get their acreage allotments well in advance of planting time."[39]

The AAA's scheduling of the next marketing-quota referendum for December 10 was another important reason for the agency's efforts to have individual allotments ready in late 1938. In the December vote, Texas support for marketing quotas dropped from the March referendum's numbers: 148,159 growers out of 191,973, or 77.2 percent, voted in favor of continuing quotas; 43,814 voted against them. This result, while still impressive, showed a decline from the 88.4 percent approval rate in March. Overall, American cotton growers voted 983,903–185,760, or 84.1 percent, in favor of continuing the marketing quotas (down from the 92.1 percent approval given by the growers in March.) Despite discontent with the delays and administrative difficulties, Texas' cotton producers strongly supported marketing quotas for another season. By doing so, they avoided the chaos that tobacco producers encountered in 1939, after they failed to support quotas for their crop.[40]

The AAA announced the details of the 1939 cotton program in mid-August 1938. The agency preserved the essentials of the previous year's plan, with the only changes involving modifications in payments. Because of funding considerations, the AAA lowered the maximum conservation payments for cotton growers from 2.4 cents per pound on the normal yield per acre of the acreage allotment to 1.8 cents per pound. Also, under terms of the Price Adjustment Act of 1938, Congress appropriated $212 million in price-adjustment parity payments to all cotton, wheat, corn, tobacco, and rice producers who remained within their allotted acreage. This appropriation added another payment at the rate of 1.6 cents per pound on the normal production of the cotton farmers' allotments. The AAA disbursed a total of $96.2 million to cotton farmers in 1939, with Texans receiving $24.9 million.[41]

In October 1938, the AAA experienced an administrative change for the 1939 season when Secretary Wallace announced a reorganization. Howard Tolley left to become the new head of the Bureau of Agricultural Economics (BAE). Wallace replaced him with R. M. "Spike" Evans, an Iowa stock feeder who had been one of his special assistants since 1936 and was a more inspiring figure to most ordinary farmers. Although Tolley had proved an excellent economic planner, the secretary believed he lacked the administrative and political skills needed to run the New Deal's most important agricultural agency. Cully Cobb thought he was "a complete flop" as AAA administrator. According to Dean Albertson, "Tolley looked more like a genuine dirt farmer and thought less like one" than any man in the USDA, and his inability to "speak the farmer's language" hindered the AAA's efforts on some occasions.[42]

As AAA officials and extension agents hoped, the administration of the 1939 cotton program was much more efficient than the previous year's program. Most Texas agents cited growers' receiving their allotments far in advance of planting time as a major reason for fewer complaints and better producer reception of the plan. Improved comprehension of the program's workings under the new farm act also accounted for greater acceptance. Farmers began to understand that they would receive greater compensation through government conservation and subsidy checks than through noncompliance with the program.[43]

In 1939, Texas growers harvested 2,846,000 bales on 8,520,000 acres (even fewer acres than in 1938), though the state allotment was 10,137,157 acres. The average price of cotton rose 2 cents per pound from the previous season, to 10.3 cents. The state's cotton crop brought in $124 million, which was supplemented by $30,730,000 in conservation payments and $24,898,000 in price adjustment payments.[44]

With the outbreak of war in Europe near the end of the 1939 growing season, consumers and commodity producers alike began to speculate on the conflict's ramifications. On September 1, 1939, soon after the initiation of hostilities, Henry Wallace issued a statement in an attempt to reassure the public that they had no need to panic: ample supplies of American agricultural products were available for consumers, and commodity loans were in effect to prevent price collapses. For Wallace, the beginning of World War II showed the importance of having a flexible, long-term national farm program. The same ever-normal granary machinery that farmers used to adjust production to decreased demand in peacetime could be utilized in wartime to stimulate increased production, if needed.[45]

Before stating my conclusions about the AAA's efforts to aid Texas cotton growers, in the next chapter I will break away from the chronological arrangement to devote attention to the important topic of tenant and sharecropper displacement. No aspect of the agency's operations generated as much criticism; thus an evaluation of the AAA would be incomplete without addressing it.

CHAPTER 6

TENANT AND SHARECROPPER
DISPLACEMENT IN TEXAS

On the evening of October 31, 1933, twenty-three-year-old Gib Womack and his twenty-four-year-old cousin Coleman Miller strolled down the main street of Paradise, Texas, in Wise County. Earlier in the day, the two men had forcibly ejected a tenant family from a farm owned by their grandfather, J. F. Womack. Suddenly, the head of the evicted tenant family, Tim Harlan, a forty-year-old father of four, approached Womack and Miller. After an angry exchange of words, Harlan whipped out a pistol and shot both men dead. The disgruntled tenant promptly surrendered himself to a deputy sheriff who had witnessed the shooting.[1]

While dramatic, this incident differs in two main ways from the normal pattern of tenant and sharecropper displacement in Texas during the 1930s. First, this event took place early in the decade. As will be shown, a majority of displacement cases took place in the latter half of the decade. Second, the Harlan case ended with brutal violence. Unlike the quarrels between evicted tenants and landlords in the Mississippi Delta region, Texas displacement incidents usually were characterized by a noticeable lack of violence. Nevertheless, the Harlan eviction represents an early example of an important externality growing out of the AAA's crop-reduction policy, namely, as planters were paid for planting fewer acres and increasingly used government money to purchase farm equipment and to pay wage laborers, there would be less need for tenant and sharecropper labor. As will be shown, the government's response to this consequence was totally inadequate.[2]

The Government's Response and the AAA's Defense

The 1930s proved to be a transitional period between the old and the modern agricultural systems of the Lone Star State. As table 1 demonstrates, the number of Texas tenants and sharecroppers increased in every census from 1880 to 1930, and then markedly decreased beginning with the 1940 decennial census. For Texas, the state with the most tenants and sharecroppers, the censuses show that between 1930 and 1940 the number of tenants and croppers declined by 32.2 percent and 62.1 percent, respectively, with a majority of the decline occurring after 1935. The institution of sharecropping continued well into the 1950s, when it was supplanted by technological advances, including the mechanical cotton picker and the development of efficient herbicides and pesticides. However, the 1930s marked the initial decline of sharecropping and tenancy in Texas and most sections of the Cotton Belt.

During the Great Depression, no cotton growers suffered more than tenant farmers and sharecroppers. Although the AAA cotton programs provided much-needed relief for a great number of Texas' producers, they did little to prevent tens of thousands of tenants and sharecroppers from being displaced by their landlords. Roosevelt administration officials were aware that tenants and croppers were leaving the land in large numbers by the late 1930s, but they were either unwilling to admit that AAA policies were to blame or felt too constrained by the political power of southern politicians (who could effectively block other New Deal measures) to make any concrete efforts on their behalf. The result was an often-schizophrenic public response to the problem. While there was much investigation of alleged injustices caused by AAA policies, there was also much effort expended to throw blame elsewhere, even when partial culpability was unavoidable. As Pete Daniel has written, although the AAA considered itself "innocent of displacing tenants, it favored programs that displaced tenants, and it washed its hands of the conflicting results."[3]

An early example of the AAA's neglect took place in 1935, when Henry Wallace and Chester Davis asked AAA economic adviser Calvin B. Hoover to conduct a survey of the agency's impact on tenant farmers and sharecroppers. Publicly, Hoover reported that large numbers of tenants were not receiving their fair share of payments. He also stated that the cotton programs had created an incentive for planters to reduce the number of tenants (though he noted that he was not convinced that AAA policies had caused much dis-

Sharecroppers gathering cotton on a plantation near Dallas, Texas, 1907. Courtesy Center for American History, University of Texas–Austin, Prints and Photographs Collection, CN No. 01281.

placement). Nevertheless, Hoover concluded that the cotton programs had benefits for the South as a whole that far outweighed individual injustices. Privately, however, Hoover reversed his public stance. In a letter sent to Wallace after the report was released, he revealed his belief that there was indeed much evidence to show that the acreage-reduction programs were precipitating evictions. Hoover recommended more accountability to ensure that tenants were paid properly, as well as better assurances that planters were maintaining the proper number of tenants and croppers on their land.[4]

One reason for the AAA's mixed response to tenant problems was a schism among top agency officials. Until 1935, the AAA's Washington staff was polarized between two major groups of individuals often labeled by historians as the "agrarians" and the "liberals." AAA agrarians were those officials who came from an agricultural background and tended to hold an inherent prolandlord bias. Men such as Cully Cobb, Oscar Johnston, George Peek, and many close assistants certainly fit this mold. While paying lip service to the concerns of tenants, these conservatives tended to discount criticism of the AAA as being the work of rabble-rousers or communist agitators. They sought to keep the agency's focus on economic recovery, not on the structural inadequacies of southern agricultural society. At the opposite end of the spectrum were the liberals who staffed the AAA's Legal Division. Although not astute in agricultural matters, these principled urban men—Legal Division chief Jerome Frank and his cadre of lawyers—felt that they knew injustice when they saw it and often protested various AAA procedures that they believed discriminated against the interest of tenants and sharecroppers.[5]

The two groups had a cantankerous relationship until early 1935, when Secretary Wallace fired the liberal lawyers at the request of Chester Davis. The precipitating event for this much-publicized "purge" was an administrative ruling made by the Legal Division stating that Paragraph 7a of the 1935 cotton contract should be interpreted as meaning that planters must retain the *exact* tenants and sharecroppers who occupied the land as during the previous year, rather than just the same *number* of tenants and croppers, as had been the usual practice. This ruling, which was propagated and distributed to the localities while Davis was out of Washington, infuriated the administrator. Up to this point he had tried to hold the middle ground between the agrarians and the liberals (though he personally leaned toward the agrarian view on most matters). Certainly the planters and their representatives in Washington would not stand for this blatant intrusion into landlord-tenant matters and they made their complaints known. Davis threatened to resign if Wallace did not fire the whole lot of lawyers. The secretary reluctantly acquiesced. With these bureaucratic evictions, tenants and sharecroppers lost their staunchest supporters in the AAA and their best protection from future evictions. President Roosevelt, ever mindful of the political power of the southerners in Congress, registered no objection.[6]

Politics was also an important factor behind Roosevelt's creation of a commission chaired by Secretary Wallace (and staffed by many notable agriculturalists, such as M. L. Wilson, Rexford Tugwell, Mordecai Ezekiel, and John Black) to study farm tenancy problems. If anything, the Special Committee on Farm Tenancy—an entity that the president had promised to create during his reelection campaign—would give the impression that the administration was aware that tenant problems existed while continuing to deny that AAA policies contributed to them.[7]

The committee's report (and FDR's endorsement of its contents) resulted in passage of the Bankhead-Jones Farm Security Act of 1937 and the creation of the Farm Security Administration (FSA). Part of the FSA's mandate was a loan program for displaced tenants desiring to purchase family farms. Scant appropriations and rigid acceptance criteria, however, meant that only one in twenty-two applicants ever received financing. From 1938 to 1940, the FSA made only 8,045 loans to southern tenants wishing to purchase land. In Texas, only 542 of over 15,000 applicants, or fewer than 4 percent, received FSA financing.[8]

Despite the creation of the FSA and statements issued by the AAA and USDA guaranteeing that tenants would receive justice and protection, large numbers of Texas tenants and sharecroppers (as elsewhere in the Cotton Belt) were systematically displaced from the land in the late 1930s. Quantitative research suggests that this displacement was not uniform throughout Texas: some areas suffered more displacement, and for different reasons, than others. Nevertheless, when we look at displacement statewide, the impact was immense and marked the beginning of a new agricultural era in the Lone Star State.[9]

Throughout the late 1930s, AAA and USDA officials neglected to adequately help huge numbers of evicted tenants and croppers while avoiding culpability for the displacement. One of the main reasons for inadequate assistance was an overreliance on the county committees to carry out the tenant provisions of the programs. Often praised by Henry Wallace, Cully Cobb, and M. L. Wilson as "agrarian democracy," the localized management system was anything but democratic in most parts of Texas and the South, because landlords dominated the committees and consistently worked to protect their interests (thus often working against tenant and cropper interests). Further, county agents did little to rankle the landlords, who had influence over payment of salaries and future employment.

AAA and USDA officials also tended to have two strongly held beliefs that made them less than eager to protect tenants from displacement. First, many believed that there were too many poor farmers on the land. Wallace, Cobb, and others believed that there was simply not enough wealth on the land to support all who were engaged in farming. Thus, they thought that many tenants and croppers would be better off elsewhere, probably in the nation's growing cities. Second, these officials were reluctant to impede farm-labor reductions resulting from increased mechanization of southern farming operations. To do so, in their minds, would be tantamount to inhibiting progress itself.

A statement of the official AAA position on the displacement issue can be found in a June 1940 pamphlet prepared by the agency's Division of Information. In "Questions and Answers about the AAA Farm Program" the following question is asked: "Has not the Triple-A program injured sharecroppers and farm laborers generally?" In response, the pamphlet's writers state that American agriculture had a sharecropper and tenancy problem long before the AAA programs. The main problem, according to the pamphlet, was too many farmers for the available land. The pamphlet also notes that the agency was set up to generate agricultural recovery, not to solve the tenant and sharecropper problem. With regard to the accusation that the AAA was not doing enough to prevent unlawful dislocations of tenants and sharecroppers, the writers asserted that tenants and croppers were given adequate legal protection. Although there may have been instances when landlords illegally reduced the number of tenants and croppers, such occurrences of "unjustified" evictions were rare, the pamphlet's writers claimed.[10]

In the final analysis, the dividing line between a "justified" and an "unjustified" reduction of farm laborers during the later AAA programs depended on the landlord's *intent,* as determined by the county committees. Under the SCDAA and the Agricultural Adjustment Act of 1938, if county committees determined that a tenant reduction was made *solely* to increase the landlord's share of government payments, then the reduction was illegal. However, if the reductions were made, in whole or in part, as a result of improved farming techniques, such as utilization of new farm machinery, the reduction could be legally justified. Of course, because the New Deal farm laws delegated so much power to the landlord-dominated county committees, landlords had little trouble dislocating their tenants, whether doing so was legally "justified" or not.

A round of correspondence between Rep. George Mahon of Lubbock, AAA officials, and Secretary Wallace reveals much about the manner in which AAA officials excused the agency from any responsibility in the dislocation of thousands of southern tenants and sharecroppers during the 1930s. In late 1938, Mahon wrote Southern Division director Ivy Duggan to express his concern that the AAA was not doing enough to ensure that tenants living in his southern High Plains district were protected from unwarranted displacement by their landlords. "I am constantly told that this man or that man is closing out some eight or ten tenants this year in order that he may get the Government check next year," Mahon explained. He asked Duggan to check on the situation to "discover whether or not the various counties . . . will make an accurate check in order to see it that the provision of the law . . . is strictly carried out."[11]

Duggan noted in his reply that the AAA had recently received "more than the usual number of complaints regarding the displacement of tenants." He then proceeded to relate his belief that much of the displacement was occurring because there was insufficient income from cotton farming to maintain all the growers who wished to remain on the land. He also expressed his understanding that the Cotton Belt was facing years of reconstruction and re-organization of its economy due to mechanization:

> I am convinced that many who have been pushed back on the farms because of technological changes in industry and because of the depression will find it increasingly difficult to remain on farms. I am also convinced that technological changes on the farm itself, such as have already occurred in wheat production, will very likely decrease the demand for labor and will cause some displacement on farms. I am hopin[g] that this will be gradual and that we can make some adjustments as it develops. On the other hand, I do not think that anything we might do will permanently stop technological developments either in industry or on the farm. Nationally, we need to devote our brains and energy to getting the greater use out of mechanization and make it serve us rather than enslave us. These improvements should be the means of a higher standard of living for all. Yet as I have already said, it is a problem we have not solved.[12]

Reminding Mahon that Congress left final responsibility for matters relating to the displacement of tenants to the county committees, Duggan continued: "This would seem to indicate that the Congress preferred to leave the question of the displacement of tenants to local determination." In a final defense of the AAA, he concluded: "I doubt if as many tenants are being displaced as would have been displaced without the farm programs." Nevertheless, the director assured Mahon that AAA field workers would investigate and verify that county committees were performing their responsibilities as mandated in the 1938 farm act.[13]

Before receiving Duggan's reply, Mahon wrote Marvin Jones to share his thoughts on tenant displacement, as well as his belief that the AAA was not doing enough to stop it: "The great complaint which I have heard in my District from tenants against the farm program is that it is a contributing factor to displacing many of the tenants and sending them to town and placing them on relief. Of course, the tractors have played a big part in this, but I think the farm program is in part responsible. Of course, if we had no farm program, they might all be on relief, but the point is I feel we ought to do everything possible to encourage landlords to keep their tenants and discourage their displacement."[14]

Mahon then related to Jones the results of a disappointing meeting with AAA officials in Lubbock. At the conference, the congressman tried to garner promises from officials that the county committees would follow the 1938 farm law by protecting tenants from illegal displacement. They refused to give Mahon any guarantees: "I asked them if an accurate check-up would be made in order to ascertain if landlords were displacing their tenants before the issuance of soil conservation checks on the 1938 crop. I got the impression from them that no great effort would be made to enforce the particular provision of the law . . . *They seemed to recognize the problem all right but seemed to feel that the county committees will not under the circumstances have the courage and inclination to enforce this provision of the law.*"[15]

In concluding his letter, Mahon displayed not only his genuine concern for displaced tenants, but also his respect for landlord power in his district. He appealed for some type of statement to be sent out to county agents and committeemen reminding them of their duty to enforce the law: "I do not know of anything you and I can do about it [displacement]—*I certainly am not going to make any speeches about it*—but if you could prevail on Secretary Wallace or Mr. Duggan to get out a strong letter to the County Agents and county committees on this subject it might do a world of good."[16]

Jones agreed with Mahon, writing to Duggan that a "good, strong letter" should be sent to county agents and committeemen asking them to enforce the tenant-displacement provision of the 1938 farm act. Duggan's reply was very similar to his response to Mahon's earlier letter. It contained an expression of his belief that the income from cotton was insufficient to support the present farm population, an affirmation that it was not AAA policy to stifle improved farming methods (especially with regard to mechanization), a statement reminding Jones that Congress left the question of tenant reductions to local determination, and an assurance that AAA field investigators were verifying that committeemen properly performed their assignments as prescribed by the law.[17]

Sensing that he was not getting anywhere with AAA officials, Mahon, in one last effort on behalf of displaced tenants, directed an appeal to Secretary Wallace. He reiterated concerns for the displaced tenant farmers in his district, as well as his desire for rigid enforcement of the 1938 farm law's tenant provisions: "I have upon several occasions called the attention of your Department to the fact that hundreds of people on tenant farms are being displaced by their landlords partially because of the fact that the landlord hoped thereby to secure additional Government benefit payments. I know that the tractor has contributed to this displacement of tenants. Perhaps there is nothing we can do about the tractor, but I do feel that every effort ought to be made to see to it that the farm program does not operate against the best interest of thousands of tenant farmers."[18]

As an example, Mahon presented the secretary with the case of nine Lynn County tenant families from his district. The families had farmed for a San Antonio lumber company for several years without any complaint from the owners. Nevertheless, all of the families received the following notice and were ordered to vacate within a month:

Dear Sir:

You are hereby notified that I will want possession of the property which you are renting from me at expiration of your present rental agreement with me, and in no event later than December 31st, 1938. If you can possibly arrange to give me full possession at an earlier date, your consideration will be a favor and very sincerely appreciated.

Inasmuch as this request is first and final notice, I respectfully urge that you immediately commence making arrangements to deliver possession of this property on the date specified. I will not, under any circumstances, be in position to grant any extension of time.

I assure you that I have no complaint to make of the way or manner in which you have farmed the land which you have rented from me, and I sincerely hope that you will be able to locate other land equally or more suitable to your needs without difficulty.

With kindest regards and best wishes, I am

Respectfully yours,

E. L. Powell

Vice President, Alamo Lumber Company

Mahon requested that Wallace issue a press release to explain that the AAA looked with disfavor on such indiscriminate displacement of tenants and that the tenant provisions of the farm act would be strictly enforced. If that was done, the congressman hoped, many more tenants who might have been displaced would be retained on the land.

Wallace's reply was little different from Duggan's earlier responses to Mahon and Marvin Jones. He defended the AAA by reiterating previous arguments that Duggan had made earlier: Congress left final responsibility for displacement to the county committees, which were properly performing their tasks; displacement to some extent occurred naturally, because there was not enough income in cotton farming to sustain the current farm population; and farm mechanization might be causing some displacement, but this development should not be impeded. In short, Wallace gave Mahon the traditional AAA defense regarding the displacement issue.[19]

The AAA never issued any statement or press release. As the decade wore on, Texas landlords displaced tens of thousands of tenants and sharecroppers, and the agency did little to stop it. AAA officials were not willing to interfere with the landlords' efforts to reorient their use of the land. They were convinced that, in the long run, this reorganization was a positive thing for Texas and the entire Cotton Belt. Although many government officials viewed farm-labor displacement as inevitable and as progress, the tenants and croppers who were affected by this modern enclosure movement experienced great confusion, fear, and anxiety as their traditional way of life began to disappear before their eyes.

The Tenant and Sharecropper View of Displacement

During the early New Deal, the main complaint of most Texas tenants and sharecroppers against the AAA was not displacement, but the failure of many landlords to share benefits with tenants and croppers as specified in their contracts. The response of many tenants and sharecroppers, however, was similar to their reaction to displacement later. Very few resorted to any form of violence. A large majority simply grumbled, thinking there was nothing they could do, but others took up their pens or pencils and wrote to government officials.

In scattered Texas archives, but especially among the voluminous AAA Papers in the National Archives, a researcher can find scores of dispatches written by displaced Texas sharecroppers and tenant farmers. The letters, though certainly not the most articulate expressions one may encounter, are a record of honest attempts by displaced farmers to describe how their lives had been turned upside down. Many of the messages reflect the fears of tenants about life away from farming. The vast majority of the letters ask government officials for help and usually request an opportunity to get off the relief rolls and return to the land. Many of the letters characterize landlords as dispassionate, even heartless, while stressing a belief that the government did not seem to understand what was happening down on the farm.

Some of the tenants' letters are short, straightforward pleas for help. For example, a recently evicted tenant farmer from the Clarksville area wrote: "Gentlemen, advise me what to do. I cant get any land to work. my understanding when this plowup began the landlord had to keep same amount of tenants and shearcroppers. I have farmed in Texas 55 years and farming is all I can do. if the government is going to fix it all for the landlord it beats me."[20]

When the USDA failed to send him a prompt response, the tenant sent another concise message: "Gentlemen. wat does the government aim to do with the sharecropper and s[m]all tenant farmer? do they intend to put on relief? it looks that way. there is thousands of them begging for land and cant get even a place to have a garden and some landlord say they will let the [l]and layout. I have farmed 55 years in Texas and have bin on all govement plans to [19]38 and couldant get any land to work. I wrote you about this a few days ago and you dont seem to understand."[21]

Other letters are lengthy and appear to be attempts by desperate people to describe their plight to someone in a position of power and to inform officials about what was occurring in the countryside. One mother of two young boys who was displaced from her farm in 1936 wrote a long letter to Henry Wallace trying to do just that:

I ofton wonder as thousand of other people do if you Realised the condition of the world under the present Sistem.

Wee know you and all that are helping mean well but it seems like every step makes it worse on the poore class of people.

First a few men have rented land In Hundreds of acers each and work this land with one hired hand at Same time putting other Families of[f] farm Forceing them to go to town to live in any kind of a place and work on relief at a very low price while thire Family suffer for want . . .

Thousands of Families would be on Farms if could rent land and grow a big part of thire living If the Big men were forced to work just a reasonable amount [of their land].

I am a widow with 2 Boys age 13 and 16 years of age. We were farming making a good living three years ago . . . I were forced to give up Farming and move to town. do what ever I can to exzist. I am 55 years old. No jobs for surch people. My boys tried to get Farm work. The Big men would Say you are to[o] light. I wont use any one under 18 years of age. so I am forced to keep my boys out of school to rome streets as thousand of other Boys are forced to do when if they were on farm could Bee making a living . . . My Boys are not old enuff to go to C.C. [Civilian Conservation Corps] Camp so what are people in my class to do? suffer and Beg, steal or anything. it is filling the jail[s] every where.

A great Dr. told me why the Goverment dont realise the condit[i]on. This is Just the cry from thousands. This man I were renting from are Just one of a thousand that are doing the Same thing. In less than 2 hours I could have 75 names of Families that would go Back on Farms in this little town of only a few hundred Popalation.[22]

A Floyd County sharecropper who was abruptly evicted by his landlord wrote another long letter to the secretary, not only to describe his situation, but to reiterate his strong desire to get off the relief rolls and to remain on the land:

I am writing you a few lines in regards to the farm that I am renting. I work the place last year on the halves. The landlord never said any thing about me not staying here this year until yesterday the 9th. That he wanted the place to handle him self. That he was going to have it work diff[erent] this year. They would not let me sind up for eny off the cotton reduction . . .

So I am forced to move to a town and get on the releif, something I have never in all off my life had to do, unless the goverment help a little farmer. I have a wife and six children age 18 to 2 years old. We want to stay on the farm but how can we, with such landlords?[23]

Some of the displaced tenants and sharecroppers expressed continued support for the AAA, despite the negative impact that the agency's policies had had on their lives. For example, a displaced farmer in Hale Center, Texas, supported the AAA's goals while requesting another chance to participate in the program:

in reguard to the triple A Plan I cant say I am against it. But Will Say this. it has Put more Families on the relief than any one thing Because the man that has got the lan[d] wont let a man have any of it Because he want[s] all of those check[s] that he gets from the goverment to run his Big Auto. then in the fall he get[s] a Big Bunch of Mexicans to gather the cotton and wont hardly hire a white Family. it wood Bea all right if a man could get some land to work . . . I am with my wife and three groan girl[s] and cant get no land to work. Some men work in 2 and 3 Section[s] and wont let a man have any of it on the account of them checks he gets from the Goverment. So you See that puts lots of Families on the releaf. I have farmed all of my life But cant get any land now. But I aint the only one. there are thousands in the same Fix I am in now. Mr Wallace you studdy this over and see what you think about it.[24]

Viewed collectively, these letters reveal that Texas' tenant farmers and sharecroppers did attempt to describe their problems to the government. Just as important, they demonstrate that large numbers of tenants and croppers sought to return to the land, make their own way through the Depression by farming, and live as they were accustomed to living—even if that meant perpetuating an impoverished lifestyle. Many of them, especially those who had farmed for most of their lives, abhorred the thought of giving up and moving to the city. Instead, they longed for a return to the rural way of life that provided them with inner peace.

George Sessions Perry captures this attitude in a memorable moment in *Hold Autumn in Your Hand*. While on a hunting trip, Sam Tucker reflects about a brief period in his youth when he tried working in a Houston auto factory. He labored hard for good pay, but he despised the work so much that he quit after two weeks. Sam thought about the experience often, and was doing so again because once more he was feeling the pressure to give up farming and take up a better-paying job in the city. Ultimately, the tenant farmer decides, as he always does when he mulls it over, that he simply cannot stomach the idea of going back to work in any factory with its repetitive, dehumanizing routine, no matter how much they pay him. At least for now he is lucky because he is still on the land. "Then with almost a feeling of shame for the richness of his own way of life," Perry narrates, "when so many thousands of other men must undergo the steady desiccation of the spirit that factories impose upon them, he would flip his cigarette into the weeds and walk down to the red boat, get into it, and start smoothly up the river."[25]

Possible Alternatives

Even if Franklin Roosevelt wanted to ensure that the AAA did not unfairly displace any tenants or sharecroppers, the president certainly would have encountered a brick wall of political opposition from the South because such an action would have meant intervening directly in the landlord-tenant relationship. Any effort perceived as being too "pro-tenant" would have been viewed equally as being "anti-landlord," resulting in a backlash against the New Deal even stronger than the conservative resistance that was already forming by the late 1930s. Chester Davis made his awareness of this political reality (as well as his belief that there were too many farmers on the land) perfectly clear in a 1936 memo to Henry Wallace:

> It seems to be that most of the discussions of the social and economic problem of the sharecropper overlook two fundamental factors in the situation.

The first of these is the large number of people engaged in cotton production in relation to the total income from cotton production . . .

The second factor of importance is the necessity for local cooperation in any Federal program. The Federal Government could not superimpose by the administration of any law a new social order upon the South. That is one way of saying that the march of social and economic progress of the sharecroppers can not be forced by the Federal Government to proceed much faster than the rate that Southern opinion and Southern leadership will heartily support. To try to force a faster pace would merely be to insure violent controversy, lack of local cooperation in administration, evasion, and ineffectiveness for the plan. We have found from long hard work and gruelling experience in the AAA that there are limits beyond which we could not go, without precipitating a conflict, in which even our slow progress would be turned into chaos and retrogression.[26]

In the memo, Davis stated the dilemma for those desiring to aid southern tenant farmers and sharecroppers during the Great Depression. The active cooperation of southern cotton producers with AAA programs was necessary to forestall economic chaos. Yet, the programs would fail without the cooperation of the large landlords, whose actions directly led to chaos for tenants and croppers who were displaced. The AAA never challenged landlord power because of the agency's own biases and because officials feared that if landlord cooperation was not obtained the programs would likely fail and nobody would be helped. During a conversation with Socialist Party leader Norman Thomas (a strong tenant and sharecropper supporter), FDR revealed his understanding of the situation and frankly explained his willingness to compromise with southern leaders: "I know the South and we've got to be patient."[27]

Despite many government bureaucrats' myriad of political constraints and ideological biases, what else could have been expected of the AAA regarding tenant displacement? What *were* some possible alternatives to simply ignoring the problem?

A modernist approach might call for the government to admit its role in contributing to the loss of jobs. Then, if the officials did not restore the tenants to their former work, they could at least have assumed more responsibility for easing the displaced workers' transition out of agriculture, perhaps through sponsorship of work-training programs. That idea was ahead of its time and not seriously considered, but some contemporaries mentioned this option—the most noteworthy being Eleanor Roosevelt. In a 1939 letter to Henry Wallace concerning a highly publicized demonstration organized by displaced Missouri sharecroppers, she called attention to the fact that nothing was being done for over a thousand of these desperate farmers who had camped out in dismal conditions alongside two major highways in the Missouri Bootheel to protest their plight. Wallace acknowledged that sharecropper displacement was taking place in Missouri and other southern states and then launched into a lengthy defense of the AAA, explaining that the displacement was due to mechanization and the "historical and continuing off-throwing of population from the farms." Probably feeling that she was not getting anywhere, the First Lady responded with a brief note, politely thanking him for the explanation, but then tersely inquiring: "Should we be developing more industries and services? Should we practice birth control or drown the surplus population?"[28]

Another approach, mentioned once by Mordecai Ezekiel, would have enhanced the role of tenants and sharecroppers within the existing AAA structure in order to provide them with better protection. Ezekiel proposed guaranteeing tenant and cropper representation in the policy-making and implementation processes. In a 1936 memo to Secretary Wallace, he laid out the problem simply enough:

> There can be no question that the farm owners, constituting less than half of those engaged in agriculture, have been the dominant element in the preparation and administration of AAA programs heretofore. In certain commodities, notably cotton, this has resulted in their receiving the lion's share of the benefits resulting from the programs. Under the new soil conservation approach, it will be even more difficult to maintain equity in the treatment of these weaker groups in farming than it has been in the past, and there may be even less likelihood of their participating fairly in the advantages accruing to agriculture in their region.

He then proposed a bold remedy: "One method of trying to see that they get a fair break would be to create a farm tenant and laborer representative to participate in the development of the future programs, with the duty of representing these groups. It might also be well to ask each county association in areas with heavy tenancy or many farm laborers to have an auxiliary tenant and farm laborer committee or association, and then to have auxiliary state committees representing tenants and laborers selected by these county groups." Anticipating possible criticism of his plan, the economist simply stated: "It might be argued against this suggestion that it will create conflicts . . . That is true. Each would represent certain interests; efforts to speak for them would raise problems. But the problems do exist in agriculture. If we give them expression here, we may help to solve them. Certainly we cannot solve them by refusing to face them."[29]

Ezekiel was correct when he wrote that tenant and sharecropper problems could not be solved if the AAA ignored them. He erred, however, in assuming that AAA, USDA, and Extension Service officials truly desired to solve them. Stimulating economic recovery was foremost in their minds. Wallace simply filed Ezekiel's proposal, and it never received any serious consideration. Later, when Gardner Jackson (one of the purged AAA lawyers) toured the South, he asked a county agent why there were no sharecroppers on any county committees. The agent answered: "Hell! You wouldn't put a chicken on a poultry board, would you?"[30]

If one looks away from the AAA and toward the tenant farmers and sharecroppers themselves, one might ask: Could Texas tenants and croppers have organized themselves into some form of union? Many farm laborers residing in the Mississippi River Delta had attempted this solution (and suffered violent repression for doing so) when they formed the Southern Tenant Farmers Union (STFU). Could such a course of action have worked in Texas?

In fact, the STFU did attempt to gain tenant and sharecropper support in Texas, but its efforts proved disappointing. Neil Foley devotes an entire chapter of *The White Scourge* to the STFU's efforts to organize in Texas. He concludes that the union was not successful in most parts of Texas mainly because the structure of cotton agriculture was different from agriculture in the Mississippi Delta, where the union had better organizational success. In the Delta, immense factory farms were dominant. The STFU formed among plantation laborers who increasingly viewed themselves as "proletarianized farm workers" with concerns about wages and working conditions. Most Texas tenants, however, worked on family farms or plots on small plantations, thought of themselves as farmers just beneath the status of owners, and felt little brotherhood with farmworkers, whom they viewed as beneath them on the agricultural ladder.

Despite this prevailing mentality, the STFU still made efforts to organize farm laborers in the largest cotton-producing state. Nevertheless, the factory farms of southeastern Texas proved inadequate recruiting grounds because owners could take advantage of their closeness to the Mexico border to get fresh workers if trouble emerged with existing ones.

The STFU achieved marginal success on the large operations of the northwest Texas Panhandle near Lubbock. Only eight local chapters were formed, however, with a total membership of fewer than five hundred. Regarding possible farm-labor trouble, it was indeed a case of "all quiet on the southwestern front of Texas." No cotton strike took place in the Lone Star State throughout the 1930s.[31]

Criticism of the AAA's negative impact on the lives of tenants and sharecroppers continued throughout the Depression. The AAA's leaders felt the pressure, but almost always tried to place a positive spin on their actions, even in their interoffice communications. At the conclusion of a memo to Henry Wallace, Chester Davis acknowledged the criticism of his agency for allegedly harming tenants and croppers, but still denied that the AAA was responsible. Instead, he tried to keep the focus on the grand goal of raising overall farm prices to generate economic recovery: "I have never been able to agree . . . with those critics who considered the AAA entirely worthless so long as it did not result in a social revolution in the South, and who now judge the entire soil conservation program solely on the basis of its contribution to the income of the sharecroppers." Davis was correct: the Agricultural Adjustment Administration's performance should not be judged a failure simply because it did not do enough for southern tenants and sharecroppers. Nevertheless, in looking back on the AAA experience, that failure to help tenants and croppers will always be the proverbial albatross around the agency's neck.[32]

CHAPTER 7

CONCLUSION

By the end of 1939, the AAA had generated only a partial agricultural recovery. Prices for most commodities remained far below parity levels. Cotton was selling for ten cents per pound, or 66 percent of parity. Any chance for achieving parity prices by the end of the decade was all but eliminated after the huge 1937 harvest greatly enlarged the carryover of unconsumed cotton. Some historians have cited the large surplus at the end of the decade as proof that the cotton programs simply did not work as production-control measures, but the carryover situation throughout the entire New Deal should be studied before definite judgments are made about the AAA's efforts. Before the Supreme Court in effect ended the first AAA, the cotton programs (coupled with the 1934 drought) did, in fact, reduce the surplus of American cotton. As table 2 shows, only after the record 1937 crop, under the purely voluntary features of the SCDAA, did the carryover become extremely burdensome and wipe out the gains of the previous three years. One is left to ponder how effective the original AAA would have been if allowed to continue throughout the decade.

The United States' entry into the Second World War instigated a quick reversal of Depression-era farm policy. In 1942, the government began to encourage increased production to meet wartime needs, even guaranteeing commodity producers prices at 110 percent of parity. Thus, it was World War II, rather than the peacetime crop-adjustment policies of the AAA, that used up the vast accumulated surpluses and allowed southern cotton farmers to escape the Great Depression.[1]

Although it was the war that spawned agricultural recovery, it would be a mistake to label the AAA cotton programs as an unmitigated failure. At the least, they succeeded in providing an important relief function for a majority

Table 2
Carryover of American Cotton, 1932–40

Year	Carryover on August 1 (thousands of bales)
1932	9,581
1933	8,081
1934	7,648
1935	7,138
1936	5,336
1937	4,387
1938	11,446
1939	12,956
1940	10,469

Source: U.S. Department of Agriculture, Economic Research Service, "Statistics on Cotton and Related Data, 1930–67," 65.

of Texas cotton producers. While obtaining cash benefits surpassing $300 million, growers consistently received higher prices than the six cents per pound they got during Herbert Hoover's last year in office. The programs also contributed to the maintenance of independently owned farms in Texas. In 1930, 193,829 Texans owned farms. By 1940, the number of farm owners in the Lone Star State had increased to 213,540 (see table 1). The New Deal proved to be, as Anthony Badger has called it, a "holding operation" for American agricultural producers during hard economic times. It enabled millions of growers to survive and to remain on the land when they had few alternatives for employment elsewhere.[2]

Farmers continued to support the AAA because the agency was successful in helping so many of them survive during the Great Depression, and it did it without resorting to dictatorship. Indeed, grower cooperation was absolutely essential to the government's efforts. Producers could have thwarted the cotton programs on numerous occasions, but most enthusiastically accepted them (though they often complained about certain administrative aspects). Farmers could have refused to participate in the plow-up campaign, for example, but most concurred with the administration's goals and joined the movement. After the plow-up, they could have refused to take part in the 1934–35 program, but not only did the growers provide support, they also put pressure on FDR to accept the Bankhead Cotton Control Act while voting in the 1934 referendum to continue the program for another year. Further, after Congress passed the Agricultural Adjustment Act of 1938, producers voted to accept the legislation's cotton provisions in every referendum held until U.S. entry into World War II. Some growers did emphatically oppose the AAA, but an overwhelming majority, including most Texas cotton farmers, backed the Roosevelt administration and cooperated with the government's labors to steer agricultural producers from the shoals of economic ruin.

Not all Texans benefited from the AAA. Ginners and export merchants were negatively affected by the cotton programs, just as other underrepresented groups fared under Franklin Roosevelt's approach to governance. Because the administration chose to work with the highly organized and politically power-ful farmers, volume-oriented businesses were hit hard by AAA production controls and suffered accordingly. Less cotton harvested simply meant less fiber to gin and ship. Unable to change a policy so detrimental to their trade, many ginners and exporters had to close their doors permanently. As evidence of the AAA's impact on Texas export merchants, one can compare the 1933 and the 1940 membership lists of their trade association—the Texas Cotton As-sociation. The records reveal that only half the members from the 1933 list were still on the 1940 rolls. Nevertheless, New Dealers argued, with much justification, that the needs of the more numerous cotton growers outweighed the concerns of the less numerous middlemen. As Roosevelt explained to an adviser: "I prefer to help the 90 percent at the expense of the 10 percent." There is also little doubt that the president was well aware of the positive po-litical benefits of adopting such a position.[3]

Tenant farmers and sharecroppers were another underrepresented group to which the AAA cotton programs offered little security. Despite scattered ap-peals from tenants and croppers, landlords often cheated large numbers of them out of government money. Worse, by the late 1930s, tens of thousands of Texas tenants and croppers were displaced by their landlords and forced to find alternative employment. USDA officials other than the purged AAA lawyers either assigned blame elsewhere or looked the other way, viewing landlord-tenant troubles as local problems that the federal government should stay out of.

Contributing to the unprotected situation of the tenant farmers and sharecroppers was the fact that the AAA delegated too much authority to the land-lord-dominated committees. The agency expected county committeemen and extension agents to resolve disputes within their localities, even when there were obvious conflicts of interest. M. L. Wilson, Henry Wallace, and other administration officials liked to praise the AAA as an example of grass-roots agrarian democracy in action. While the agency's decentralized bureaucracy may have been well suited for Wilson and Wallace's more egalitarian Mid-west, the reality of the AAA's system when transplanted to the South was that the local power structure—landlords, bankers, and merchants—exerted pri-mary control over the cotton programs. Celebrated for its efficiency and def-erence to local expertise, the AAA was often criticized, and justly so, for its lack of accountability. Committeemen and extension agents were regularly accused of siding with landlords in tenant disputes and favoring certain grow-ers in various endeavors. There is no way to assess accurately how often fraud or favoritism occurred, but the flaws in the system are readily apparent. The AAA's decentralized administration encouraged the establishment of govern-ment-sanctioned fiefdoms in the southern countryside, and many tenants, croppers, and small farmers suffered as a result.[4]

The New Deal's efforts to aid Texas' cotton farmers mirrored many of the Roosevelt administration's other activities to help Americans during the Great Depression. The haste that characterized the plow-up campaign, for example, was matched by the hurriedness of the March 1933 operations to save the na-tion's banks. In 1934, political pressure exerted by farmers and their represen-tatives convinced FDR to switch positions and endorse the Bankhead Act. Similarly, Roosevelt felt compelled by citizens and their congressmen to sup-port federal bank deposit insurance legislation that he had originally opposed. Just as New Dealers had to alter their plans after the Supreme Court ruled against such measures as the National Industrial Recovery Act, the AAA en-countered legal challenges and had to change tack after the High Court ruled against the Agricultural Adjustment Act of 1933. Finally, FDR's deference to the political power of southern conservatives in Congress regarding tenant matters paralleled his failure to act more boldly on civil rights issues for the same reason.

In the final analysis, the Roosevelt administration's efforts to save Texas cot-ton farmers were muddled. New Dealers sailed uncharted waters, gaining from experience while maneuvering through numerous political and legal shoals. Along the way, the government asked for, and largely received, the growers' cooperation. Ultimately, the AAA cotton programs succeeded in saving a majority of Texas farm owners and many lucky tenant farmers and sharecroppers from economic collapse. The regrettable aspect of this story is that the programs actually hurt many unfortunate Texas tenants, croppers, ginners, and shippers.

NOTES

Preface

1. Robert A. Calvert, "Agrarian Texas," 227.

2. John Braeman, "The New Deal and the 'Broker State:' A Review of the Recent Scholarly Literature."

3. Anthony J. Badger, *Prosperity Road: The New Deal, Tobacco, and North Carolina,* xvii.

Chapter 1

1. George Sessions Perry, *Hold Autumn in Your Hand,* 133.

2. Alvar Núñez Cabeza de Vaca, *Castaways: The Narrative of Alvar Núñez Cabeza de Vaca,* 101, 103–104; Karen Gerhardt Britton, Fred C. Elliott, and E. A. Miller, "Cotton Culture."

3. Gregg Cantrell, *Stephen F. Austin: Empresario of Texas;* Randolph B. Campbell, *An Empire for Slavery: The Peculiar Institution in Texas, 1821–1865.*

4. *Texas Almanac and State Industrial Guide, 1941–42,* 204; Sitton and Utley, *From Can See to Can't: Texas Cotton Farmers on the Southern Prairies,* 16.

5. Joseph F. Gordon, "The History and Development of Irrigated Cotton on the High Plains of Texas," chaps. 3 and 4; Neil Foley, "Mexicans, Mechanization, and the Growth of Corporate Cotton Culture in South Texas: The Taft Ranch, 1900–1930." The 1926–30 state average was 4.6 million bales annually on 16.7 million acres.

6. Rupert B. Vance, *Human Factors in Cotton Culture: A Study in the Social Geography of the American South,* chaps. 6, 7, 9; Harold D. Woodman, *King Cotton and His Retainers: Financing and Marketing the Cotton Crop of the South, 1800–1925,* chap. 24; idem, *New South—New Law: The Legal Foundations of Credit and Labor Relations in the Postbellum Agricultural South,* 59, 79.

7. Foley, *The White Scourge: Mexicans, Blacks, and Poor Whites in Texas Cotton Culture,* chap. 3.

8. Sitton and Utley, *From Can See to Can't,* 116–17; Samuel Lee Evans, "Texas Agriculture, 1880–1930," 19; Robert A. Calvert, "Nineteenth-Century Farmers, Cotton, and Prosperity," 513.

9. Sitton and Utley, *From Can See to Can't,* 118–22; Evans, "Texas Agriculture," 20–27; Vance, *Human Factors in Cotton Culture,* 159; Harry Bates Brown, *Cotton: History, Species, Varieties, Morphology, Breeding, Culture, Diseases, Marketing, and Uses,* 285–87.

10. Sitton and Utley, *From Can See to Can't,* 152–53; Evans, "Texas Agriculture," 30–35; Brown, *Cotton,* 289–96.

11. Sitton and Utley, *From Can See to Can't,* 153.

12. Sharpless, *Fertile Ground, Narrow Choices: Women on Texas Cotton Farms, 1900–1940,* 165–68; Sitton and Utley, *From Can See to Can't,* 160.

13. Sitton and Utley, *From Can See to Can't,* 156–65; Evans, "Texas Agriculture," 35–39; Sharpless, *Fertile Ground, Narrow Choices,* 171–74; Brown, *Cotton,* 296–302; Calvert, "Nineteenth-Century Farmers, Cotton, and Prosperity," 514–15.

14. For extensive discussions on the threats to cotton plants presented by various diseases and insects, see Brown, *Cotton,* chaps. 14 and 15; Evans, "Texas Agriculture," chap. 2.

15. Brown, *Cotton,* 339–44; Vance, *Human Factors in Cotton Culture,* 89 (quotation); Douglas Helms, "Just Lookin' for a Home: The Cotton Boll Weevil and the South."

16. Sitton and Utley, *From Can See to Can't,* 186–203; Sharpless, *Fertile Ground, Narrow Choices,* 174–75; for information on food production, preparation, and preservation, see chap. 3.

17. Sitton and Utley, *From Can See to Can't;* 207–10; Sharpless, *Fertile Ground, Narrow Choices,* 179–83; Foley, *White Scourge,* 42–53; Evans, "Texas Agriculture," 40–41.

18. Sitton and Utley, *From Can See to Can't,* 208 (first quotation), 209–11; Sharpless, *Fertile Ground, Narrow Choices,* 179–86; Evans, "Texas Agriculture," 40–45; Brown, *Cotton,* 377–80; Vance, *Human Factors in Cotton Culture,* 166. In large parts of the southern High Plains of Northwest Texas, cotton picking was performed differently from the rest of the state. Chronic labor shortages led to a picking method known as "snapping." A laborer simply pulled the entire cotton boll off the stalk and threw it into a sack. The flat terrain of the Plains, coupled with the existing labor shortage, led to the development of the "stripper"—the only practical advance in cotton harvesting before the invention of the mechanical cotton picker in the 1940s. The most popular form of stripper was the "finger" type—basically a wooden box that contained an open front with iron rods, or "fingers," projecting outward. As work stock pulled the contraption over the cotton rows, the stripper pulled the stalks through the finger grooves and "stripped" the bolls right off the plants. The device, in a sense, was a type of mechanical snapper. Both snapping and the use of the stripper resulted in quicker harvesting and reduced labor costs, but a lower grade of cotton due to the additional trash mixed with the lint. In 1926, southern High Plains farmers harvested an estimated 185,000 bales out of a total production of 375,000 bales by stripping. See Evans, "Texas Agriculture," 41, 45–47; Brown, *Cotton,* 381–87; D. L. Jones, W. M. Hurst, and D. Scoates, "Mechanical Harvesting of Cotton in Northwest Texas."

19. Sitton and Utley, *From Can See to Can't,* 222–33; Evans, "Texas Agriculture," 47–49; Brown, *Cotton,* 399–411, 499–524. Ginners sold the collected seed to cottonseed oil companies, which processed the meat, hulls, and small fibers remaining on the seeds (known as "linters") for use as major ingredients in a host of products ranging from animal feed and fertilizer to soap and oleomargarine. For information on the cottonseed industry, see Lynette B. Wrenn, *Cinderella of the New South: A History of the Cottonseed Industry, 1855–1955.* For detailed information on cotton ginning, see Karen Britton, *Bale o' Cotton: The Mechanical Art of Cotton Ginning.* The diesel-powered gin at Burton, Texas,

is one of the few operational gins from the pre-Depression era still in the South. It functions as a museum artifact and educational tool. The gin building is open for tours, and the gin itself is fired up annually at the Burton Cotton Gin Festival, to the delight of curious onlookers.

20. Alston Hill Garside, *Cotton Goes to Market: A Graphic Description of a Great Industry*, 170–76; Sitton and Utley, *From Can See to Can't*, 233–36; Brown, *Cotton*, 439–40; Vance, *Human Factors in Cotton Culture*, 170.

21. Brown, *Cotton*, 439–42; Garside, *Cotton Goes to Market*, 176–86. For information on Anderson, Clayton and Company, see Lamar Fleming, Jr., *Growth of the Business of Anderson, Clayton and Company*. In 1927, Anderson, Clayton and Company bought 2.6 million bales of the 13 million–bale total produced by American cotton farmers.

22. *Texas Almanac and State Industrial Guide, 1931*, 166.

23. Henry I. Richards, *Cotton and the AAA*, 10–11.

24. Van L. Perkins, *Crisis in Agriculture: The Agricultural Adjustment Administration and the New Deal, 1933*, 19–20.

25. Richards, *Cotton and the AAA*, 24–26.

26. Perkins, *Crisis in Agriculture*, 11.

27. Gilbert C. Fite, "Voluntary Attempts to Reduce Cotton Acreage in the South, 1914–1933," 481–85.

28. Ibid., 486–87.

29. Ibid., 487–92.

30. Ibid., 494–97.

31. Gilbert C. Fite, *George N. Peek and the Fight for Farm Parity*, 21–37; John Kennedy Ohl, *Hugh S. Johnson and the New Deal*, 36–57. Johnson served as the first head of the National Recovery Administration (NRA).

32. Fite, *George N. Peek*, 38–58; Ohl, *Hugh S. Johnson*, 59–64.

33. Fite, *George N. Peek*, 59–76; Ohl, *Hugh S. Johnson*, 57–59, 64–69.

34. Fite, *George N. Peek*, 59–168; Christiana McFadyen Campbell, *The Farm Bureau and the New Deal: A Study of the Making of National Farm Policy, 1933–1940*, 35–42; Grant McConnell, *The Decline of Agrarian Democracy*, 61–64.

35. Fite, *George N. Peek*, 169–202. For a pro-Coolidge view, see Donald R. McCoy, *Calvin Coolidge: The Quiet President*, 322–28.

36. Fite, *George N. Peek*, 203–20.

37. David E. Hamilton, *From New Day to New Deal: American Farm Policy from Hoover to Roosevelt, 1928–1933*, 27–42; Albert Romasco, *The Poverty of Abundance: Hoover, the Nation, the Depression*, 20–23.

38. Hamilton, *From New Day to New Deal*, 42–49.

39. Ibid., 50–108.

40. Federal Farm Board press release, August 12, 1931, Agriculture—Cotton folder, Box 19, Agricultural Material, Marvin Jones, Papers, Southwest Collection, Texas Tech University, Lubbock (cited hereafter as Marvin Jones Papers); Hamilton, *From New Day to New Deal*, 122–25; Fite, "Voluntary Efforts to Reduce Cotton Acreage," 497.

41. Donald Snyder, *Cotton Crisis*, 3–4.

42. Snyder, *Cotton Crisis*, 36; T. Harry Williams, *Huey Long*, 531; Alan Brinkley, *Voices of Protest: Huey Long, Father Coughlin, and the Great Depression*, 37; William Ivy Hair, *The Kingfish and His Realm: The Life and Times of Huey Long*, 214.

43. *Dallas Morning News,* August 19, 1931; Snyder, *Cotton Crisis,* 40–43.

44. Donald W. Whisenhunt, "Huey Long and the Texas Cotton Acreage Control Law of 1931," 144; Snyder, *Cotton Crisis,* 93–97 (quotation); Brinkley, *Voices of Protest,* 39.

45. Karl E. Ashburn, "The Texas Cotton Acreage Control Law of 1931–32," 116–17.

46. Ashburn, "Texas Cotton Acreage Control Law," 124; Snyder, *Cotton Crisis,* 124–27.

47. W. J. Spillman, *Balancing the Farm Output: A Statement of the Present Deplorable Conditions of Farming, Its Causes, and Suggested Remedies;* William D. Rowley, *M. L. Wilson and the Campaign for the Domestic Allotment,* 33–39; Perkins, *Crisis in Agriculture,* 27.

48. John D. Black, *Agricultural Reform in the United States;* Hamilton, *From New Day to New Deal,* 182; Rowley, *M. L. Wilson,* 53–60. Hamilton notes the irony of Black's role in promoting the allotment plan: the economist was never very enthused with the idea; he included it in his book as a favor to Beardsley Ruml, the head of the Laura Spelman Rockefeller Foundation, who gave Black a grant to support his research. Unaware of Spillman's work, Ruml had independently conceived an allotment plan and wished to underwrite Black's book in hopes of promoting the idea. Black used an outline provided by Ruml (along with his own knowledge of Spillman's book) to formulate a domestic allotment program for the book (Hamilton, *From New Day to New Deal,* 297–98n31).

49. Rowley, *M. L. Wilson,* 2–5; Richard S. Kirkendall, *Social Scientists and Farm Politics in the Age of Roosevelt,* 11–15.

50. Rowley, *M. L. Wilson,* 5–7, 48–49, 57–60; Kirkendall, *Social Scientists and Farm Politics,* 25; Hamilton, *From New Day to New Deal,* 182–86.

51. Hamilton, *From New Day to New Deal,* 186–90. Ezekiel was serving as the assistant chief economist for Hoover's Farm Board at the time he and Wilson collaborated on their version of the allotment plan.

52. Hamilton, *From New Day to New Deal,* 190–94; Perkins, *Crisis in Agriculture,* 28; Kirkendall, *Social Scientists and Farm Politics,* 25–26.

53. Hamilton, *From New Day to New Deal,* 190–94. For information on associationalism during the interwar period, see Ellis Hawley, *The Great War and the Search for a Modern Order: A History of the American People and Their Institutions, 1917–1933,* especially chap. 6.

54. Rowley, *M. L. Wilson,* 107–36; Hamilton, *From New Day to New Deal,* 204; Fite, *George N. Peek,* 230–34; Edward L. Schapsmeier and Frederick H. Schapsmeier, *Henry A. Wallace of Iowa: The Agrarian Years, 1910–1940,* 126–30.

55. Henry C. Wallace primarily handled the paper's business affairs while the elder Wallace used the editorial section as his personal pulpit to teach about God and scientific agricultural principles until his death in 1916. For information on the lives of Henry Wallace and Henry Cantwell Wallace and their influence on Henry A. Wallace, see John C. Culver and John Hyde, *American Dreamer: The Life and Times of Henry A. Wallace,* 3–65; Russell Lord, *The Wallaces of Iowa,* 1–258; Schapsmeier and Schapsmeier, *Henry A. Wallace,* 2–15, 48–80.

56. On the early life of Henry A. Wallace, see Culver and Hyde, *American Dreamer,* 11–101; Lord, *Wallaces of Iowa,* 107–312; Schapsmeier and Schapsmeier, *Henry A. Wallace,* 17–142.

57. Perkins, *Crisis in Agriculture,* 29–30. In his acceptance speech at the Republican national convention, Hoover made his beliefs on any type of acreage-reduction plan per-

fectly clear: "There is no relief to the farmer by extending government bureaucracy to control his production and thus curtail his liberties, nor by subsidies that bring only more bureaucracy and ultimate collapse. I shall oppose them" *(New York Times,* August 12, 1932; see also *Dallas Morning News,* August 12, 1932).

58. Rowley, *M. L. Wilson,* 150–63; Kirkendall, *Social Scientists and Farm Politics,* 41–47; for background information on Rexford Tugwell and analysis on his influence as a member of the Brain Trust, see Bernard Sternsher, *Rexford Tugwell and the New Deal,* 3–90; Elliot A. Rosen, *Hoover, Roosevelt, and the Brains Trust: From Depression to New Deal,* 151–94.

59. Irvin M. May, Jr., *Marvin Jones: The Public Life of an Agrarian Advocate,* 94; Perkins, *Crisis in Agriculture,* 32; Kirkendall, *Social Scientists and Farm Politics,* 50–51.

60. May, *Marvin Jones,* 95–96; Kirkendall, *Social Scientists and Farm Politics,* 50–53; *Dallas Morning News,* January 4, 1933; *Houston Post,* January 4, 1933; *New York Times,* January 5, 13, 1933. Rep. Fritz G. Lanham of Fort Worth cast the only dissenting vote from Texas' eighteen-member House delegation.

Chapter 2

1. Franklin Roosevelt to Henry Wallace, February 3, 1933, Henry A. Wallace, Papers (hereafter cited as Wallace Papers). For information on the political aspects of Wallace's appointment as secretary of agriculture, see David M. Kennedy, *Freedom from Fear: The American People in Depression and War, 1929–1945,* 127; Raymond Moley, *After Seven Years,* 123–24n12; and Schapsmeier and Schapsmeier, *Henry A. Wallace,* 160–61. On George Peek's attitude regarding the post, see Fite, *George N. Peek,* 241–42. On the broad southern support for Cully Cobb's appointment, see Roy V. Scott and J. G. Shoalmire, *The Public Career of Cully A. Cobb: A Study in Agricultural Leadership,* 194–98. For the efforts of Texans on Cobb's behalf, see H. H. Williamson [vice-director of Texas Extension Service] to Cobb, November 10, 1932; Cobb to Williamson, November 21, 1932; and O. B. Martin [director of Texas Extension Service] to Cobb, January 12, 1933 (all in Box 1, Folder 1, Cully A. Cobb, Papers, Mitchell Memorial Library, Mississippi State University, Starkville; cited hereafter as Cully Cobb Papers). For Cobb's belief that it would not be "good politics to appoint any Republican to a cabinet post," see Cobb to T. O. Walton [president of Texas A&M College], December 7, 1932, Box 1, Folder 5, Cully Cobb Papers.

2. Washington Conference Report, Box 43, Agricultural Adjustment Act folder, Subject Files, Rexford G. Tugwell, Papers, Franklin D. Roosevelt Presidential Library, Hyde Park, N.Y. (cited hereafter as Rexford Tugwell Papers). The best summary of the farm bill's drafting is found in Perkins, *Crisis in Agriculture,* 36–48. The following sketch is based on Perkins's description.

3. Frederick E. Hosen, *The Great Depression and the New Deal: Legislative Acts in Their Entirety (1932–1933) and Statistical Economic Data (1926–1946),* 61–62 (quotation). The base period for tobacco was later changed by amendment to the August 1919–July 1929 period.

4. Cattle and sheep were later removed from the 1933 farm bill by amendment.

5. The bill stated that "in the case of cotton, the term 'processing' means the spinning, manufacturing, or other processing (except ginning) of cotton." See Hosen, *Great Depression and the New Deal,* 67. The processing tax was to equal the difference between

the parity price and the current market price of the commodity. Although many expected that processors would simply pass the tax on to consumers, most agricultural spokespersons argued that any increase in the retail price of finished goods would be minimal.

6. Marvin Jones, "The Reminiscences of Marvin Jones," Oral History Research Office Collection, 582 (quotation), Columbia University, New York (quotation). For conflicting evaluations of Cotton Ed Smith's political career, see Allan A. Michie and Frank Rhylick, *Dixie Demagogues,* 265–85; Daniel W. Hollis, "Cotton Ed Smith—Showman or Statesman?"

7. A bill based on the option plan passed both houses of Congress at the end of the 1932 lame-duck session, but President Hoover used a pocket veto on the measure. Smith lobbied adamantly for his plan's inclusion in the 1933 farm bill. Administration officials, needing Smith's acquiescence on the bill, agreed to include the cotton option as one possible method available to the secretary of agriculture to induce reduced cotton production. As Marvin Jones remembered: "[The Cotton Option Plan] was put in because we wanted Senator Smith to go along with the program. By putting his pet bill, which he had been introducing in different forms for two or three years, in to the act, it would help get him, as chairman of the committee, interested in supporting the bill" (Jones, "Reminiscences of Marvin Jones," 583). In a memo to Paul Appleby, assistant to Secretary Wallace, Mordecai Ezekiel referred to the inclusion of the cotton option as a "swap" for Smith's support of the farm bill. See Ezekiel to Appleby, June 27, 1933, "Agriculture, U.S. Department of, 1932–33" file, Box 1, Subject Files, Mordecai Ezekiel, Papers, Franklin D. Roosevelt Presidential Library, Hyde Park, N.Y. (cited hereafter as Mordecai Ezekiel Papers).

8. Message to Congress, March 16, 1933, Box 14, FDR Speech File, President's Personal File (cited hereafter as PPF) 1820, Franklin D. Roosevelt, Papers, Franklin D. Roosevelt Presidential Library, Hyde Park, New York (cited hereafter as FDR Papers).

9. On the early life of Marvin Jones and his views on agricultural problems, see May, *Marvin Jones,* 3–78.

10. Jones wrote the president-elect before the lame-duck session to explain his views on the problems of agriculture and possible solutions. In no part of the letter does he mention overproduction as a major problem or acreage curtailment as a proposed solution. See Jones to Roosevelt, November 29, 1932, PPF 2736, FDR Papers.

11. May, *Marvin Jones,* 102; Perkins, *Crisis in Agriculture,* 52; *Dallas Morning News,* March 21, 22 (quotation), 1933; *Houston Post,* March 21, 1933; *New York Times,* March 21, 1933.

12. *Congressional Record,* House, 73d Cong., 1st sess., pt. 1, 673–74 (quotation). Jones outlined his preferred program for farm relief, similar to the one that he presented on the House floor, in a letter to President-elect Roosevelt in late November 1932. See Jones to Roosevelt, November 29, 1932, PPF 2736, FDR Papers. For the remarks of the other Texas congressmen, see *Congressional Record,* House, 73d Cong., 1st sess., pt. 1, 685–86, 736–37, 756–57, 764–65.

13. *Congressional Record,* House, 73d Cong., 1st sess., pt. 1, 751–52 (quotations); *Dallas Morning News,* March 23, 1933. The bill passed by a vote of 315–98. Fifteen members of the Texas delegation voted for the measure, while only two members, Joseph W. Bailey, Jr., and Fritz D. Lanham, joined George Terrell in voting against the bill. Perkins, *Crisis in Agriculture,* 49–78, contains the best summary of the farm bill debate in both houses.

14. *Congressional Record,* Senate, 73d Cong., 1st sess., pt. 2, 1646 (quotation); *Dallas Morning News,* April 29, 1933; *Houston Post,* April 29, 1933.

15. *Dallas Morning News,* May 13, 1933; *New York Times,* May 13, 1933.

16. Arthur M. Schlesinger, Jr., *The Age of Roosevelt: The Coming of the New Deal,* 47 (quotation).

17. Fite, *George N. Peek,* 251–57; Perkins, *Crisis in Agriculture,* 55–56, 82–90; Schlesinger, *Age of Roosevelt,* 48. For a detailed look at the tobacco agreement, see Badger, *Prosperity Road,* 57–71.

18. Perkins, *Crisis in Agriculture,* 92–93; Theodore Saloutos, *The American Farmer and the New Deal,* 56–58; Scott and Shoalmire, *Cully A. Cobb,* 199; *New York Times,* May 23, 1933.

19. For biographical information on Cully Cobb before he became AAA Cotton Section chief, see Scott and Shoalmire, *Cully A. Cobb,* 3–199.

20. For background information on Oscar Johnston's life before joining the AAA, see Lawrence J. Nelson, *King Cotton's Advocate: Oscar G. Johnston and the New Deal,* 1–48.

21. The first bale of Texas cotton, produced by Teófilo García, a Lower Rio Grande Valley farmer, reached the Houston Cotton Exchange in the early morning hours of June 13 (*Houston Post,* June 14, 1933).

22. Richards, *Cotton and the AAA,* 28; Perkins, *Crisis in Agriculture,* 102–103.

23. Proceedings of Washington Cotton Conference, June 3, 1933, Conferences and Meetings—1933 file, Box 12, Docket Files, Agricultural Adjustment Administration, Records of the Agricultural Stabilization and Conservation Service, Record Group 145, National Archives II, College Park, Md. (cited hereafter as AAA, RG 145, NA).

24. *Houston Post,* June 6, 1933.

25. Clayton to Peek, June 7, 1933 (first quotation); memo, Johnston to Peek, June 7, 1933 (second quotation); Peek to Clayton, June 7, 1933 (third quotation) (all in Box 18, Cotton file, Central Correspondence Files arranged by subject [cited hereafter as SC] 1933–35, AAA, RG 145, NA).

26. The full text of Wallace's announcement appears in the *New York Times,* June 20, 1933. The processing tax was subsequently set at 4.2 cents per pound (*New York Times,* July 15, 1933; *Dallas Morning News,* July 15, 1933).

27. The Cotton Section decided against accepting contracts for land with an average yield under one hundred pounds per acre. For a justification of the payment schedule eventually approved by the AAA, see "Memorandum on Basis for Recommending Schedule of Payments for Cotton," "Agriculture, U.S. Dept. of, 1932–33" file, Box 1, Subject Files, Mordecai Ezekiel Papers.

28. The Cotton Section favored equal acceptance of the two plans by cotton farmers. As Cobb wired state Extension Service directors: "Desirable that we obtain equal number of contracts for both plan number one and plan number two. We believe limitations and element of risk surrounding option on cotton will make the all cash plan number two more attractive to the smaller producers than plan number one. Neither plan should be sold at the expense of the other" (Cobb to state extension directors, June 26, 1933, Cotton—Blanket Wires file, Box 24, SC 1933–35, AAA, RG 145, NA).

29. Henry A. Wallace, *New Frontiers,* 174–75 (quotation).

30. Demonstration work involved county agents inviting growers to observe a patch

of land where farmers were following prescribed cultivation methods. USDA officials hoped that growers who saw positive results on a neighbor's farm would be more likely to adopt recommended practices. The Smith-Lever Act of 1914 established the Federal Extension Service and provided for federal grants-in-aid to states for "extension work," as demonstration work became to be called, because the service would "extend" the latest research from the agricultural colleges to local farmers. See Roy V. Scott, *The Reluctant Farmer: The Rise of Agricultural Extension to 1914,* 206–36; Evans, "Texas Agriculture," 71; Louis Franke, "How the Extension Service Came to Be," 1–4; Gladys Baker, *The County Agent,* 25–45; McConnell, *Decline of Agrarian Democracy,* 44–54.

31. Scott and Shoalmire, *Cully A. Cobb,* 211–12.

32. Lord, *Wallaces of Iowa,* 382 (quotation); Perkins, *Crisis in Agriculture,* 97–98.

33. Press release of the Agricultural Adjustment Administration (cited hereafter as AAA R.), 1410–33, Box 1, Entry 6, AAA, RG 145, NA.

34. Martin to Cobb, May 26, 1933, Texas A&M College—O. B. Martin file, Box 1074, Central Correspondence Files (arranged alphabetically by correspondent; cited hereafter as AC) 1933–35, AAA, RG 145, NA.

35. Cully Cobb was especially happy that Martin chose Williamson, an old friend and colleague, to head the plow-up campaign in Texas. For an expression of Cobb's high confidence in Williamson's ability to run the cotton program in the Lone Star State, see Cobb to Chester Davis, June 27, 1933, Reports—Volume 3 file, Box 12, Docket Files, AAA, RG 145, NA. In 1933, Texas farmers devoted approximately 16,050,000 acres to cotton; the 1933 acreage for all American cotton growers was estimated to be 40,852,000 (Henry I. Richards, *Cotton under the Agricultural Adjustment Act: Developments up to July 1934,* 37).

36. Cobb to state extension directors, June 27, 1933, Cotton—Blanket Wires file, Box 24, SC 1933–35, (quotation); AAA R. 1421–33, Box 1, Entry 6 (both in AAA, RG 145, NA).

37. *Houston Post,* June 21, 1933; AAA R. 31–34, Box 1, Entry 6, AAA, RG 145, NA.

38. Cobb to Martin, June 16, 1933, Cotton—A.R. [Acreage Reduction] file, Box 20, SC 1933–35, AAA, RG 145, NA (quotation).

39. Richards, *Cotton under the Agricultural Adjustment Act,* 18. When I could ascertain the occupation of county committeemen from county agent reports or newspaper stories, I found that the arrangement of having one banker, one merchant, and one farmer on the committee was generally followed in Texas. It should also be noted that I never came across the name of a female county or local committee memeber, hence, I have continued to use the contemporary term "committeemen."

40. Texas county agents divided up the jurisdictions of the local committees in numerous ways based on convenience. Many agents simply assigned committees to areas organized by rural communities, as occurred in Brown and Harrison counties. Several agents partitioned their counties by school district, as in Hockley, Jones, Lamb, Lubbock, and Shelby counties. Many other agents simply grouped their committeemen to cover equal numbers of farmers within more or less arbitrary geographical divisions. See microfilmed 1933 annual narrative reports of Texas county agents, Texas Agricultural Extension Service, Historical Records, Texas A&M University, College Station (cited hereafter as TAES Historical Records).

41. The AAA implored the Extension Service to keep the estimated average yields for the counties in 1933 within each county's five-year average for the 1928–32 period, as com-

piled by the USDA Division of Crop and Livestock Estimates. For example, see Tugwell to Martin, June 27, 1933, Texas A&M—O. B. Martin file, Box 1074, AC 1933–35, AAA, RG 145, NA.

42. See annual narrative reports for county agents of Garza, Hockley, and Palo Pinto counties, microfilm reels 86, 87, 89, TAES Historical Records.

43. For example, see the editorials in *Houston Post,* June 22, 1933; *Dallas Morning News,* June 24, 1933.

44. AAA R. 1403–33, Box 1, Entry 6, AAA, RG 145, NA.

45. For newspaper accounts of McDonald's tour, see *Austin Statesman,* June 20, 1933; *Dallas Morning News,* June 20, 22, 24, 1933; *Austin Statesman,* June 26, 1933; and *Houston Post,* June 27, 1933.

46. AAA R. 1403–33, Box 1, Entry 6, AAA, RG 145, NA (quotation).

47. Era Lane to the author. Mrs. Lane was thirty-three years old at the time of the plow-up. See also *Dallas Morning News,* June 25, 1933; annual narrative report of Cedar A. Walton, Negro county agent for Dallas County, 1933, microfilm reel 85, TAES Historical Records.

48. Annual narrative report of V. T. Kallus, county agent for Atascosa County, 1933, microfilm reel 84, TAES Historical Records. Agent Kallus noted: "One must admit that [the success of the sign-up] is largely due to the number of meetings held and meeting demands peculiar to every nationality." See also annual narrative report of D. W. Brown, county agent for Williamson County, 1933, microfilm reel 90, TAES Historical Records.

49. Annual narrative report of W. B. Frederick, county agent for Freestone County, 1933, microfilm reel 86; see also annual narrative reports of S. Goen, county agent for Sabine County, 1933, microfilm reel 89, and W. M. Burks, county agent for Upshur County, 1933, microfilm reel 90 (all in TAES Historical Records).

50. Williamson to Cobb, June 27, 1933, H.H. Williamson file, Box 1186, AC 1933–35 (first quotation); Williamson to Cobb, July 5, 1933; J. E. McDonald to Peek, July 10, 1933, Texas State Department of Agriculture file, Box 1077 (second quotation) (all in AAA, RG 145, NA). See also 1933 annual narrative report of Robert Lancaster, District 5 (South Texas) agent, microfilm reel 84, TAES Historical Records; annual narrative reports of county agents from Angelina, Comal, Gray, Howard, Jones, and Stephens counties, microfilm reels 84–87, 89, 1933 TAES Historical Records; *San Antonio Express,* July 3, 1933; *Houston Post,* July 4, 7, 1933; *Bryan Daily Eagle,* July 7, 1933.

51. Annual narrative report of K. C. Edwards, county agent for Goliad County, 1933, microfilm reel 86, TAES Historical Records; letter to the editor [from a Hillsboro, Texas, cotton farmer] in *Dallas Morning News,* June 23, 1933; Rev. Emil Listman to Cobb, September 1, 1933, Cotton—A.R. file, Box 21, SC 1933–35, AAA, RG 145, NA.

52. Annual narrative report of Ross B. Jenkins, county agent for Callahan County, 1933, microfilm reel 85 (quotation); see also annual narrative reports of county agents from Atascosa, Goliad, Houston, and Limestone counties, 1933, microfilm reels 84–88 (all in TAES Historical Records).

53. H. Helpin to Wallace, July 21, 1933, Cotton—A.R. file, Box 21, SC 1933–35, AAA, RG 145, NA (quotation).

54. Aron Weaver to Roosevelt, n.d., Cotton—A.R. file, Box 21, SC 1933–35, AAA, RG 145, NA (quotation). For other protests from Texas growers complaining about their estimated yield, see letters in Cotton—A.R. file, Box 21, SC 1933–35, AAA, RG 145, NA,

and narrative annual reports from county agents in Jones, Stephens, Throckmorton, and Wilbarger counties, 1933, microfilm reels 87, 89, 90, TAES Historical Records.

55. For a discussion of the speculative rise in the price of cotton during this period, see Perkins, *Crisis in Agriculture, 101–103.* For comments on the effects of the price rise on the sign-up, see annual narrative reports of county agents for Goliad and Limestone counties, 1933, microfilm reels 86, 88, TAES Historical Records; *Dallas Morning News,* July 2, 1933; *Bryan Daily Eagle,* July 5, 1933.

56. AAA R. 36–34, Box 1, Entry 6; Cobb to state extension directors, July 8, 1933, Cotton—A.R. file, Box 20, SC 1933–35 (both in AAA, RG 145, NA). By July 8, Texas farmers had signed up only 2,494,872 acres of cotton for destruction.

57. Memo, "Recommendations for Carrying Out the 1933 Cotton Adjustment Program," Cobb to Wallace, n.d., Cotton—A.R. file, Box 20, SC 1933–35; Cobb to state extension directors, July 14, 1933, Cotton—Blanket Wires file, Box 24; AAA R. 80–34, Box 1, Entry 6 (all in AAA, RG 145, NA); *Dallas Morning News,* July 15, 1933; *Houston Post,* July 15, 1933; *New York Times,* July 15, 1933.

58. *Bryan Daily Eagle,* July 14 (first quotation), 15, 1933; Richards, *Cotton under the Agricultural Adjustment Act,* 36–37; press release, July 20, 1933, March–August 1933 folder, Box 1, President's Official File (cited hereafter as OF) 258, FDR Papers (second quotation).

59. Memo, Davis to Jerome Frank, July 27, 1933, Cotton—A.R. file, Box 21, SC 1933–35; Cobb to state extension directors, July 18, 1933; AAA R. 133–34, Box 1, Entry 6 (all in AAA, RG 145, NA).

60. Memo, Cobb to Davis, July 26, 1933, Cotton—A.R. file, Box 21, SC 1933–35 (first quotation); Miller to Williamson, July 25, 1933, H. H. Williamson file, Box 1186, AC, 1933–35 (second quotation) (both in AAA, RG 145, NA).

61. Richards, *Cotton under the Agricultural Adjustment Act,* 48–49; Perkins, *Crisis in Agriculture,* 109. See also annual narrative reports of county agents from Angelina, Montague, and Panola counties, 1933, microfilm reels 84, 88, 89, TAES Historical Records; AAA R. 353–34, 401–34 (both in Box 1, Entry 6, AAA, RG 145, NA).

62. Williamson to Cobb, August 17, 1933, H. H. Williamson file; Cobb to Williamson, August 17, 1933 (first quotation) (both in Box 1186, AC 1933–35, AAA, RG 145, NA). See also annual narrative report of F. O. Montague, county agent for Matagorda County, 1933, microfilm reel 88 (second quotation); annual narrative report of T. A. Adams, county agent in charge of the plow-up campaign in Aransas, Refugio, and San Patricio counties, 1933, microfilm reel 89 (all in TAES Historical Records). For news stories on the storms' effects on the plow-up efforts, see *Austin Statesman,* August 10, 1933; *San Antonio Express,* July 31, August 12, 1933.

63. Dies to Wallace, August 10, 1933; Wallace to Dies, August 17, 1933 (both in Cotton—A.R. file, Box 21, SC 1933–35, AAA, RG 145, NA); annual narrative report of S. Goen, county agent for Sabine County, 1933, microfilm reel 89, TAES Historical Records.

64. *Dallas Morning News,* August 27, 1933 (quotation). For news stories of "balking mules" in Texas, see *San Antonio Express,* August 2, 1933; *Dallas Morning News,* August 27, 1933. For related incidents in other parts of the South, see *New York Times,* August 10, 1933; Michael S. Holmes, *The New Deal in Georgia: An Administrative History,* 219.

65. *Terry County Herald,* September 22, 1933; annual narrative report of T. A. Adams, county agent in charge of plow-up campaign in Aransas, Refugio, and San Patricio counties, 1933, microfilm reel 89, TAES Historical Records; Cobb to state extension directors,

August 22, 1933, Cotton—A.R. file, Box 21, SC 1933–35; AAA R. 401–35, Box 1, Entry 6 (both in AAA, RG 145, NA).

66. Annual narrative report of E. C. Jameson, county agent for Montague County, 1933, microfilm reel 88, TAES Historical Records (quotation).

67. *Dallas Morning News*, July 29, 1933; *New York Times*, July 29, 1933; *San Antonio Express*, July 29, 1933.

68. See especially the annual narrative reports of the county agents from Callahan, Castro, Comal, Gray, Montague, and San Saba counties, 1933, microfilm reels, 85, 86, 88, 89, TAES Historical Records.

69. Annual narrative report of R. B. Tate, county agent for Mason County, 1933, microfilm reel 88, TAES Historical Records (quotation; emphasis mine).

70. Morgan Sanders to Sam Rayburn, September 8, 1933, "1933 Farm Legislation and Farm Problems" file, "Correspondence, 1914–39" drawer, Sam Rayburn, Papers, Sam Rayburn Library, Bonham, Tex. (cited hereafter as Sam Rayburn Papers) (quotation). For a summary of the USDA forecast, see *Dallas Morning News*, August 8, 1933. On the growing price-cost squeeze experienced by farmers in the late summer months of 1933, see Perkins, *Crisis in Agriculture*, 168–71; *Dallas Morning News*, August 27, September 9, 11, 1933.

71. James Buchanan to Henry Wallace, August 14, 1933, James Buchanan file, Box 140, James Buchanan file, AC 1933–35, AAA, RG 145, NA; *New York Times*, August 16, 1933.

72. McDonald to Roosevelt, August 14, 1933, Cotton file, Box 18, SC 1933–35, AAA, RG 145, NA; *Dallas Morning News*, August 17, 1933; *Houston Post*, August 18, 1933.

73. McDonald to Roosevelt, August 15, 1933, "Farm Relief—Cotton" file, Box 1817, General Correspondence of the Secretary of Agriculture, Secretary of Agriculture, Office of the, Records, National Archives II, College Park, Md., Record Group 16 (cited hereafter as GC, USDA, RG 16), NA; *Houston Post*, August 15, September 16, 1933; *Dallas Morning News*, August 18, 1933.

74. Bankhead to Roosevelt, August 21, 1933; Roosevelt to Bankhead, September 13, 1933 (both in Cotton file, Box 18, SC 1933–35, AAA, RG 145, NA).

75. Perkins, *Crisis in Agriculture*, 168–72; *Dallas Morning News*, September 19, 20, 21, 22, 1933; *Houston Post*, September 19, 20, 21, 22, 1933; *New York Times*, September 19, 20, 21, 22, 1933.

76. Memo, Johnston to George Peek, September 22, 1933, Cotton file, Box 1, OF 258, FDR Papers; "Memorandum on Ten Cent Cotton Loan," Box 1, "Agriculture, U.S. Department of, 1932–33" file, Subject Files, Mordecai Ezekiel Papers; Nelson, *King Cotton's Advocate*, 55–58.

77. Samuel Rosenman, ed., *The Public Papers of Franklin D. Roosevelt*, vol. 2: *The Year of Crisis, 1933*, 404–407; AAA R. 679–34, 698–34, 806–34, 890–34, Box 1, Entry 6, AAA, RG 145, NA; *Dallas Morning News*, September 23, 24, 25, October 7, 9 (quotation), 18, 20, 1933; *Houston Post*, September 23, 24, 25, 30, October 7, 8, 18, 1933; *New York Times*, September 23, 24, 28, October 7, 18, 1933; Nelson, *King Cotton's Advocate*, 58–62; Perkins, *Crisis in Agriculture*, 173–74; Richards, *Cotton and the AAA*, 212–17.

78. *Dallas Morning News*, September 5, 23, October 8, 21, 1933. See also Sanders to Wallace, August 26, 1933, Morgan Sanders file, Box 944 (quotation); Johnson to Chester Davis, September 21, 1933, Luther Johnson file, Box 543; Thomason to Wallace, Septem-

ber 23, 1933, R. E. Thomason file, Box 1082; Patman to Cobb, October 25, 1933, Wright Patman file, Box 832 (all in AC 1933–35, AAA, RG 145, NA); Patman to Rayburn, October 10, 1933, Congressional Correspondence—1933 file, "Correspondence, 1914–39" drawer, Sam Rayburn Papers.

79. For farmers' complaints about payment delays stretching into 1934, see Lee Walden to James Buchanan, January 25, 1934, James Buchanan file, Box 140, AC 1933–35, AAA, RG 145, NA; and J. E. Burkhalter to Miriam Ferguson, March 20, 1934, Cotton Reduction Plan file, Folder 2, Subject Files 1929–35, Records of Miriam Amanda Ferguson, Governor's Papers, Record Group 301, Texas State Archives, Austin (cited hereafter as Miriam Ferguson Papers). In a February 19, 1934, letter to National Extension director C. W. Warburton, H. H. Williamson listed 962 Texas farmers who had signed cotton contracts in 1933, but who had yet to receive a check in payment (Warburton to Williamson, February 24, 1934, Texas Director file, Box 275, General Correspondence of the Extension Service, Federal Extension Service, Records, Record Group 33, National Archives II, College Park, Md. Cited hereafter as GC, FES, RG 33, NA).

80. USDA, *Agricultural Adjustment: A Report on the Agricultural Adjustment Administration, May 1933 to Feb. 1934,* 316. Fifty-two percent of Texas farmers chose the cash-and-option plan, while 48 percent chose the cash-only plan (Richards, *Cotton under the Agricultural Adjustment Act,* 45). In order to keep the option bales from being thrown on the market too abruptly, Oscar Johnston developed a plan for a "cotton option pool" whereby farmers would be advanced an additional four cents per pound on their option cotton (to equal the current CCC loan rate), minus nominal holding fees, in exchange for storing the option cotton. Participating producers basically trusted the pool manager (Johnston) to use his expertise to gradually liquidate the pool's holdings at opportune times in order to maximize profits. Three-quarters of the South's option holders placed their cotton in the pool, which Johnston finally "drained" completely by July 1936. For general information on the option-cotton pool, see Richards, *Cotton and the AAA,* 196–212; for an excellent discussion of Johnston's management of the option pool, see Nelson, *King Cotton's Advocate,* 62–65, 132–56.

81. See most annual narrative reports of the Texas county agents (TAES Historical Records) for comments on the improved attitude of the people toward the government and life in general as a result of the plow-up campaign.

82. Annual report of vice-director and county agent leader H. H. Williamson, 1933, microfilm reel 84 and annual report of Texas state director O. B. Martin, 1933, microfilm reel 84 (both in TAES Historical Records).

83. Annual narrative report of K. C. Edwards, county agent for Goliad County, 1933, microfilm reel 86, TAES Historical Records (quotation).

84. Annual narrative report of B. C. Colgin, county agent for Baylor County, 1933, microfilm reel 84, TAES Historical Records. The extension agent of Kent County in northwest Texas was very blunt in his annual report on the subject of where the credit belonged for the success of the cotton plow-up campaign in his county: "It is by the Grace of God and the efforts of the Federal Government that the Kent County farmer is on his feet again" (annual narrative report of W. C. Hale, county agent for Kent County, 1933, microfilm reel 87, TAES Historical Records).

85. For example, see J. H. Townley to Wallace, July 7, 1933, Cotton—A.R. file, Box

20; and Charles E. Jackson to Cobb, July 10, 1933, Box 21 (both in SC 1933–35, AAA, RG 145, NA).

86. Luther Johnson to Cobb, June 28, 1933, and Cobb to Johnson, June 28, 1933 (both in Cotton—A.R. file, Box 20, SC 1933–35, AAA, RG 145, NA); M. L. Walker to Ferguson, July 3, 1933, Cotton—General file, Folder 21; Ida and Early Leonard to Ferguson, October 10, 1933, Cotton—General file, Folder 24; James Wilrich to Ferguson, November 4, 1933 Cotton—General file, Folder 21 (all in Box 479, Miriam Ferguson Papers).

87. Allison to Miller, November 29, 1933, A. A. Allison file, Box 20, AC 1933–35, AAA, RG 145, NA (quotation).

88. Allison's handwritten message to Cobb (quotation) appears on Gladys Little to Alifonzo Escamilla, December 5, 1933, A. A. Allison file, Box 20, AC 1933–35, AAA, RG 145, NA.

89. Allison to Miller, November 29, 1933 (first quotation); Miller to Allison, December 6, 1933 (second quotation; emphasis mine) (both in A. A. Allison file, Box 20, AC 1933–35, AAA, RG 145, NA).

90. Allison to Miller, November 29, 1933 (quotations); see also Allison to Miller, December 16, 1933 (both in A. A. Allison file, Box 20, AC 1933–35, AAA, RG 145, NA).

Chapter 3

1. Annual narrative report of George E. Ehlinger, county agent for Comal County, 1933, microfilm reel 85, TAES Historical Records (quotation).

2. Transcript, "Conference with the Secretary of Agriculture and the Directors of Extension of the Cotton States to Discuss the Tentative Plans for Cotton Acreage Reduction in 1934 and 1935," "Agricultural Adjustment Administration: General, July–December 1933" folder, Box 1, Cully A. Cobb/Ruralist Press, Papers, Mitchell Memorial Library, Mississippi State University, Starkville (cited hereafter as Cobb/Ruralist Press Papers); David Conrad, *The Forgotten Farmers: The Story of Sharecroppers in the New Deal,* 54; Nelson, *King Cotton's Advocate,* 67. See also memo, Cobb to Chester Davis, August 25, 1933, Cotton—A.R. file, Box 22, SC 1933–35; AAA R. 453–34, Box 1, Entry 6 (both in AAA, RG 145, NA); *New York Times,* August 29, 1933; *Houston Post,* August 29, September 2, 1933; *Dallas Morning News,* August 31, September 1, 1933.

3. Transcript, "Report of Meeting Held at the Baker Hotel, Dallas, Texas, September 5th, 1933, in re: 'Tentative Plan for Cotton Acreage Reduction in 1934 and 1935,'" "Agricultural Adjustment Administration: Cotton Conference, September 5, 1933" folder, Box 1, Cobb/Ruralist Press Papers; *Dallas Morning News,* September 6, 1933; *Houston Post,* September 7, 1933; *New York Times,* September 6, 1933.

4. "Tentative Plan for Cotton Acreage Reduction in 1934 and 1935," September–December 1933 folder, Box 1, OF 258, FDR Papers; Allison to Chester Davis, September 5, 1933, A. A. Allison file, Box 20, AC 1933–1935, AAA, RG 145, NA; J. E. McDonald to Cobb, September 6, 1933, Texas State Department of Agriculture file, Box 1077, AC 1933–1935, AAA, RG 145, NA; Richards, *Cotton and the AAA,* 351–54; *Dallas Morning News,* September 6, 1933; *New York Times,* September 6, 8, 1933; *Houston Post,* September 7, 1933. The AAA suggested that the rental payments be a sliding scale based on the estimated yield of the farmer's land, ranging from three dollars per acre (for land yielding 75 to 125 pounds

per acre) to eleven dollars per acre (for land yielding 400 pounds per acre and over). As will be noted, the Cotton Section eventually shifted to a flat rate for rental payments under the official 1934–35 program.

5. Memo, Cobb to Davis, September 8, 1933, "Agricultural Adjustment Administration: Memoranda to Chester Davis" folder, Box 1, Cobb/Ruralist Press Papers; Conrad, *Forgotten Farmers,* 54. Soon after the Dallas conference, concerns emerged among many Texas tenants and sharecroppers about the possible impact that the new cotton program might have on their employment prospects. State and federal officials began receiving reports from various parts of Texas indicating that landlords were refusing to sign on tenants and sharecroppers for the coming year until they knew how many laborers would be needed. Many bankers and merchants also voiced concern because a reduction in tenants and croppers would mean a reduction in business for these providers of credit and merchandise. Editors speculated frankly about the detrimental impact the reduction in cotton acreage would have on the employment possibilities of Texas farm laborers. See R. L. Mullins to Rayburn, September 26, 1933, "General Correspondence 1933, M-P" file, "Correspondence 1914–39" drawer, Sam Rayburn Papers; Cross to Wallace, October 6, 1933, O. H. Cross file, Box 256, AC 1933–35, AAA, RG 145, NA; A. Agan to Ferguson, October 26, 1933, "Dept. of Agriculture (3)" file, Box 473, Miriam Ferguson Papers; *Texas Weekly,* September 9, 1933; *Houston Post,* September 13, October 27, 1933.

6. AAA R. 1228–34, Box 2, Entry 6, AAA, RG 145, NA; *Dallas Morning News,* November 30, 1933; *New York Times,* November 30, 1933.

7. AAA R. 1228–34, Box 2, Entry 6, AAA, RG 145, NA.

8. Memo, Cobb to Davis, September 28, 1933; memo, Cobb to Davis, February 6, 1935 (both in "Agricultural Adjustment Administration: Cobb memoranda to Davis" folder, Box 1, Cobb/Ruralist Press Papers); Conrad, *Forgotten Farmers,* 59–61; Schlesinger, *The Age of Roosevelt,* 77.

9. Conrad, *Forgotten Farmers,* 59–61. Conrad presents a hypothetical example involving a nonmanaging share tenant operating a forty-acre farm yielding two hundred pounds of lint cotton per acre. The example assumes an agreement between the tenant and landlord stating that the two parties would divide the crop equally at the end of the season. Although the landlord would receive close to 80 percent of the government payments, the tenant would still benefit from the program because of the increased price of cotton (12.6 cents per pound on average in 1934). If cotton remained at the 1932 level of 6.5 cents per pound without any government program, the participating tenant would enjoy a 22.4 percent increase in revenue (from $260.00 to $318.40), though the landlord's income would increase 65.5 percent (from $260.00 to $430.40). The example also assumes that the landlord (who legally received all AAA checks) distributed the government money fairly to his tenant. For a strong critique of the division of payments, see Donald Grubbs, *Cry from the Cotton: The Southern Tenant Farmers' Union and the New Deal,* 19–20.

10. Petition, Tenant Farmers' Association, Local No. 1, Lamesa, Texas, to Wallace, n.d. (first and second quotations); Cobb to W. A. Cook, December 16, 1933 (third quotation). See also Ernest Norman to Cobb, January 17, 1934 (all in Cotton—A.R. file, Box 22, SC 1933–35, AAA, RG 145, NA).

11. AAA R. 1228–34, Box 2, Entry 6, AAA, RG 145, NA (emphasis mine).

12. Conrad, *Forgotten Farmers,* 59 (first quotation); Nelson, *King Cotton's Advocate,*

79–81; Richards, *Cotton and the AAA*, 138–40. I examine Texas tenant and sharecropper displacement in chap. 6.

13. Allison to Cobb, December 6, 1933, A. A. Allison file, Cobb to Allison, December 15, 1933 (both in Box 20, AC 1933–35); W. D. McFarlane to Wallace, December 16, 1933, Wallace to McFarlane, January 4, 1934 (both in Cotton—A.R. file, Box 23, SC 1933–35); Buchanan to Wallace, January 26, 1934, Tugwell to Buchanan, February 16, 1934 (both in J. Buchanan file, Box 68, AC 1933–35); Tugwell to Morris Sheppard, January 30, 1934, Cobb to Marvin Jones, February 7, 1934, Cotton—A.R. file, Box 22, SC 1933–35 (all in AAA, RG 145, NA).

14. AAA R. 1403–34, 1412–34, 1502–34, Box 3, Entry 6, AAA, RG 145, NA; *Dallas Morning News,* December 19, 1933. For a discussion of Wallace's disagreements with Peek, see Fite, *George N. Peek,* 243–66; Saloutos, *American Farmer and the New Deal,* 87–97; Rexford G. Tugwell, *Roosevelt's Revolution: The First Year—A Personal Perspective,* 122–26, 191–204. On Peek's tenure as the president's special adviser on foreign trade, see Fite, *George N. Peek,* 267–81. Peek clashed over trade policy with Roosevelt's secretary of state, Cordell Hull, and resigned his post as special adviser in July 1935, eventually becoming a staunch critic of the New Deal.

15. Richards, *Cotton and the AAA,* 75–76.

16. Annual narrative reports of county agents from Cameron, Duval, Hockley, Howard, Jones, Lubbock, and Scurry counties, 1934, microfilm reels 91–95, TAES Historical Records.

17. Petition of 44 Jim Wells County farmers to Cotton Section, January 13, 1934; R. C. Miller to Cotton Section, January 13, 1934 (quotations); E. A. Miller to R. C. Miller, January 19, 1934 (all in Cotton—A.R. file, Box 22, SC 1933–35, AAA, RG 145, NA).

18. For information on the educational meetings, see 1934 annual narrative reports of Texas county agents, TAES Historical Records. After the meetings, local committees employed a variety of means to contact farmers about signing a contract. Committeemen in some locales, such as Donley, Taylor, and Victoria counties, actively engaged farmers in the field to solicit their cooperation. Other committees, such as those in Anderson and Kaufman counties, set up shop in locations scattered about their counties so that producers could come to them with their crop data. Farmers in Stephens County turned in their production information and signed contracts only at the county agent's office. Meanwhile, the Howard County agent mailed survey cards to all growers in his county who had cooperated with the plow-up campaign asking them to join the new program and provide relevant crop data (annual narrative reports for county agents from Anderson, Donley, Howard, Kaufman, Stephens, Taylor, and Victoria counties, 1934, microfilm reels 91–96, TAES Historical Records).

19. Williamson to Cobb, January 2, 1934, H. H. Williamson file, Box 1186, AC 1933–35 (quotation).

20. Allison to Cully Cobb, January 7, 19, 23, 1934 (all in A. A. Allison file, Box 20, AC 1933–35); E. Ruhman to Cobb, January 16, 1934, Cotton—A.R. file, Box 23, SC 1933–35; C. H. Alvord to Ruhman, January 25, 1934, Cotton—A.R. file, Box 23, SC 1933–35 (all in AAA, RG 145, NA); *Dallas Morning News,* January 14, 18 (quotation), 1934. Many USDA officials believed that the Cotton Section worded the cotton contract poorly. See memo, George Bishop to Henry Wallace, February 21, 1934; Mordecai Ezekiel to Wallace,

March 5, 1934 (both in "Farm Relief—Cotton Acreage Reduction" file, Box 1985); memo, D. Trent to Paul Appleby, June 14, 1934, "Farm Relief—Cotton, January–July 1934" file, Box 1984 (all in GC, USDA, RG 16, NA).

21. In August 1933, Mordecai Ezekiel warned Henry Wallace that a per acre limit of one hundred pounds was too high and might exclude up to one-third of Texas producers. In order to guarantee the effectiveness of the program, the economist advised Wallace to lower the limit to seventy-five pounds per acre (Ezekiel to Wallace, August 22, 1933, "Agriculture, U.S. Department of, 1932–33" file, Box 1, Subject Files, Mordecai Ezekiel Papers).

22. R. L. Mullins et al. to Rayburn, January 26, 1934, Sam Rayburn file, Box 894, AC 1933–35; McDonald to Wallace, January 29, 1934, Texas State Dept. of Agriculture file, Box 1077, Box 894, AC 1933–35; Martin to Cobb, January 24, 1934, Texas A&M College—O. B. Martin file, Box 1074, Box 894, AC 1933–35 (quotation); Allison to Cobb, January 23, 1934, A. A. Allison file, Box 20, Box 894, AC 1933–35; A. O. Hebel to James Buchanan, January 17, 1934, Cotton—A.R. file, Box 23, SC 1933–35 (all in AAA, RG 145, NA); *Dallas Morning News,* January 19, 1934.

23. Williamson to Cobb, January 25, 1934, H. H. Williamson file (first quotation); Cobb to Williamson, January 26, 1934 (second quotation) (both in Box 1186, AC 1933–35, AAA, RG 145, NA); *Dallas Morning News,* January 28, 1934 (third quotation). For coverage of the sign-up campaign's slowness in Texas, see *Dallas Morning News,* January 23, 24, 28, 29, 30, 31, 1934.

24. AAA R. 1738–34, 1828–34, 1853–34, Box 3, Entry 6; memo, Cobb to Davis, February 15, 1934, Chester Davis file, Box 273, AC 1933–35 (both in AAA, RG 145, NA); *Dallas Morning News,* February 1, 1934; annual report of E. A. Miller, Texas state agronomist, 1934, microfilm reel 90, TAES Historical Records. Early in 1934, there was talk in administration circles of employing an AAA insignia, similar to the National Recovery Administration's "Blue Eagle," to identify participating farmers. Some producers and government officials argued that use of some sign of cooperation might boost the pride of participants as well as apply pressure on nonsigners to join the campaign. Henry Wallace and Chester Davis nixed the idea, however, believing that employing such an insignia might result in detrimental consequences for farmers who were sympathetic to the government program but could not sign cotton contracts for various reasons. Because feelings in many communities ran very high against noncooperators, those farmers who could not join the program might be lumped unfairly into the same category as belligerent noncooperators and unjustly ostracized. See C. W. Warburton to H. H. Williamson, March 10, 1934, Texas Director file, Box 275, GC, FES, RG 33, NA.

25. Williamson to Martin, January 10, 1934; Martin to Cully Cobb, January 15, 1934; Cobb to Martin, January 22, 1934 (all in Texas A&M College—O. B. Martin file, Box 1074, AC 1933–35, AAA, RG 145, NA); Williamson to county agents, February 14, 1934, Texas Director file, Box 275, GC, FES, RG 33, NA.

26. Annual narrative reports of county agents, 1934, TAES Historical Records; Richards, *Cotton and the AAA,* 103–108.

27. Annual narrative reports for county agents from Bell, Duval, Henderson, Hopkins, Lamb, Lubbock, Nueces, and Victoria counties, 1934, microfilm reels 94–95; annual narrative report of E. C. Jameson, county agent for Montague County, microfilm reel 94 (quotation) (all in TAES Historical Records).

28. Annual narrative report of W. M. Sellers, county agent for Nueces County, 1934,

microfilm reel 95, TAES Historical Records (quotation); petition, citizens of Nueces County to Connally, n.d., Tom Connally file, Box 233; Shirley Yregg to Cully Cobb, May 10, 1934, Box 1214; J. Ross Bell to Yregg, ibid.; J. A. Coleman to Jones, May 19, 1934, Marvin Jones file, Box 551; E. L. McGaugh to Cobb, June 5, 1934, Box 681; Henry Wallace to Cross, September 26, 1934, O. H. Cross file, Box 256; A. Epps to McFarlane, October 20, 1934, W. D. McFarlane file, Box 683; Cobb to McFarlane, October 31, 1934, ibid. (all in AC 1933–35, AAA, RG 145, NA).

29. Annual narrative report of H. M. Haswell, county agent for Trinity County, 1934, microfilm reel 96, TAES Historical Records; *Dallas Morning News,* May 23, June 8, 29, July 15, 24, August 8, 1934; 1934 annual narrative reports of Texas county agents, TAES Historical Records.

30. Richards, *Cotton and the AAA,* 66–79; Ezekiel to Wallace, June 15, 1933, "Agriculture, U.S. Department of, 1932–33" folder, Box 1, Subject Files, Mordecai Ezekiel Papers (quotation; emphasis in original).

31. See Henry Clay to Henry Wallace, July 17, 1933, Box 21; H. W. Tolson to Wallace, October 31, 1933, Box 22; Otis Miller to Cully Cobb, November 2, 1933, Box 22; Abe Rabinowitz to Wallace, November 17, 1933, Box 22; M. L. MacDonald to Wallace, December 11, 1933, Box 22 (all in SC 1933–35, Cotton—A.R. file, AAA, RG 145, NA).

32. Wallace to Roosevelt, June 7, 1933; Bankhead to Roosevelt, August 21, 1933; Roosevelt to Bankhead September 18, 1933 (all in September–December 1933 folder, Box 1, OF 258, FDR Papers); Bankhead to Wallace, August 22, 1933; Wallace to Bankhead, September 5, 1933 (both in John Bankhead file, Box 68, AC 1933–35, AAA, RG 145, NA); Bankhead to Wallace, November 17, 1933; Wallace to Bankhead, December 5, 1933 (both in "Farm Relief—Cotton, October–December 1933" file, GC, USDA, RG 16, NA); Jack Brien Key, "John H. Bankhead, Jr.: Creative Conservative," 147–48, 152–56.

33. For background information on John Bankhead, see Evans C. Johnson, "John H. Bankhead 2d: Advocate of Cotton"; Sidney Baldwin, *Poverty and Politics: The Rise and Decline of the Farm Security Administration,* 132–33; and Key, "John H. Bankhead, Jr.," 1–48.

34. Key, "John H. Bankhead, Jr.," 157–58; *Dallas Morning News,* January 14, 1934. For information about Bankhead's brother, see Walter J. Heacock, "William B. Bankhead and the New Deal."

35. *Dallas Morning News,* January 16 (first and second quotations), 30 (third quotation), 1934.

36. J. M. Bevers to Wallace, January 3, 1934, Cotton—A.R. file, Box 23, SC 1933–35 (quotation). See also J. E. Junker to Morris Sheppard, January 10, 1934; I. H. Terry to Wallace, January 18, 1934; Walter G. Burkholder to Wallace, January 18, 1934; C. A. Craven to Wallace, January 29, 1934 (all in Cotton file, Box 19, SC 1933–35); petition, 32 farmers of Dime Box, Texas, to Buchanan, January 27, 1934, J. Buchanan file, Box 140, AC 1933–35; and petition, 75 farmers of Lynn County, Texas, to Jones, n.d., Marvin Jones file, Box 551, AC 1933–35 (all in AAA, RG 145, NA).

37. "A Comparison of Two Plans Designated to Control the Production of Cotton," January 15, 1934, Chester Davis file, Box 272, AC 1933–35, AAA, RG 145, NA.

38. *Dallas Morning News,* January 27, 1934; *New York Times,* January 27, 1934.

39. AAA R. 1706–34, Box 3, Entry 6; memo, Paul Porter to Wallace, February 8, 1934, Cotton file, Box 19, SC 1933–35; memo, Cobb to Wallace, February 26, 1934, Cotton—A.R. file, Box 22 (all in AAA, RG 145, NA). Anthony Badger has called the questionnaire

results "something of a self-fulfilling prophesy" because of the selective nature of the survey's participants. See Badger, *Prosperity Road,* 249n14.

40. AAA R. 1807–34, Box 3, Entry 6, AAA, RG 145, NA; *New York Times,* February 7 and 8, 1934; *Dallas Morning News,* February 8, 9, 10, 1934.

41. Roosevelt to Jones, February 16, 1934, "White House Correspondence, 1933–37" folder, Box 22, Political Material, Marvin Jones Papers (quotation). See also Roosevelt to Smith, February 16, 1934, "January–June, 1934" folder, Box 2, OF 258, FDR Papers; *New York Times,* February 18, 1934.

42. May, *Marvin Jones,* 118–19.

43. *Congressional Record,* House, 73d Cong., 2d sess., 4207 (first quotation), 4208, 4645 (second quotation).

44. *Congressional Record,* House, 73d Cong., 2d sess., 4431.

45. Ibid. (quotation).

46. *Congressional Record,* House, 73d Cong., 2d sess., 4434–35.

47. *Dallas Morning News,* March 16, 17, 18, 19, 20, 30, April 5, 10, 11, 12, 13, 14, 15, 16, 17, 18, 19, 20, 21, 22, 1934; *New York Times,* March 20, 30, April 13, 15, 18, 22, 1934. George Terrell was the only Representative from the entire Cotton Belt to vote against the Bankhead bill. He did not run for reelection in 1934.

48. Seven-eighths-inch middling was the most common grade of cotton sold in American markets. The length of its fibers, or "staple length," was seven-eighths of an inch. "Middling" refers to the fibers' overall condition based on color, amount of foreign impurities, and quality of ginning. Middling was the basic grade with respect to market price and to the measuring of other grades of cotton. For an excellent discussion of how cotton was classified during the 1930s, see Harry Brown, *Cotton,* 413–33.

49. Memo, Chester Davis to Cobb, May 3, 1934, Cully Cobb, 1933–35 file, Box 216, AC 1933–35, AAA, RG 145, NA; Richards, *Cotton and the AAA,* 163–68. On May 26, 1934, Wallace declared that the first ginning tax would be 5.67 cents per pound. He would modify the amount of the tax twice during the life of the Bankhead Act, to six cents per pound on June 18, 1935, and 5.45 cents on October 21, 1935 (AAA R. 2677–34, Box 4, Entry 6, AAA, RG 145, NA).

50. Many Texas noncooperators protested this procedure, arguing that their local committeemen discriminated against them in determining their Bankhead quotas. See J. W. Fletcher, F. W. Gibbs, and twenty-two others to Wallace, September 30, 1934, Luther Johnson file, Box 543; Henry Greener to Cross, n.d., O. H. Cross file, Box 256 (both in AC 1933–35, AAA, RG 145, NA); J. W. Crider to *Semi-Weekly News,* November 14, 1935, "Bills—Farm Tenantry" folder, Box 334, Legislation Files, James V. Allred, Papers, Special Collections and Archives, University of Houston, Houston (cited hereafter as James Allred Papers, UH).

As a hypothetical example of how quotas were determined: suppose the Secretary of Agriculture announced a national quota of 10 million bales. If a state's share of the national production during the 1928–32 base period was 20 percent, its Bankhead allotment would be 2 million bales. This amount would then be subdivided into a regular allotment of 1.8 million bales and a state reserve of 200,000 bales. Assuming a particular county had a 1 percent share of state production during the base period, it would receive a county allotment of 18,000 bales to be distributed among individual farmers.

51. Farmers could qualify for a portion of the state reserve if they operated units

which fell under one of the following four categories: (1) farms which had less than one-third of cultivated land devoted to cotton during the preceding three years; (2) farms producing cotton in 1933 or 1934 for the first time since 1927; (3) farms on which normal cotton production during any one or more years during the base period had been reduced by reason of drought, storm, flood, insects, or other uncontrollable natural cause; (4) farms on which the acreage planted to cotton during 1930–32 had been reduced voluntarily by an amount greater than the secretary of agriculture decided would have been equitable in carrying out a reasonable voluntary-reduction program (Richards, *Cotton and the AAA*, 168–69, 360–65).

52. Bankhead to Davis, May 28, 1934, John Bankhead file, Box 68, AC 1933–35 (quotations); AAA R. 2900–34, Box 5, Entry 6 (both in AAA, RG 145, NA); *Dallas Morning News*, June 22, 1934.

53. F. W. Spencer to Hopkins County Committee, July 16, 1934; Spencer to A. V. Bullock, July 17, 1934 (both in Cotton—A.R. file, Box 23, SC 1933–35); Cully Cobb to Milton West, September 27, 1934, Cotton—Bankhead file, Box 23, SC 1933–35, Buchanan to Cobb, September 10, 1934; Cobb to Buchanan, September 21, 1934 (both in J. Buchanan file, Box 140, AC 1933–35); and numerous petitions to Chairman Jones in Marvin Jones file, Box 551, AC 1933–35 (all in AAA, RG 145, NA).

54. See 1934 annual narrative reports of Texas county agents, TAES Historical Records. Some agents and committeemen, such as those in Chambers, Scurry, and Stephens counties, announced local meeting areas where farmers could present their crop information and sign their applications. In many other areas, such as Angelina, Burnet, Howard, and Victoria counties, agents and county committeemen used existing data sheets to fill out the applications for acreage-reduction contract signers, then sent local committeemen out to get signatures. These local committees also performed crop estimations for the farms of noncontract signers and sought their signatures on applications so they could also receive their share of tax-exemption certificates, if they wanted them (1934 annual narrative reports of county agents from Angelina, Burnet, Chambers, Howard, Scurry, Stephens, and Victoria counties, microfilm reels 91–93, 95–96, TAES Historical Records).

55. Richards, *Cotton and the AAA*, 80; *Dallas Morning News*, July 15, 1934.

56. Annual narrative report of E. W. Thomas, county agent for Castro County, 1934, microfilm reel 91; annual narrative report of L. T. Stone, county agent for Cochran County, microfilm reel 92; see other 1934 annual narrative reports of Texas county agents (all in TAES Historical Records).

57. Lawler to Rayburn, September 19, 1934, Sam Rayburn file, Box 894, AC 1933–35, AAA, RG 145, NA.

58. Annual narrative report of Robert R. Lancaster, District 5 agent, 1934, microfilm reel 91; 1934 annual narrative reports of county agents from Cameron, Hidalgo, and Willacy counties, microfilm reels 91, 93, 96 (all in TAES Historical Records); Connally to Cully Cobb, July 16, 1934; Cobb to Connally, July 16, 1934; Connally to Henry Wallace, July 23, 1934; Wallace to Connally, July 26, 1934 (all in Tom Connally file, Box 233, AC 1933–35, AAA, RG 145, NA); *Dallas Morning News*, July 22, 26, 28, August 17, 22, 29, September 21, 1934; *New York Times*, September 16, 1934.

59. Buchanan to Wallace, July 30, 1934, J. Buchanan file, Box 140; Sheppard to Chester Davis, August 2, 1934, Morris Sheppard file, Box 978; Connally to Henry Wallace, August 2, 1934, Tom Connally file, Box 233; Johnson to Cully Cobb, August 10, 1934,

Luther Johnson file, Box 543; Mansfield to Wallace, August 12, 1934, J. J. Mansfield file, Box 653; Rayburn to Wallace, August 15, 1934, Sam Rayburn file, Box 894; Cross to Cobb, September 28 and August 4, 1934, O. H. Cross file, Box 256 (all in AC 1933–35, AAA, RG 145, NA); *Dallas Morning News,* August 11–12, 26, 1934.

60. Rexford Tugwell to Buchanan, July 31, 1934, J. Buchanan file, Box 140; D. W. Watkins to Sheppard, August 3, 4, 1934, Morris Sheppard file, Box 978; Cully Cobb to Johnson, August 10, 1934, Luther Johnson file, Box 543 (all in AC 1933–35, AAA, RG 145, NA); annual narrative report of W. M. Sellers, county agent for Nueces County, 1934, microfilm reel 95 (quotation), and 1934 annual narrative reports of Texas county agents (all in TAES Historical Records); H. H. Williamson to Cobb, August 10, 1934, "Agricultural Adjustment Administration: General, June–December, 1934" folder, Box 1, Cobb/Ruralist Press Papers; Richards, *Cotton and the AAA,* 174.

61. USDA, Economic Research Service, "Statistics on Cotton and Related Data, 1930–67," 94; *New York Times,* August 19, 1934; *Dallas Morning News,* November 10, December 9, 10, 1934.

62. Patman to Wallace, August 10, 1934, Wright Patman file, Box 832; Sheppard to Wallace, August 28, 1934, Morris Sheppard file, Box 978 (both in AC 1933–35); Nueces County Cotton Control Committee to Wallace, August 15, 1934; Tugwell to Marvin Jones, August 21, 1934 (both in Cotton Certificates file, Box 23, SC 1933–35); Wallace to Connally, August 14, 1934, Cotton—Bankhead file, Box 23, SC 1933–35 (all in AAA, RG 145, NA).

63. AAA R. 671–35, Box 6, Entry 6; memo, D. W. Watkins to Chester Davis, August 24, 1934; Cully Cobb to State Extension Directors, October 1, 1934; memo, Cobb to D. Trent, December 5, 1934 (all in Cotton Certificates file, Box 23, SC 1933–35, AAA, RG 145, NA); *Dallas Morning News,* September 14, 16, 21, 1934; Key, "John H. Bankhead, Jr.," 167 (quotation). After the 1934 growing season, Texas farmers held an estimated surplus of tax-exemption certificates equivalent to 831,000 bales and surrendered certificates equal to approximately 734,000 bales to the national pool (Richards, *Cotton and the AAA,* 175–81).

64. Bankhead to Cobb, July 30, 1934, John Bankhead file, AC 1933–35, AAA, RG 145, NA (quotation).

65. Key, "John H. Bankhead, Jr.," 165–67.

66. Henry Wallace to Roosevelt, September 5, 1934; Roosevelt to Bankhead, September 8, 1934 (quotation); Bankhead to Roosevelt, September 12, 1934 (all in PPF 1362, FDR Papers).

67. *Dallas Morning News,* September 20, 1934.

68. Bankhead to Roosevelt, September 18, 1934, John Bankhead file, Box 68, AC 1933–35, AAA, RG 145, NA (quotation; emphasis mine). See also Bankhead to Wallace, September 12, 1934, PPF 1362, FDR Papers.

69. *Dallas Morning News,* September 20, 21, 22, 1934; *New York Times,* September 20, 1934. Jones believed that the administration should discontinue the Bankhead law after 1934, because he felt that the combination of acreage-control efforts and the drought had reduced the surplus to acceptable levels. The agriculture committee chairman had an inherent fear that if production were reduced too much, more foreign markets might be lost. Nevertheless, Jones very strongly believed that the administration should guarantee compensation to all holders of surplus certificates. See also Jones to Wallace, July 30, 1934, Marvin Jones file, Box 551, AC 1933–35, AAA, RG 145, NA; and Jones to Roosevelt, January 19, 1935, "White House Correspondence, 1933–37" folder, Box 22, Political Material, Marvin Jones Papers.

70. Sam Tarkington to Mansfield, September 21, 1934, J. J. Mansfield file, Box 653 (quotation). See also Sheppard to Henry Wallace, September 20, 1934; Sheppard to Chester Davis, September 21, 22, 1934 (all in Box 978, Morris Sheppard file); Thomason to Davis, September 21, 22, 1934 (both in R. E. Thomason file, Box 1082); Kleberg to Wallace, September 22, 1934, Richard Kleberg file, Box 582; Sumners to Wallace, September 22, 1934, Hatton Sumners file, Box 1049; and Buchanan to Wallace, September 23, 1934, J. Buchanan file, Box 140 (all in AC 1933–35, AAA, RG 145, NA).

71. *Dallas Morning News,* September 23, 1934; *New York Times,* September 23, 1934. See also Wallace to Buchanan, October 2, 1934, J. Buchanan file, Box 140, AC 1933–35; Wallace to Luther Johnson, October 2, 1934, Cotton—Bankhead file, Box 23, SC 1933–35 (both in AAA, RG 145, NA).

72. AAA R. 939–35, 1048–35 (both in Box 7, Entry 6, AAA, RG 145, NA); *Dallas Morning News,* November 24, 1934; Richards, *Cotton and the AAA,* 188.

73. Letter to the editor, K. Roberts, *Dallas Morning News,* October 9, 1934 (quotations). For other letters to the editor expressing similar views, see *Dallas Morning News,* November 11, 21, 23, 1934.

74. USDA, *Agricultural Adjustment in 1934: A Report of the Administration of the Agricultural Adjustment Act, 15 Feb. 1934 to 31 Dec. 1934,* 54. All farmers who planned to produce cotton during the 1935 season were allowed to vote in the referendum.

75. Annual narrative reports of county agents from Cameron, Cochran, Gillespie, Stephens, Tyler, and Willacy counties, 1934, microfilm reels 92, 93, 95, 96, TAES Historical Records. See also Jones to Cobb, February 2, 1935, Marvin Jones file, AC 1933–35, AAA, RG 145, NA.

76. It must be noted, however, that numerous tenants and sharecroppers complained to government officials that in 1934 their landlords either refused to hire them unless they agreed to relinquish their share of the AAA payments, or refused to give them their fair share of the payments after promising to do so. See John Bialas to Ferguson, September 2, 1934, Cotton Reduction Plan file, Box 480, Miriam Ferguson Papers; Juan Gutiérrez to Allred, State Agencies and Departments—Cotton file, Box 364, James Allred Papers, UH; D. M. Allen to Cully Cobb, July 4, 1934, Box 17; Perry Johnson to Henry Wallace, October 21, 1935, Box 541 (both in AC 1933–35, AAA, RG 145, NA).

77. USDA, *Agricultural Adjustment in 1934,* 50. The total value of the Texas cotton crop produced in 1934 was approximately $150 million (USDA, "Statistics on Cotton," 206). The 1934 price-support loan for cotton was set at 12 cents per pound. For details on the 1934 loan, see Nelson, *King Cotton's Advocate,* 135–36; Richards, *Cotton and the AAA,* 217–24. For a listing of parity prices, 1920–38, see *Texas Almanac and State Industrial Guide, 1939,* 181.

78. As in 1934, numerous farmers wrote government officials in 1935 to protest their individual and county allotments of Bankhead certificates. See, for example, petition, fifteen Fisher County farmers to Blanton, November 23, 1935, Thomas Blanton file, Box 105; petition, seventy-eight Cochran County farmers to Connally, n.d., Tom Connally file, Box 233; N. F. Johnson to Luther Johnson, August 25, 1935, Luther Johnson file, Box 543; M. G. Buchanan to Johnson, August 26, 1935, ibid.; petition, sixty-three Starr County farmers to Milton West, n.d., Box 653; Jasper Taylor to G. E. Adams, April 24, 1935, A. L. Smith file, Box 995; S. J. Stone to Wallace, July 26, 1935, ibid. (all in AC 1933–35, AAA, RG 145, NA). See also Mrs. J. J. Rogers to Allred, July 19, 1935; Bennie Steptoe to Allred, Sep-

tember 6, 1935; Herman Toll to Allred, September 12, 1935 (all in Cotton file, Box 208, James V. Allred, Governor's Papers, RG 301, Texas State Archives, Austin; cited hereafter as James Allred Papers, TSA).

79. Bankhead to Cobb, October 31, 1934; Bankhead to Wallace, November 7, 1934; Bankhead to Wallace, November 8, 1934 (all in John Bankhead file, Box 68, AC 1933–35, AAA, RG 145, NA); Bankhead to Roosevelt, November 5, 1934, October–December 1934 folder, Box 2, OF 258, FDR Papers. Cobb and Wallace initially replied to Bankhead's suggestions by stating that the administration was unwilling to risk continuing the sharp reduction rate of the previous two years because of the possibility that such an action would stimulate foreign production. They also cited certain financial constraints. Because the current program was already placing a strain on what the Cotton Section considered satisfactory rental and benefit payments, the AAA was initially reluctant to stretch resources further with additional payments to cover increased acreage reduction. See Cobb to Bankhead, November 8, 1934, John Bankhead file, Box 68, AC 1933–35, AAA, RG 145, NA; Wallace to Bankhead, November 13, 1934, October–December 1934 folder, Box 2, OF 258, FDR Papers.

80. USDA, *Agricultural Adjustment, 1933–35: A Report of the Administration of the Agricultural Adjustment Act, 12 May 1933 to 31 Dec. 1935,* 125; AAA R. 1071–35, 1393–35, Box 7, Entry 6, AAA, RG 145, NA; *Dallas Morning News,* November 29, 1934, January 18, 1935; *New York Times,* November 29, 1934, January 18, 1935.

81. AAA R. 1393–35, 1663–35 (both in Box 8, Entry 6, AAA, RG 145, NA); *New York Times,* March 2, 1935.

82. *Dallas Morning News,* July 1, 1935. See also Williamson to C. W. Warburton, July 1, 1935; Warburton to Williamson, July 11, 1935; Williamson to Warburton, July 20, 1935 (all in Texas Director file, Box 425, GC, FES, RG 33, NA); Cully Cobb to Williamson, July 10, 1935, Texas A&M College—H. H. Williamson file, Box 1075, AC 1933–35, AAA, RG 145, NA; Richards, *Cotton and the AAA,* 77.

83. Memo, Cully Cobb to Chester Davis, May 29, 1935, Cotton Loan file, Box 27, SC 1933–35; memo, Johnston to Davis, August 26, 1935, Chester Davis file, Box 274, AC 1933–35; AAA R. 1819–35, Box 8, Entry 6; 331–36, 349–36, 355–36, Box 9, Entry 6 (all in AAA, RG 145, NA); *Dallas Morning News,* August 28, 1935; Richards, *Cotton and the AAA,* 224–27; Murray R. Benedict and Oscar C. Stine, *The Agricultural Commodity Programs: Two Decades of Experience,* 12; USDA, *Agricultural Adjustment in 1934: A Report of the Administration of the Agricultural Adjustment Act, 15 Feb. 1934 to 31 Dec. 1934,* 426; USDA, *Agricultural Adjustment, 1933–35,* 296; USDA, "Statistics on Cotton," 93–94, 206. Section 32 of the Agricultural Adjustment Amendment Act, authored by Marvin Jones, provided funding for the 1935 cotton subsidy through customs receipts. For an excellent summary of Oscar Johnston's role in developing the 1935 loan-subsidy plan, see Nelson, *King Cotton's Advocate,* 139–43.

84. USDA, *Yearbook of Agriculture, 1936,* 11–12; Saloutos, *American Farmer and the New Deal,* 126–29.

85. H. H. Williamson, interview by E. N. Holmgreen, transcript, n.d., item 13, microfilm reel 2, TAES Historical Records (hereafter cited as Williamson interview); Scott and Shoalmire, *Cully A. Cobb,* 232.

86. Williamson interview; *Dallas Morning News,* April 19, 1935; Scott and Shoalmire, *Cully A. Cobb,* 234.

87. *Dallas Morning News,* April 24, May 13, 14, 1935; *New York Times,* May 12 (quotation), 14, 1935.

88. Williamson interview; Scott and Shoalmire, *Cully A. Cobb,* 235; *Dallas Morning News,* May 15, 1935; *New York Times,* May 15, 1935. Initially, Roosevelt had agreed to see only five cotton farmers, but he evidently changed his mind when he realized that the size of the gathering was going to be much larger than anticipated (Wallace to Ed O'Neal, May 4, 1935, 1935 folder, Box 2, OF 227, FDR Papers).

89. May 14, 1935 speech, No. 779, Box 21, PPF 1820, FDR Papers (quotation); *Dallas Morning News,* May 15, 1935; *New York Times,* May 15, 1935; Scott and Shoalmire, *Cully A. Cobb,* 235.

90. *Dallas Morning News,* May 28, 29, June 6, 14, August 25, 1935; *New York Times,* May 28, June 1, 6, 15, 19, 30, July 7, August 25, 1935.

91. *Dallas Morning News,* July 16, October 15, 1935; *New York Times,* July 16 (quotation), October 15, 1935. While the justices deliberated, the AAA announced a new four-year cotton program that it planned to offer growers if the Court accepted the AAA amendments and ruled favorably on the processing taxes. Under the proposed plan, the AAA would allow State Allotment Boards the right to choose from one of five possible base periods for allocating acreage to counties and individual producers, instead of the fixed 1928–32 period used in the previous two yeas. (The provision reflected the incessant lobbying of John Bankhead against the rigid 1928–32 base period used previously.) See Bankhead to Chester Davis, September 25, 1935; Bankhead to Henry Wallace, October 3, 1935; Bankhead to Davis, October 3, 1935; Bankhead to Davis, October 5, 1935; Bankhead to Wallace, October 10, 1935; Bankhead to Davis, October 14, 1935; Bankhead to Wallace, October 16, 1935 (all in John Bankhead file, Box 68, AC 1933–35, AAA, RG 145, NA).

The AAA decided to allow individual reductions in acreage ranging from 35 percent to 45 percent. The agency would issue a single adjustment payment of not less than five cents per pound on the average yield of the land to be taken out of production. The division of payments between landlords and their tenants and sharecroppers would provide more to the tenants and croppers than the previous two-year program had: 37.5 percent of the payment would go to the person furnishing the land; 12.5 percent to the individual providing the work stock and equipment; and the remaining 50 percent would be divided in proportion to the interest in the crop agreed on by the landlord and his tenants or croppers (AAA R. 993–36, Box 9, Entry 6, AAA, RG 145, NA; *Dallas Morning News,* December 14, 1935; Richards, *Cotton and the AAA,* 54–56). Previous to the AAA's release of its proposed program, on December 4, President Roosevelt announced his intention to ask Congress to support an exemption from the tax provisions of the Cotton Control Act for all growers producing fewer than two bales (*Dallas Morning News,* December 5, 1935; Richards, *Cotton and the AAA,* 192–93).

92. AAA R. 994–36, Box 9, Entry 6, AAA, RG 145, NA; May, *Marvin Jones,* 140; *Dallas Morning News,* December 11, 14, 1935; *New York Times,* December 31, 1935.

Chapter 4

1. *New York Times,* January 6, 1936 (quotations); *Dallas Morning News,* January 6, 1936; Paul L. Murphy, "The New Deal Agricultural Program and the Constitution," 161–62.

2. Memo, Davis to Wallace, January 7, 1936, "Agricultural Adjustment Act, 1936" Wle, Box 2265, GC, USDA, RG 16, NA; *New York Times,* January 7, 1936; May, *Marvin Jones,* 140–41.

3. *Congressional Record,* 74th Cong., 2nd sess., pt. 1, 199–204; *Dallas Morning News,* January 8, 12, 1936.

4. Wallace Radio Address, "The Supreme Court Decision," folder 32, Speeches Collected—General, Box 19, Agricultural Material, Marvin Jones Papers (first quotation); Henry A. Wallace, *Whose Constitution: An Inquiry into the General Welfare,* 103 (second quotation). See also Schapsmeier and Schapsmeier, *Henry A. Wallace,* 221; Culver and Hyde, *American Dreamer,* 162.

5. *New York Times,* January 9, 1936 (quotation).

6. Memo for AAA File, January 24, 1936, 1936 folder, Box 13, OF 1-k, FDR Papers (quotation).

7. Roosevelt to Congress, February 3, 1936, White House Correspondence—1933–37 folder, Box 22, Political Material, Marvin Jones Papers. For Bankhead certificate repayment requests, see E. L. Deal to Morgan Sanders, March 21, 1936, Cotton Certificates file, Box 156, SC 1936–38; Deal to Tom Connally, December 7, 1936; Deal to Wright Patman, December 8, 1936; Cully Cobb to Marvin Jones, February 10, 1937; Henry Wallace to Morris Sheppard, December 21, 1937; I. W. Duggan to J. L. Alderdice, October 12, 1938; Duggan to Will Matus, December 14, 1938; Patman to Cobb, January 21, 1937, Box 719, Wright Patman file, AC 1936–38; Deal to Jones, Feb 27, 1937, Box 441, Marvin Jones file (all in AAA, RG 145, NA).

8. *Dallas Morning News,* January 8, 1936; *New York Times,* January 8, 1936.

9. Richard S. Kirkendall, "Howard Tolley and Agricultural Planning in the 1930s," 28; idem, *Social Scientists and Farm Politics,* 135; Murray R. Benedict, *Farm Policies of the United States, 1790–1950: A Study of Their Origins and Development,* 348; USDA, *Agricultural Conservation, 1936: A Report of the Agricultural Adjustment Administration under the Provisions of the Agricultural Adjustment Act and the Soil Conservation and Domestic Allotment Act and Related Legislation from 1 Jan. 1936 to 31 Dec. 1936,* 1.

10. Kirkendall, "Howard Tolley and Agricultural Planning," 25–26; idem, *Social Scientists and Farm Politics,* 15–16, 135–36.

11. Kirkendall, "Howard Tolley and Agricultural Planning," 28–29; idem, *Social Scientists and Farm Politics,* 138.

12. Peter Farb, "Hugh Bennett: Messiah of the Soil," 40 (quotation). For a biography of Bennett, see Wellington Brink, *Big Hugh: The Father of Soil Conservation.* For a history of the SCS, see Robert J. Morgan, *Governing Soil Conservation: Thirty Years of the New Decentralization.* Among the best works on the Dust Bowl are R. Douglas Hurt, *The Dust Bowl: An Agricultural and Social History,* and Donald Worster, *The Dust Bowl: The Southern Plains in the 1930s.*

13. Kirkendall, "Howard Tolley and Agricultural Planning," 29 (quotation); idem, *Social Scientists and Farm Politics,* 144–45.

14. Transcript, "Talks Given by Secretary of Agriculture Henry A. Wallace and Agricultural Adjustment Administrator Chester C. Davis before Opening Session of Farm Leaders' Conference in Washington," "Meetings, Farm Leaders Conferences, 1936" file; copies of AAA R. 1237–36, 1245–36 (all in Box 2382, GC, USDA, RG 16, NA); Minutes, Proceedings of Washington Farm Leaders Conference, January 10–11, 1936, "1936–40"

folder, Box 2, OF 227, FDR Papers; *Dallas Morning News,* January 11, 12, 1936; *New York Times,* January 11, 12, 1936.

15. *Dallas Morning News,* January 17, 22, 1936; *New York Times,* January 17, 18, 19, 22, 1936. For a preconference briefing from Secretary Wallace to FDR, see Wallace to Roosevelt, January 16, 1936, "Farm Relief, January 1936" file, Box 2343, GC, USDA, RG 16, NA.

16. *Dallas Morning News,* January 23, 24, 25, 26, 30, February 6, 12, 16, 22, 24, 25, 28, 1936; *New York Times,* January 23, 24, 25, 26, 30, 31, February 6, 16, 22, 23, 26, 27, 28, 1936.

17. *Dallas Morning News,* March 2, 1936; *New York Times,* March 1, 2, 1936.

18. *Dallas Morning News,* March 3, 1936; *New York Times,* March 1, 5, 1936. The other regional meetings were held in Chicago, New York City, and Salt Lake City.

19. *Dallas Morning News,* March 6, 1936; *New York Times,* March 6, 7, 8, 1936. For information on the development of the tentative cotton plan, see memo, Claude Wickard to Davis, January 31, 1936, Chester Davis file, Box 187, AC 1936–38, AAA, RG 145, NA.

20. AAA R. 1539–36, 1542–36, Box 10, Entry 6, AAA, RG 145, NA; *New York Times,* March 11, June 6, 1936; Kirkendall, *Social Scientists and Farm Politics,* 145.

21. Memo, H. R. Tolley to Henry Wallace, March 16, 1936, "Farm Relief, March–August, 1936" file, Box 2344, GC, USDA, RG 16, NA; *Dallas Morning News,* March 18, 1936; *New York Times,* March 18, 1936; USDA, *Agricultural Conservation, 1936,* 58.

22. AAA R. 1579–36, Box 10, Entry 6, AAA, RG 145, NA; USDA, *Agricultural Conservation, 1936,* 41–44; *Dallas Morning News,* March 21, 1936; *New York Times,* March 21, 1936. On April 26, the Southern Division announced the payment rates that Wallace had approved for planting soil-building crops and performing soil-conserving practices in the Southern Region. For the extensive payment schedule, see AAA R. 1739–36, Box 10, Entry 6, AAA, RG 145, NA.

23. AAA R. 1591–36, Box 10, Entry 6, AAA, RG 145, NA; USDA, *Agricultural Conservation, 1936,* 57–60; *Dallas Morning News,* March 26, April 2, 1936; *New York Times,* March 29, 1936; 1936 annual narrative reports of Texas county agents, TAES Historical Records.

24. See especially the 1936 annual narrative reports of county agents from Comal, Hunt, and Terry counties, microfilm reels 104, 106, 109, TAES Historical Records.

25. Annual narrative report of Edmund Singleton, county agent for Bell County, 1936, microfilm reel 104 (quotation); see especially 1936 annual narrative reports of county agents for Montague, Palo Pinto, and Stephens counties, microfilm reels 108–09 (all in TAES Historical Records).

26. See especially the 1936 annual narrative reports of county agents from Knox, Lavaca, Madison, Morris, and Palo Pinto counties, microfilm reels 107–08, TAES Historical Records. See also USDA, *Agricultural Conservation, 1936,* 45.

27. AAA R. 1940–36, Box 10, Entry 6, AAA, RG 145, NA.

28. See 1936 annual narrative reports of Texas county agents, TAES Historical Records.

29. Cobb to Williamson, March 10, 1937; memo, Cobb to Tolley, March 29, 1937, H. R. Tolley file, Box 933 (both in Texas A&M College—H. H. Williamson file, Box 918, AC 1936–38, AAA, RG 145, NA). See also annual narrative report of William N. Williamson, county agent for Franklin County, 1936, microfilm reel 105, TAES Historical Records. For other accounts describing the use of aerial surveying in 1936, see annual reports of county agents from Harrison and Karnes counties, microfilm reels 106–107,

TAES Historical Records. On Cobb's role in initiating aerial surveying, see Scott and Shoalmire, *Cully A. Cobb*, 236.

30. USDA, *Agricultural Conservation, 1936,* 13, 55; 1936 and 1937 annual narrative reports of Texas county agents, TAES Historical Records.

31. USDA, *Agricultural Adjustment, 1937–38: A Report of the Activities Carried on by the Agricultural Adjustment Administration under the Provisions of the Agricultural Adjustment Act of 1938, the Soil Conservation and Domestic Allotment Act, the Marketing Act of 1937, the Sugar Act of 1937, and Related Legislation, from 1 Jan. 1937 through 30 June 1938,* 259, 289. For evidence of tenant and sharecropper complaints, see Curt Woodall to Roosevelt, November 5, 1936; I. W. Duggan to Williamson, February 6, 1937; and R. F. Croom to Williamson, March 19, 1937 (all in Texas A&M College—H. H. Williamson file, Box 918, AC 1936–38, AAA, RG 145, NA).

32. USDA, "Statistics on Cotton," 93–95, 206; *Texas Almanac, 1941–42,* 207; *Dallas Morning News,* October 9, November 10, December 10, 1936.

33. Anthony J. Badger, *The New Deal: The Depression Years, 1933–1940,* 160–61; USDA, "Statistics on Cotton," 93–94; USDA, *Agricultural Adjustment, 1937–38,* 42.

34. AAA R. 868–37, Box 11, Entry 6; Cobb to county and local committeemen, Box 213, AC 1936–38 (all in AAA, RG 145, NA AAA). See also *Dallas Morning News,* December 10, 1936; USDA, *Agricultural Adjustment, 1937–38,* 35. In 1937, the AAA expanded its use of aerial photography in Texas to check compliance (Texas Agricultural Extension Service, *Annual Report: Agricultural Conservation Program, 1937,* microfilm reel 111, TAES Historical Records).

35. Wallace to Rayburn, June 9, 1937, "Presidential Letters/Letters from Prominent People" binder, Sam Rayburn Papers; annual narrative report of E. C. Jameson, county agent for Montague County, 1937, microfilm reel 116; Texas Agricultural Extension Service, *1937 Annual Report,* microfilm reel 111 (both in TAES Historical Records).

36. Memo, Cobb to Tolley, July 31, 1937, Cully Cobb file, Box 142, AC 1936–38; AAA R. 818–37, 147–38, 1299–38, Box 11, Entry 6 (all in AAA, RG 145, NA). See also *New York Times,* August 3, 1937; Scott and Shoalmire, *Cully A. Cobb,* 237–38.

37. Cobb to Williamson, March 15, 1937, Texas A&M College—H. H. Williamson file, Box 918, AC 1936–38, AAA, RG 145, NA (quotations). The average price received for cotton in 1937 was 8.4 cents per pound (*Texas Almanac, 1941–42,* 207).

38. Orville Merton Kile, *The Farm Bureau through Three Decades,* 236; Badger, *Prosperity Road,* 144; Don F. Hadwiger, *Federal Wheat Commodity Programs,* 149–50.

39. Schapsmeier and Schapsmeier, *Henry A. Wallace,* 236–37; Culver and Hyde, *American Dreamer,* 57; Russell Lord, *Wallaces of Iowa,* 233–34.

40. AAA R. 1110–37, 1143–37 (both in Box 11, Entry 6, AAA, RG 145, NA); May, *Marvin Jones,* 160; Kile, *Farm Bureau,* 237.

41. AAA R. 1142–37, Box 11, Entry 6, AAA, RG 145, NA (quotations); *Dallas Morning News,* February 9, 1937; *New York Times,* February 9, 1937; Michael W. Schuyler, "The Politics of Change: The Battle for the Agricultural Adjustment Act of 1938," 166.

42. AAA R. 1153–37, Box 11, Entry 6, AAA, RG 145, NA; *Dallas Morning News,* February 10, 1937 (quotations); *New York Times,* February 10, 1937; Don F. Hadwiger, *Federal Wheat Commodity Programs,* 150; Kile, *Farm Bureau,* 237.

43. *New York Times,* May 15, 16, 17, 1937; Campbell, *Farm Bureau and the New Deal,*

113; Schuyler, "Politics of Change," 167–69; Hadwiger, *Federal Wheat Commodity Programs,* 150; Kile, *Farm Bureau,* 238–39; May, *Marvin Jones,* 160–61.

44. May, *Marvin Jones,* 161–64; Badger, *Prosperity Road,* 145. The best works on the court-packing plan are William E. Leuchtenburg's "The Origins of Franklin D. Roosevelt's 'Court-Packing' Plan," 352–99, and "Franklin D. Roosevelt's Supreme Court 'Packing' Plan," 69–115. The most authoritative book on Roosevelt's dealings with the Supreme Court is Leuchtenburg's *The Supreme Court Reborn: The Constitutional Revolution in the Age of Roosevelt.* For an overview of the congressional opposition to Roosevelt's court-packing effort, see James T. Patterson, *Congressional Conservatism and the New Deal: The Growth of the Conservative Coalition in Congress, 1933–1939,* 86–127.

45. *New York Times,* May 1 (quotations), 9, 1937.

46. *Dallas Morning News,* May 18, 1937; *New York Times,* May 18 (first quotation), 19, 22 (second quotation), 1937; Badger, *Prosperity Road,* 145; Hadwiger, *Federal Wheat Commodity Programs,* 150; May, *Marvin Jones,* 160; Campbell, *Farm Bureau and the New Deal,* 112.

47. *New York Times,* May 28, 29, (first quotation), June 12 (second, third, and fourth quotations), 1937; Badger, *Prosperity Road,* 145; May, *Marvin Jones,* 161.

48. *New York Times,* June 15, 29, 1937.

49. Roosevelt to Jones, July 12, 1937, "White House Correspondence, 1933–37" folder, Box 22, Political Material, Marvin Jones Papers (quotations). See also Jones to Smith, July 12, 1937, July–August 1937 folder, Box 3, OF 1, FDR Papers; *New York Times,* July 4, 13, 1937; and May, *Marvin Jones,* 162.

50. *New York Times,* July 7, 18, 21, 22, 24 (quotation), 25, 1937; Badger, *Prosperity Road,* 145; Hadwiger, *Federal Wheat Commodity Programs,* 150; May, *Marvin Jones,* 162–63.

51. *New York Times,* July 28, 29, 1937.

Chapter 5

1. Patton to Roosevelt, August 7, 1937, "January–August 1937" folder, Box 3, OF 258, FDR Papers (quotations).

2. *Dallas Morning News,* August 10, 1937; *New York Times,* August 10, 1937.

3. *Dallas Morning News,* August 10, 1937; *New York Times,* August 10, 1937. The August estimate for Texas was 4,314,000 bales, which would have made it the state's largest cotton crop since 1933.

4. *Dallas Morning News,* August 11, 1937; *New York Times,* August 11, 1937.

5. *Dallas Morning News,* August 12, 1937; *New York Times,* August 12, 1937 (quotation).

6. *Dallas Morning News,* August 14, 1937; *New York Times,* August 14, 26, 1937; Badger, *Prosperity Road,* 145; Hadwiger, *Federal Wheat Commodity Programs,* 150–51; Kile, *Farm Bureau,* 240. Due to financial constraints, the Commodity Credit Corporation lent only 9 cents per pound to farmers who stored the "domestically-consumed" portion (about 60 percent) of their crop in warehouses. In addition, producers received subsidy payments on the domestically consumed portion of their crop to provide them with a guaranteed price of 12 cents per pound. As in 1935, the government determined the amount of the subsidy by calculating the difference between the average price of cotton

on ten spot markets and 12 cents per pound when the farmer sold his cotton. Thus, if a grower sold his crop on a day when the average price was 10.5 cents per pound, he would eventually receive a payment of 1.5 cents per pound on his cotton. The payment was to be made in late 1938, after verification that the grower had fully participated in the 1938 program. See Wallace to Bankhead, September 18, 1937, John Bankhead file, Box 48, AC 1936–38, AAA, RG 145, NA; *Dallas Morning News,* August 22, 1937; *New York Times,* August 21, 22, 1937.

7. *Dallas Morning News,* August 25, 1937; *New York Times,* August 24, 25, 1937; Badger, *Prosperity Road,* 145; Hadwiger, *Federal Wheat Commodity Programs,* 151; Kile, *Farm Bureau,* 240.

8. *Dallas Morning News,* October 13, 1937; *New York Times,* October 13, 1937; Bankhead to Roosevelt, October 13, 1937, John Bankhead file, PPF 1362, FDR Papers (quotation).

9. Roosevelt to Jones, October 20, 1937, "White House Correspondence, 1933–37" folder, Box 22, Political Material, Marvin Jones Papers (quotations); Roosevelt to Smith, October 20, 1937, July–August 1937 folder, Box 3, OF 1, FDR Papers; May, *Marvin Jones,* 164–65.

10. May, *Marvin Jones,* 69–70, 118, 161–64.

11. *Dallas Morning News,* October 15, 1937 (quotation); *New York Times,* October 15, 1937; May, *Marvin Jones,* 164.

12. *New York Times,* October 28, November 4, 5, 11, 13, 15, 1937.

13. Bankhead to Roosevelt, September 16, 1937, "1935–42" folder, Box 1, OF 2960, FDR Papers (quotations; emphasis mine).

14. *New York Times,* November 16, 18, 21, 22, 24, 25, 26, 27, 1937; Schuyler, "Politics of Change," 177; Hadwiger, *Federal Wheat Commodity Programs,* 151; May, *Marvin Jones,* 166.

15. *New York Times,* December 11, 12, 18, 1937.

16. *Dallas Morning News,* February 7, 8, 1938; *New York Times,* December 19, 1937, January 9, 19, 25, February 3, 7, 8, 1938.

17. *Dallas Morning News,* February 9, 10, 15, 1938; *New York Times,* February 9, 10, 13, 15, 1938; press release, February 16, 1938, 1938 folder, Box 14, OF 1–k, FDR Papers (quotation). Kleberg's negative vote reflected his resistance to marketing quotas. Thomas agreed with Houston merchant, labor, and shipping interests who opposed reduced cotton production because of its effect on their volume-oriented businesses. West's vote reflected his Lower Rio Grande Valley constituents' long-standing antagonism to crop-reduction plans based on prior production and the disadvantages they had suffered in past programs because of the early start of their growing season.

18. In a letter to Oscar Johnston (who by now had left the AAA to return to the presidency of the Delta and Pine Land Company), Cully Cobb expressed his belief that the 1937 division of payments between landlords and tenants was the best that could be devised. He believed the new, more equitable division of payments proposed in the farm bill to be "not only inexcusable" but also "most unjust." Cobb attributed the new division-of-payment scheme to "the social reform element which has always felt that in some way the landlords of the South should be punished" (Cobb to Johnston, September 27, 1937, "Oscar G. Johnston [Delta and Pine Land Company/National Cotton Council]" folder, Box 8, Cobb/Ruralist Press Papers [quotations]). In his response, Johnston agreed with Cobb,

stating that the new division of payments was "clumsy and uneconomic" and the work of individuals with sincerity of purpose but with unsound judgment. Nevertheless, Johnston pointed out that his personal inclination was to favor the general principles embodied in the farm bill (Johnston to Cobb, September 24, 1937, "Oscar G. Johnston [Delta and Pine Land Company/National Cotton Council]" folder, Box 8, Cobb/Ruralist Press Papers).

19. "Statement to District Agents with Reference to Relationships between the Texas Extension Service and the State A.A.A. Program," Box 628, GC, FES, RG 33, NA; USDA, *Agricultural Adjustment, 1937–38*, 100–22; USDA, *Agricultural Adjustment, 1938–39: A Report of the Activities Carried on by the Agricultural Adjustment Administration, 1 July 1938 through 30 June 1939*, 15–29, 49–52, 97–118; AAA R. 1262–38, Box 12, Entry 6, AAA, RG 145, NA; see also "Explanation of the Main Provisions of the Agricultural Adjustment Act of 1938," n.d., January–April 1938 folder, Box 3, OF 1, FDR Papers.

20. *Dallas Morning News,* February 16, 1938.

21. Jones to editor, *Dallas Morning News,* February 19, 1938, Marvin Jones file, Box 441, AC 1936–38, AAA, RG 145, NA (quotations).

22. Jones to editor, *Dallas Morning News,* February 19, 1938, Marvin Jones file, Box 441, AC 1936–38, AAA, RG 145, NA (quotations).

23. Annual narrative report of C. L. Beason, county agent for Brazos County, 1938, microfilm reel 120, TAES Historical Records.

24. *Dallas Morning News,* March 12, 13, 14, 1938; USDA, *Agricultural Adjustment, 1937–38,* 110–11; AAA R. 1483–38, Box 12, Entry 6, AAA, RG 145, NA. The votes for the three dissenting Texas counties were as follows: Cameron—488 for, 583 against; Throckmorton—139–178; Willacy—193–297.

25. Annual narrative report of G. C. King, county agent for Lavaca County, 1938, microfilm reel 125 (quotation), TAES Historical Records.

26. Memo, F. E. Elliot to Evans, December 19, 1938, R. M. Evans file, Box 233, AC 1936–38, AAA, RG 145, NA (quotations).

27. See, for example, 100 Austin County farmers to J. J. Mansfield, March 30, 1938; Wallace to Connally, April 28, May 27, June 1, 1938 (all in Tom Connally file, Box 157); Tarrant County Committee to Lanham, May 24, 1938, Fritz Lanham file, Box 491; and Shackelford County Committee to Sheppard, April 26, 1938, Morris Sheppard file, Box 829 (all in AC 1936–38, AAA, RG 145, NA).

28. V. H. Hurland to Mahon, March 28, 1938 (first quotation); W. E. Angley et al. to Mahon, March 23, 1938 (second quotation); R. B. Gladden to Mahon, March 23, 1938; Lewis Owen to Mahon, March 26, 1938; Zeke Sanders to Mahon, March 26, 1938; J. E. Gibbs to Mahon, April 1, 1938 (all in "Farm Problems—Cotton Allotments—Cochran, 1938" folder). See also Mrs. C. W. Vanlandingham to Mahon, March 26, 1938; William J. Kennedy et al. to Wallace, April 5, 1938 (both in "Farm Problems—Cotton Allotments—Bailey County, 1938" folder). All citations in Box 86, George Mahon, Papers, Southwest Collection, Texas Tech University, Lubbock.

29. AAA R. 1566–38, Box 12, Entry 6, AAA, RG 145, NA.

30. Wallace to Milton West, July 15, 1938; Paul Appleby to John C. Myrick, July 26, 1938 (all in Cotton file, Box 154, SC 1936–38, AAA, RG 145, NA). See annual narrative reports of county agents for Bexar, Brazos, Cameron, Hood, San Saba, Scurry, and Shelby counties, 1938, microfilm reels 120, 121, 124, 127, TAES Historical Records.

31. George Marburger to AAA, May 4, 1938; I. W. Duggan to Marburger, May 12,

1938 (both in bulk files, Box 765, AC 1936–38). See also W. F. Hartfield to Connally, June 3, 1938; W. A. Klaus to Connally, n.d.; Wallace to Connally, June 27, 1938; Duggan to Connally, June 15, 1938 (all in Tom Connally file, Box 157, AC 1936–38). Also see Duggan to R. L. Graham, June 11, 1938; Harry Brown to J. J. Mansfield, July 28, 1938 (both in Box 154, Cotton file, SC 1936–38). All citations are in AAA, RG 145, NA. See also *New York Times,* May 15, 1938, and annual narrative reports of county agents for Bexar, Fayette, and Liberty counties, 1938, microfilm reels 120, 122, 125, TAES Historical Records.

32. Connally to Wallace, October 11, 1938; Wallace to Connally, November 5, 1938 (quotations). See also Wallace to Connally, September 22, 1938 (all in Tom Connally file, Box 157, AC 1936–38, AAA, RG 145, NA).

33. AAA R. 1890–38, Box 12, Entry 6, AAA, RG 145, NA; *Dallas Morning News,* June 3, 4 (quotation), 1938.

34. AAA R. 2072–38, Box 12, Entry 6, AAA, RG 145, NA; USDA, *Agricultural Adjustment, 1937–38,* 110.

35. See 1938 annual narrative reports of county agents for Austin, Jackson, Lavaca, Morris, Parmer, Refugio, and Scurry counties, microfilm reels 120, 124, 125, 126, 127, TAES Historical Records.

36. USDA, "Statistics on Cotton," 93, 94, 206; idem, *Agricultural Adjustment, 1938–39,* 88, 125; *Texas Almanac, 1941–42,* 207.

37. See 1938 annual narrative reports of county agents for Hall, Hockley, Hood, Johnson, Lavaca, and Parmer counties, microfilm reels 123–26, TAES Historical Records.

38. Bankhead to Roosevelt, October 25, 1938, 1938 folder, OF 258, FDR Papers (quotation).

39. Rayburn to Duggan, September 15, 1938 (first and second quotations); Duggan to Rayburn, September 22, 1938 (third quotation) (all in Sam Rayburn file, Box 765, AC 1936–38, AAA, RG 145, NA).

40. AAA R. 1110–39, Box 13, Entry 6, AAA, RG 145, NA. For the problems in administering the tobacco program in 1938, the December tobacco referendum in North Carolina, and the effects of the tobacco producers' failure to sanction marketing quotas in 1939, see Badger, *Prosperity Road,* 150–94.

41. USDA, *Agricultural Adjustment, 1938–39,* 28–29; *New York Times,* August 16, 1938. See also AAA R. 228–39, Box 13, Entry 6; County Committee of Burnet County to Johnson, February 27, 1939, Lyndon B. Johnson file, Box 1118, AC 1939–42 (both in AAA, RG 145, NA).

42. "Biographical Sketch of R. M. Evans, Administrator, Agricultural Adjustment Administrator," n.d., R. M. Evans file, Box 1088, AC 1939–42, AAA, RG 145, NA; Cully Cobb to W. B. Camp, November 17, 1938, "W. B. Camp and Sons" folder, Box 4, Cobb/Ruralist Press Papers (first quotation); Dean Albertson, *Roosevelt's Farmer: Claude R. Wickard in the New Deal,* 117–18 (second and third quotations); Richard S. Kirkendall, "Howard Tolley and Agricultural Planning," 30; idem, *Social Scientists and Farm Politics,* 157–64.

43. See 1939 annual narrative reports of Texas county agents, microfilm reels 129–42, TAES Historical Records.

44. USDA, "Statistics on Cotton," 93–94, 206; USDA, *Agricultural Adjustment, 1939–40: A Report of the Activities of the Agricultural Adjustment Administration, 1 July 1939 through 30 June 1940,* 42; *Texas Almanac, 1941–42,* 207. Local committees found that only

1,864 Texas cotton farms overplanted, 328 in Cameron County in the Lower Rio Grande Valley (1939 annual report of the Texas state AAA office, microfilm reel 129, TAES Historical Records).

45. AAA R. 407–40, Box 15, Entry 6, AAA, RG 145, NA.

Chapter 6

1. *Dallas Morning News,* November 1, 1933; *Houston Post,* November 1, 1933. Transcripts of Harlan's trial do not exist, but the Wise County courthouse holds some court documents from the case. The records reveal that a jury eventually acquitted Harlan, apparently on grounds of self-defense (*State of Texas v. Tim Harlan,* Case No. 5620–1936, Wise County Courthouse, Decatur, Tex.).

2. For a thorough account of the plight of tenant farmers' efforts to resist eviction in the Delta, see Grubbs, *Cry from the Cotton.*

3. Pete Daniel, *Breaking the Land: The Transformation of Cotton, Tobacco, and Rice Cultures since 1880,* 107 (quotation).

4. Conrad, *Forgotten Farmers,* 123–26. For a copy of the Hoover Report, see "Human Problems in Acreage Reduction in the South," released as AAA R. 2470–A in Box 4, Entry 6, AAA, RG 145, NA.

5. Much has been written on the agrarian-liberal split in the AAA. See relevant portions of the following works to view how this division has been described by different historians over time: Conrad, *Forgotten Farmers;* Grubbs, *Cry from the Cotton;* Lord, *Wallaces of Iowa;* Nelson, *King Cotton's Advocate;* Saloutos, *American Farmer and the New Deal;* Schlesinger, *Age of Roosevelt;* and Scott and Shoalmire, *Cully A. Cobb.*

6. For information on the AAA purge, see the works mentioned in note 5 and Richard Lowitt, "Henry A. Wallace and the 1935 Purge in the Department of Agriculture"; Lawrence J. Nelson, "The Art of the Possible: Another Look at the 'Purge' of the AAA Liberals in 1935."

7. Roosevelt to Wallace, November 16, 1936, "Tenant Farming—Special Folder," Box 1, OF 1650, FDR Papers; see also Roosevelt to Jones, September 21, 1936, "White House Correspondence, 1933–37," Folder 18, Box 22, Marvin Jones Papers.

8. Foley, *White Scourge,* 181. For information on the FSA, see Baldwin, *Poverty and Politics;* Paul E. Mertz, *New Deal Policy and Southern Rural Poverty.*

9. For a quantitative analysis of displacement in Texas, see Keith J. Volanto, "Leaving the Land: Tenant and Sharecropper Displacement in Texas during the New Deal."

10. USDA, "Questions and Answers about the AAA Farm Program," found in "Agricultural Adjustment Administration Information, 1939–41" Folder, Box 19, Agricultural Material (1928–1974), General Office Files (1931–1974), Marvin Jones Papers (quotations).

11. Mahon to Duggan, October 18, 1938, George Mahon file, Box 529, AC 1936–38, AAA, RG 145, NA (quotations).

12. Duggan to Mahon, November 12, 1938, George Mahon file, Box 529, AC 1936–38, AAA, RG 145, NA (quotation).

13. Ibid. (quotations).

14. Mahon to Jones, November 4, 1938, George Mahon file, Box 529, AC 1936–38, AAA, RG 145, NA (quotation).

15. Ibid. (emphasis mine).

16. Ibid. (emphasis mine).

17. Jones to Duggan, November 8, 1938 (quotation); Jones to Mahon, November 8, 1938, George Mahon file, Box 529; Duggan to Jones, December 12, 1938 (all in George Mahon file, Box 529, AC 1936–38, AAA, RG 145, NA).

18. Mahon to Wallace, November 29, 1938, George Mahon file, Box 529, AC 1936–38, AAA, RG 145, NA (quotation).

19. Wallace to Mahon, December 30, 1938, George Mahon file, Box 529, AC 1936–38, AAA, RG 145, NA. For other letters written by administration officials expressing the traditional AAA defense on the displacement issue, see Duggan to Connally, December 14, 1938, Tom Connally file, Box 157, AC 1936–38; Wallace to Sheppard, December 29, 1939, and February 7, 1940 (both in Morris Sheppard file, Box 1170, AC 1939–42; and Duggan to Bankhead, January 12, 1940, John Bankhead file, Box 1059A, AC 1936–38 (all in AAA, RG 145, NA).

20. A. A. Cross to USDA, October 2, 1938, Box 176, AC 1936–38, AAA, RG 145, NA (quotation).

21. A. A. Cross to USDA, October 21, 1938, Box 176, AC 1936–38, AAA, RG 145, NA (quotation).

22. Mrs. J. C. Bland to Wallace, August 21, 1936, Box 68, Box 176, AC 1936–38, AAA, RG 145, NA (quotation).

23. W. A. Harrick to Wallace, January 10, 1935, Box 442, AC 1933–35, AAA, RG 145, NA (quotation).

24. G. H. Summers to Wallace, n.d., Box 895, AC 1936–38, AAA, RG 145, NA (quotation).

25. Perry, *Hold Autumn in Your Hand,* 181–82 (quotation).

26. Memo, Davis to Wallace, February 25, 1936, "Farm Relief, February 1936" File, Box 2343, GC, RG 16, NA (quotations).

27. Nelson, *King Cotton's Advocate,* 90 (quotation).

28. Eleanor Roosevelt to Wallace, May 17, 1939; Wallace to Eleanor Roosevelt, June 7, 1939 (first quotation); Eleanor Roosevelt to Wallace, June 15, 1939 (second quotation) (all in "Henry Wallace—1939" folder, Box 335, "Correspondence with Government Departments, 1934–35" file, Eleanor Roosevelt, Papers, Franklin D. Roosevelt Presidential Library, Hyde Park, N.Y.). For information on the Missouri sharecropper protest, see Louis Cantor, *A Prologue to the Protest Movement: The Missouri Roadside Demonstration of 1939.*

29. Memo, Ezekiel to Wallace, February 5, 1936, "Tenancy, 1936" file, Box 2439, GC, RG 16, NA (quotations).

30. Conrad, *Forgotten Farmers,* 81 (quotation).

31. See Foley, *White Scourge,* chap. 8; quotation on 184.

32. Memo, Davis to Wallace, February 25, 1936, "Farm Relief, February 1936" file, Box 2343, GC, RG 16, NA (quotation).

Chapter 7

1. Benedict, *Farm Policies of the United States,* 402–30.

2. Badger, *New Deal,* 168 (quotation).

3. Texas Cotton Association Membership Lists for 1933–1940, Texas Cotton Association, Papers, Texas A&M University Archives, Cushing Memorial Library, Texas A&M

University, College Station; Roosevelt to Marvin McIntyre, December 17, 1934, September–December 1934 folder, Box 2, OF 258, FDR Papers (quotation).

4. A classic example of the accountability problem involves a complaint filed by small growers in Henderson County, Texas. In 1934, these producers wrote to their congressman, Morgan Sanders, to explain that their county agent had unfairly treated them by blatantly allowing their county committee to favor other growers with generous Bankhead quotas while sharply cutting their allotments. Sanders wrote directly to Wallace to bring the situation to the secretary's attention and to ask for an investigation of the complaint. Acting Secretary Rexford Tugwell sent Sanders's request to the AAA Cotton Division in Washington. The matter was settled when Cotton Division officials wrote to the same county agent accused of the malfeasance and asked him to investigate the allegations against himself (Sanders to Wallace, August 6, 1934; Tugwell to Sanders, August 21, 1934; and R. F. Croom to John O. Moosberg [extension agent for Henderson County], August 13, 1934. All in Morgan Sanders file, Box 944, AC 1933–35, AAA, RG 145, NA).

BIBLIOGRAPHY

Manuscripts and Archival Sources

Agricultural Stabilization and Conservation Service. Records. Record Group 145, National Archives II, College Park, Md.

Allred, James V. Governor's Papers. Texas State Archives, Austin.

———. Papers. Special Collections and Archives, University of Houston, Houston.

Cobb, Cully A. Papers. Mitchell Memorial Library, Mississippi State University, Starkville.

Cully A. Cobb/Ruralist Press. Papers. Mitchell Memorial Library, Mississippi State University, Starkville.

Evans, Samuel Lee. "Texas Agriculture, 1880–1930." University of Texas, Austin, 1960.

Ezekiel, Mordecai. Papers. Franklin D. Roosevelt Presidential Library, Hyde Park, N.Y.

Federal Extension Service. Records. Record Group 33, National Archives II, College Park, Md.

Ferguson, Miriam A. Governor's Papers. Texas State Archives, Austin.

Gordon, Joseph F. "The History and Development of Irrigated Cotton on the High Plains of Texas." Texas Technological College, Lubbock, 1961.

Helms, Douglas. "Just Lookin' for a Home: The Cotton Boll Weevil and the South." Florida State University, Tallahassee, 1977.

Jones, Marvin. Papers. Southwest Collection, Texas Tech University, Lubbock.

———. "The Reminiscences of Marvin Jones." Oral History Research Office Collection, Columbia University, New York, 1972.

Key, Jack Brien. "John H. Bankhead, Jr.: Creative Conservative." Johns Hopkins University, Baltimore, 1964.

Mahon, George. Papers. Southwest Collection, Texas Tech University, Lubbock.

Motheral, Joseph R. "Recent Trends in Land Tenure in Texas." Texas Agricultural Experiment Station Bulletin, no. 641. College Station: Texas Agricultural and Mechanical College (June, 1944).

Rayburn, Sam. Papers. Sam Rayburn Library, Bonham, Tex.

Roosevelt, Eleanor. Papers. Franklin D. Roosevelt Presidential Library, Hyde Park, N.Y.

Roosevelt, Franklin D. Papers. Franklin D. Roosevelt Presidential Library, Hyde Park, N.Y.

Secretary of Agriculture, Office of the. Records. Record Group 16, National Archives II, College Park, Md.

Texas Agricultural Extension Service. Historical Records. Texas A&M University, College Station.

Texas Cotton Association. Papers. Texas A&M University Archives, Cushing Memorial Library, College Station.

Tugwell, Rexford G. Papers. Franklin D. Roosevelt Presidential Library, Hyde Park, N.Y.

Wallace, Henry A. Papers. University of Iowa, Iowa City (microfilm, Texas A&M University, College Station).

Books and Articles

Albertson, Dean. *Roosevelt's Farmer: Claude R. Wickard in the New Deal.* New York: Columbia University Press, 1961.

Ashburn, Karl E. "The Texas Cotton Acreage Control Law of 1931–32." *Southwestern Historical Quarterly* 61 (July 1957): 116–24.

Badger, Anthony J. *The New Deal: The Depression Years, 1933–1940.* New York: Noonday Press, 1989.

———. *Prosperity Road: The New Deal, Tobacco, and North Carolina.* Chapel Hill: University of North Carolina Press, 1980.

Baker, Gladys. *The County Agent.* Chicago: University of Chicago Press, 1939.

Baldwin, Sidney. *Poverty and Politics: The Rise and Decline of the Farm Security Administration.* Chapel Hill: University of North Carolina Press, 1968.

Benedict, Murray R. *Farm Policies of the United States, 1790–1950: A Study of Their Origins and Development.* New York: Twentieth Century Fund, 1953.

———, and Oscar C. Stine, *The Agricultural Commodity Programs: Two Decades of Experience.* New York: Twentieth Century Fund, 1956.

Black, John D. *Agricultural Reform in the United States.* New York: McGraw-Hill, 1929.

Braeman, John. "The New Deal and the 'Broker State:' A Review of the Recent Scholarly Literature." *Business History Review* 46, no. 4 (Winter 1972): 409–29.

Brink, Wellington. *Big Hugh: The Father of Soil Conservation.* New York: MacMillan Co., 1951.

Brinkley, Alan. *Voices of Protest: Huey Long, Father Coughlin, and the Great Depression.* New York: Vintage Books, 1982.

Britton, Karen. *Bale o' Cotton: The Mechanical Art of Cotton Ginning.* College Station: Texas A&M University Press, 1992.

———; Fred C. Elliott; and E. A. Miller. "Cotton Culture." In *The New Handbook of Texas,* 2: 353–54. Austin: Texas State Historical Association, 1996.

Brown, Harry Bates. *Cotton: History, Species, Varieties, Morphology, Breeding, Culture, Diseases, Marketing, and Uses.* New York: McGraw-Hill, 1938.

Cabeza de Vaca, Alvar Núñez. *Castaways: The Narrative of Alvar Núñez Cabeza de Vaca,* edited by Enrique Pupo-Walker. Translated by Frances M. López-Morillas. Berkeley & Los Angeles: University of California Press, 1993.

Calvert, Robert A. "Agrarian Texas." In *Texas through Time: Evolving Interpretations,* edited by Walter L. Buenger and Robert A. Calvert, 197–228. College Station: Texas A&M University Press, 1991.

———. "Nineteenth-Century Farmers, Cotton, and Prosperity." *Southwestern Historical Quarterly* 73 (April 1970): 509–21.

Campbell, Christiana McFadyen. *The Farm Bureau and the New Deal: A Study of the Making of National Farm Policy, 1933–40.* Urbana: University of Illinois Press, 1962.

Campbell, Randolph B. *An Empire for Slavery: The Peculiar Institution in Texas, 1821–1865.* Baton Rouge: Louisiana State University Press, 1989.

Cantor, Louis. *A Prologue to the Protest Movement: The Missouri Roadside Demonstration of 1939.* Durham, N.C.: Duke University Press, 1969.

Cantrell, Gregg. *Stephen F. Austin: Empresario of Texas.* New Haven, Conn.: Yale University Press, 1999.

Conrad, David. *The Forgotten Farmers: The Story of Sharecroppers in the New Deal.* Urbana: University of Illinois Press, 1965.

Culver, John C., and John Hyde. *American Dreamer: The Life and Times of Henry A. Wallace.* New York: W. W. Norton, 2000.

Daniel, Pete. *Breaking the Land: The Transformation of Cotton, Tobacco, and Rice Cultures since 1880.* Urbana: University of Illinois Press, 1985.

Farb, Peter. "Hugh Bennett: Messiah of the Soil." *American Forests* 66 (January 1960): 18–19, 40–42.

Fite, Gilbert C. *Cotton Fields No More: Southern Agriculture, 1865–1980.* Lexington: University of Kentucky Press, 1984.

———. *George N. Peek and the Fight for Farm Parity.* Norman: University of Oklahoma Press, 1954.

———. "Voluntary Attempts to Reduce Cotton Acreage in the South, 1914–1933." *Journal of Southern History* 14 (November 1948): 481–99.

Fleming, Lamar, Jr. *Growth of the Business of Anderson, Clayton and Company,* edited by James A. Tinsley. Houston: Texas Gulf Coast Historical Association, 1966.

Foley, Neil. "Mexicans, Mechanization, and the Growth of Corporate Cotton Culture in South Texas: The Taft Ranch, 1900–1930." *Journal of Southern History* (May 1996): 275–302.

———. *The White Scourge: Mexicans, Blacks, and Poor Whites in Texas Cotton Culture.* Berkeley and Los Angeles: University of California Press, 1997.

Franke, Louis. "How the Extension Service Came to Be." *Acco Press* 17 (June 1939): 1–9.

Garside, Alston Hill. *Cotton Goes to Market: A Graphic Description of a Great Industry.* New York: Frederick A. Stokes, 1935.

Grubbs, Donald. *Cry from the Cotton: The Southern Tenant Farmers' Union and the New Deal.* Chapel Hill: University of North Carolina Press, 1971.

Hadwiger, Don F. *Federal Wheat Commodity Programs.* Ames: Iowa State University Press, 1970.

Hair, William Ivy. *The Kingfish and His Realm: The Life and Times of Huey Long.* Baton Rouge: Louisiana State University Press, 1991.

Hamilton, David E. *From New Day to New Deal: American Farm Policy from Hoover to Roosevelt, 1928–1933.* Chapel Hill: University of North Carolina Press, 1991.

Hawley, Ellis. *The Great War and the Search for a Modern Order: A History of the American People and Their Institutions, 1917–1933.* New York: St. Martin's Press, 1979.

Heacock, Walter J. "William B. Bankhead and the New Deal." *Journal of Southern History* 21 (August 1955): 347–59.

Hollis, Daniel W. "Cotton Ed Smith—Showman or Statesman?" *South Carolina Historical Magazine* 71 (October 1970): 235–56.

Holmes, Michael S. *The New Deal in Georgia: An Administrative History.* Westport, Conn.: Greenwood Press, 1975.

Hosen, Frederick E. *The Great Depression and the New Deal: Legislative Acts in Their Entirety (1932–1933) and Statistical Economic Data (1926–1946).* Jefferson, N.C.: McFarland and Company, 1992.

Hurt, R. Douglas. *The Dust Bowl: An Agricultural and Social History.* Chicago: Nelson-Hall, 1981.

Johnson, Evans C. "John H. Bankhead 2d: Advocate of Cotton." *Alabama Review* 41 (January 1988): 30–58.

Jones, D. L.; W. M. Hurst; and D. Scoates. "Mechanical Harvesting of Cotton in Northwest Texas." Texas Agricultural Experiment Station Circular, no. 52. College Station: Texas Agricultural and Mechanical College (November 1928).

Kennedy, David. M. *Freedom from Fear: The American People in Depression and War, 1929–1945.* New York: Oxford University Press, 1999.

Kile, Orville Merton. *The Farm Bureau through Three Decades.* Baltimore: Waverly Press, 1948.

Kirby, Jack Temple. *Rural Worlds Lost: The American South, 1920–1960.* Baton Rouge: Louisiana State University Press, 1987.

Kirkendall, Richard S. "Howard Tolley and Agricultural Planning in the 1930s." *Agricultural History* 39 (January 1965): 25–33.

———. *Social Scientists and Farm Politics in the Age of Roosevelt.* Columbia: University of Missouri Press, 1966.

Leuchtenburg, William E. "Franklin D. Roosevelt's Supreme Court 'Packing' Plan." In *Essays on the New Deal,* edited by Harold M. Hollingsworth and William F. Holmes, 69–115. Austin: University of Texas Press, 1969.

———. "The Origins of Franklin D. Roosevelt's 'Court-Packing' Plan." In *The Supreme Court Review,* edited by Phillip B. Kurland, 352–99. Chicago: University of Chicago Press, 1966.

———. *The Supreme Court Reborn: The Constitutional Revolution in the Age of Roosevelt.* New York: Oxford University Press, 1995.

Lord, Russell. *The Wallaces of Iowa.* Boston: Houghton Mifflin, 1947.

Lowitt, Richard. "Henry A. Wallace and the 1935 Purge in the Department of Agriculture." *Agricultural History* 53 (July 1979): 607–21.

McConnell, Grant. *The Decline of Agrarian Democracy.* Berkeley & Los Angeles: University of California Press, 1959.

McCoy, Donald R. *Calvin Coolidge: The Quiet President.* New York: Macmillan, 1967.

May, Irvin M., Jr. *Marvin Jones: The Public Life of an Agrarian Advocate.* College Station: Texas A&M University Press, 1980.

Mertz, Paul E. *New Deal Policy and Southern Rural Poverty.* Baton Rouge: Louisiana State University Press, 1978.

Michie, Allan A., and Frank Rhylick. *Dixie Demagogues.* New York: Vanguard, 1939.

Moley, Raymond. *After Seven Years.* New York: Harper and Brothers, 1939.

Morgan, Robert J. *Governing Soil Conservation: Thirty Years of the New Decentralization.* Baltimore: Johns Hopkins University Press, 1965.

Murphy, Paul L. "The New Deal Agricultural Program and the Constitution." *Agricultural History* 29 (October 1955): 160–69.

Nelson, Lawrence J. "The Art of the Possible: Another Look at the 'Purge' of the AAA Liberals in 1935." *Agricultural History* 57 (October 1983): 416–35.

———. *King Cotton's Advocate: Oscar G. Johnston and the New Deal.* Knoxville: University of Tennessee Press, 1999.

Ohl, John Kennedy. *Hugh S. Johnson and the New Deal.* DeKalb: Northern Illinois University Press, 1985.

Patterson, James T. *Congressional Conservatism and the New Deal: The Growth of the Conservative Coalition in Congress, 1933–1939.* Lexington: University of Kentucky Press, 1967.

Perkins, Van L. *Crisis in Agriculture: The Agricultural Adjustment Administration and the New Deal, 1933.* Berkeley and Los Angeles: University of California Press, 1969.

Perry, George Sessions. *Hold Autumn in Your Hand.* Albuquerque: University of New Mexico Press, 1975.

Richards, Henry I. *Cotton and the AAA.* Washington, D.C.: Brookings Institution, 1936.

———. *Cotton under the Agricultural Adjustment Act: Developments up to July 1934.* Washington, D.C.: Brookings Institution, 1934.

Romasco, Albert. *The Poverty of Abundance: Hoover, the Nation, the Depression.* New York: Oxford University Press, 1965.

Rosen, Elliot A. *Hoover, Roosevelt, and the Brains Trust: From Depression to New Deal.* New York: Columbia University Press, 1977.

Rosenman, Samuel, ed. *The Public Papers of Franklin D. Roosevelt.* Vol. 2: *The Year of Crisis, 1933.* New York: Random House, 1938.

Rowley, William D. *M. L. Wilson and the Campaign for the Domestic Allotment.* Lincoln: University of Nebraska Press, 1970.

Saloutos, Theodore. *The American Farmer and the New Deal.* Ames: Iowa State University Press, 1982.

Schapsmeier, Edward L., and Frederick H. Schapsmeier. *Henry A. Wallace of Iowa: The Agrarian Years, 1910–1940.* Ames: Iowa State University Press, 1968.

Schlesinger, Arthur, Jr. *The Age of Roosevelt: The Coming of the New Deal.* Boston: Houghton Mifflin, 1958.

Schuyler, Michael W. "The Politics of Change: The Battle for the Agricultural Adjustment Act of 1938." *Prologue: The Journal of the National Archives* 15 (Fall 1983): 165–78.

Scott, Roy V. *The Reluctant Farmer: The Rise of Agricultural Extension to 1914.* Urbana: University of Illinois Press, 1970.

———, and J. G. Shoalmire. *The Public Career of Cully A. Cobb: A Study in Agricultural Leadership.* Jackson: University and College Press of Mississippi, 1973.

Sharpless, Rebecca. *Fertile Ground, Narrow Choices: Women on Texas Cotton Farms, 1900–1940.* Chapel Hill: University of North Carolina Press, 1999.

Sitton, Thad, and Dan K. Utley. *From Can See to Can't: Texas Cotton Farmers on the Southern Prairies.* Austin: University of Texas Press, 1997.

Snyder, Donald. *Cotton Crisis.* Chapel Hill: University of North Carolina Press, 1984.

Spillman, W. J. *Balancing the Farm Output: A Statement of the Present Deplorable Conditions of Farming, Its Causes, and Suggested Remedies.* New York: Orange Judd, 1927.

Sternsher, Bernard. *Rexford Tugwell and the New Deal.* New Brunswick, N.J.: Rutgers University Press, 1964.

Texas Almanac and State Industrial Guide, 1931. Dallas: A. H. Belo, 1931.

Texas Almanac and State Industrial Guide, 1939. Dallas: A. H. Belo, 1939.

Texas Almanac and State Industrial Guide, 1941–42. Dallas: A. H. Belo, 1942.

Tugwell, Rexford G. *Roosevelt's Revolution: The First Year—A Personal Perspective.* New York: Macmillan, 1977.

United States. Congress. *Congressional Record,* vols. 77–80, 73d–74th Cong., 1933–34.

———. Department of Agriculture. *Agricultural Adjustment: A Report on the Agricultural Adjustment Administration, May 1933 to Feb. 1934.* Washington, D.C, 1934.

———. *Agricultural Adjustment in 1934: A Report of the Administration of the Agricultural Adjustment Act, 15 Feb. 1934 to 31 Dec. 1934.* Washington, D.C., 1935.

———. *Agricultural Adjustment, 1933–35. A Report of the Administration of the Agricultural Adjustment Act, 12 May 1933 to 31 Dec. 1935.* Washington, D.C., 1936.

———. *Agricultural Adjustment, 1937–38. A Report of the Activities Carried on by the Agricultural Adjustment Administration under the Provisions of the Agricultural Adjustment Act of 1938, the Soil Conservation and Domestic Allotment Act, the Marketing Act of 1937, the Sugar Act of 1937, and Related Legislation, from 1 Jan. 1937 through 30 June 1938.* Washington, D.C., 1939.

———. *Agricultural Adjustment, 1938–39. A Report of the Activities Carried on by the Agricultural Adjustment Administration, 1 July 1938 through 30 June 1939.* Washington, D.C., 1939.

———. *Agricultural Adjustment, 1939–40. A Report of the Activities of the Agricultural Adjustment Administration, 1 July 1939 through 30 June 1940.* Washington, D.C., 1940.

———. *Agricultural Conservation, 1936. A Report of the Agricultural Adjustment Administration under the Provisions of the Agricultural Adjustment Act and the Soil Conservation and Domestic Allotment Act and Related Legislation from 1 Jan. 1936 to 31 Dec. 1936.* Washington, D.C., 1937.

———. *Yearbook of Agriculture, 1936.* Washington, D.C., 1936.

———. Economic Research Service. "Statistics on Cotton and Related Data, 1930–67." Statistical Bulletin, no. 417. Washington, D.C., 1968.

———. Department of Commerce. Bureau of the Census. *Census of Agriculture: 1950, Counties and State Economic Areas.* Vol. I, Part 26. Washington, D.C., 1952.

———. *Census of Agriculture: 1959, Final Report.* Vol. I, Part 37. Washington, D.C., 1959.

———. *Sixteenth Census of the United States: 1940, Agriculture.* Vol. I, Part 5. Washington, D.C., 1942.

Vance, Rupert B. *Human Factors in Cotton Culture: A Study in the Social Geography of the American South.* Chapel Hill: University of North Carolina Press, 1929.

Volanto, Keith J. "Leaving the Land: Tenant and Sharecropper Displacement in Texas during the New Deal." *Social Science History* 20 (Winter 1996): 533–51.

———. "Burying White Gold: The AAA Plow-up Campaign in Texas." *Southwestern Historical Quarterly* 103 (January 2000): 326–55.

Wallace, Henry A. *New Frontiers.* New York: Reynal and Hitchcock, 1934.

———. *Whose Constitution: An Inquiry into the General Welfare.* New York: Reynal and Hitchcock, 1936.

Whisenhunt, Donald W. "Huey Long and the Texas Cotton Acreage Control Law of 1931." *Louisiana Studies* 13 (Summer 1974): 142–53.

Williams, T. Harry. *Huey Long.* New York: Alfred A. Knopf, 1989.

Woodman, Harold D. *King Cotton and His Retainers: Financing and Marketing the Cotton Crop of the South, 1800–1925.* Columbia: University of South Carolina Press, 1968.
———. *New South—New Law: The Legal Foundations of Credit and Labor Relations in the Postbellum Agricultural South.* Baton Rouge: Louisiana State University Press, 1995.
Worster, Donald. *The Dust Bowl: The Southern Plains in the 1930s.* New York: Oxford University Press, 1979.
Wrenn, Lynette B. *Cinderella of the New South: A History of the Cottonseed Industry, 1855–1955.* Knoxville: University of Tennessee Press, 1995.

INDEX

Italic typeface indicates pages with illustrations

ISBN 1-58544-402-2

90000